Economics Imperialism and Interdisciplinarity

Volume 1

Studies in Critical Social Sciences Book Series

Haymarket Books is proud to be working with Brill Academic Publishers (www.brill.nl) to republish the *Studies in Critical Social Sciences* book series in paperback editions. This peer-reviewed book series offers insights into our current reality by exploring the content and consequences of power relationships under capitalism, and by considering the spaces of opposition and resistance to these changes that have been defining our new age. Our full catalog of *SCSS* volumes can be viewed at https://www.haymarketbooks.org/series_collections/4-studies-in-critical-social-sciences.

Series Editor
David Fasenfest (York University, Canada)

Editorial Board
Eduardo Bonilla-Silva (Duke University)
Chris Chase-Dunn (University of California–Riverside)
William Carroll (University of Victoria)
Raewyn Connell (University of Sydney)
Kimberlé W. Crenshaw (University of California–LA and Columbia University)
Heidi Gottfried (Wayne State University)
Alfredo Saad-Filho (King's College London)
Chizuko Ueno (University of Tokyo)
Sylvia Walby (Lancaster University)
Raju Das (York University)

Economics Imperialism and Interdisciplinarity

Critical Reconstructions of Political Economy

Volume 1: Before the Watershed

Ben Fine

Haymarket Books
Chicago, IL

First published in 2023 by Brill Academic Publishers, The Netherlands
© 2023 Koninklijke Brill NV, Leiden, The Netherlands

Published in paperback in 2024 by
Haymarket Books
P.O. Box 180165
Chicago, IL 60618
773-583-7884
www.haymarketbooks.org

ISBN: 979-8-88890-333-9

Distributed to the trade in the US through Consortium Book Sales and Distribution (www.cbsd.com) and internationally through Ingram Publisher Services International (www.ingramcontent.com).

This book was published with the generous support of Lannan Foundation, Wallace Action Fund, and the Marguerite Casey Foundation.

Special discounts are available for bulk purchases by organizations and institutions. Please call 773-583-7884 or email info@haymarketbooks.org for more information.

Cover design by Jamie Kerry and Ragina Johnson.

Printed in the United States.

Library of Congress Cataloging-in-Publication data is available.

Contents

Preface VII

1 Economics Imperialism as Intellectual Revolution 1
   1   The Personal Background 1
   2   The Revolution Displayed 5
   3   From Becker to Bourdieu via Kuhn and Coleman 10
   4   The Revolution Betrayed by Way of Concluding Remarks 14

2 The Historical Approach to Rent and Price Theory Reconsidered 18
      Postscript as Personal Preamble 18
   1   Introduction 22
   2   Adam Smith's Theory of Rent 26
   3   Marginalist Rent Theory 31
   4   Compromise in Neoclassical Rent Theory 33
   5   Concluding Remarks 34

3 Landed Property and the Distinction between Royalty and Rent 39
      Postscript as Personal Preamble 39
   1   Introduction 42
   2   The Historical Background 43
   3   The Theoretical Background 50
   4   The Debate 53
   5   Concluding Remarks 56

4 The New Revolution in Economics 63
      Postscript as Personal Preamble 63
   1   POLEMIC 64

5 From Bourdieu to Becker: Economics Confronts the Social Sciences 72
      Postscript as Personal Preamble 72
   1   Introduction 74
   2   The Enigma and Fluidity of Capital 78
   3   Bourdieu's Distinction of Social Capital 85
   4   From Bourdieu to Coleman – With Intermediate Stops 93
   5   The Revolution Portrayed 99
   6   Concluding Remarks 105

6 Economics Imperialism as Kuhnian Revolution? 114
    Postscript as Personal Preamble 114
    1   Introduction 115
    2   Preliminaries 119
    3   Paradigm Lost or (Re)Gained? 124
    4   Paradigm Shift? 132
    5   Paradigm Lost, Regained or Reconstructed? 135
    6   Concluding Remarks 147

7 A Question of Economics: Is It Colonising the Social Sciences? 157
    Postscript as Personal Preamble 157
    1   Introduction 160
    2   Whither Economics? 162
    3   Economics and Economies 166
    4   Standard Theory 168
    5   Determinism 170
    6   Social Scientists: Beware Economists Bearing Gifts 173
    7   From Potential to Practice 177
    8   Concluding Remarks 182

Appendix 191
Index 196

Preface

The motivation, energy, and capacity for this volume, the first in a series, derive from both short- and long-term factors. The immediate context was the covid pandemic, which curtailed my engaging in any major new research initiative, especially as I was thrown into more than full-time care for my special needs son. This only allowed piecemeal time for reading, writing and thinking, even though I had already recently retired and was not burdened with the delivery of normal academic duties in the newly straitened circumstances. But, in general, my time was rarely my own, and it only became available with uncertainty. The situation eased but persisted after lockdown given the vagaries and generally recognised crisis of care provision – for which, things being otherwise, a major new avenue of research could well have opened up. By character, I have to have something to do, ideally with some sort of worth however defined, but it also had to be something that would fit with the heavy constraints around the doing.

Longer term, especially at an age when looking back tends to take hold, it was inevitable that I would reflect upon what I had achieved as an academic, both personally and in the wider context of ideas, policy and politics, in all of which I had been engaged. I remain to be convinced that such speculation goes beyond self-indulgence, of being more interested in self than others, and this thought has continued to plague my endeavours without impeding them. However, the positive reception to such genuflection in a lecture delivered shortly after my retirement, and the suggestion from those in the audience and beyond that I should do more of the same, set me thinking how and what (Fine 2019).

Eventually, I came up with the idea of a series of pieces surveying what had happened or was happening in the areas in which I had contributed – how had economics, policy and broader corresponding discourses changed? For a variety of reasons and from a variety of prompts, this morphed into the current project of targeting volumes of previously published journal articles on select topics and reproducing these in each volume with a newly drafted update, together with individual commentaries on each of the pieces. This had the major advantage, necessity even, of allowing me to work on this initiative as and when severe constraints allowed.

I began my plan by reviewing all of my publications, allocating select contributions to what eventually turned out to be ten projected volumes – the themes were economics imperialism, development, mainstream economics, heterodox economics, Marxist political economy, neoliberalism, South Africa, and policy. I had anticipated, from this point on, it would be plain sailing, with the major burden coming from surveying more recent literature and material and intellectual developments around the topics covered for which there had been the Global Financial Crisis, the pandemic, climate change, neoliberalism, financialisation, (post)postmodernism, etc, whether these had already been engaged or not in the articles to be included in light of timing, oversight and/or relevance.

But things did not turn out as easily as anticipated even with the first volume. First of all, the initial collection on economics imperialism turned out to be too long for a single volume, once I got to a word count. So, I split out for a separate volume those pieces dealing in economic history. Interestingly, something similar had happened when drafting what turned out to be one, then, two books on economics imperialism (Milonakis and Fine 2009 and Fine and Milonakis 2009) with our projected volume, then two volumes, on economics and economic history remaining stillborn. Even then, the first volume for this series turned out too large and it, in turn, was split into two, with reorganisation across the first three volumes to suit.

Second, some articles were published so long ago that no convenient electronic copy existed for editing. I dealt with this initially by making as best an electronic version as I could from journal downloading, and then correcting the formatting and the like, tedious but manageable. Following this, though, I then had the idea of going back to original electronic typescripts and working directly with them. This created new problems. There were multiple versions, the final ones of which would have been copy-edited and proofed without necessarily a record of what had been done. Through this route, it would have been difficult if not impossible to reproduce the copy as published.

So, I decided to make a virtue out of a necessity by editing whatever I considered to be the best or easiest version available, also bearing in mind that my electronic files of pieces only ran back to the mid-1990s, with versions at that time being in WordPerfect rather than word, creating electronic glitches of their own in the conversions, alongside those glitches from wordifying pdfs. As a result, I cheated big time with the original articles, often taking longer versions, or combining different versions together, whilst also making both minor revisions for sense and more significant additions, especially to refer to other, possibly even later literature including my own – something which would often stand out by virtue of the *ex post* dating of referenced publications relative to the edited piece in which they appear.[1]

---

1 Relatively late on, I would on occasion put out as working papers the longer versions of published pieces, designating them as "The Director's Cut", a homage to Blade Runner and more.

However, these amendments breaching with the reproduction of 'as was' pieces have not been anywhere near approaching the updating of the articles as if they were being written now, a venture both obliquely and partially engaged in the overall introductions to the volumes and the preambles to each article. I have, though, been mindful of allowing the reader to gauge the nature of my contributions to the themes as they have evolved and, to that extent, also to locate their place in the more general intellectual evolution and context. What we do and do not say now is very much highlighted by comparison with what was said, or could be said, previously. I have a sense of responsibility to convey my thoughts, and memories, over what is now more than fifty years as an academic economist – I was there, I taught or I was taught, I debated, was involved or not in this and that, and will have my own take on the evolving ethos and its connections with what was going on.

Others will have different memories and takes and, searching through my files, I find that my memory is far from perfect (as is the file record itself). But economics has a notoriously short memory of itself and of the situated economy, and what it remembers is generally partial if not wrong. Hopefully, my past meanderings will prove useful to those with some sort of curiosity about the past and how it sheds light, if not influence, upon the present.[2] What I might, immodestly, be able to claim is that my memories may be somewhat richer than those of the standard economist for I have ranged widely over numbers of topics with commitment to interdisciplinarity. I suspect that many of those who know my work only do so in part – I am particularly mindful that economists, even the heterodox, do not tend to know of major contributions to the study of consumption and the critique of social capital for example. Yet, I am acutely conscious that, whilst the different areas on which I have worked do not always have immediate connections with one another, the value added across them, taken as a whole, is significant if not vital – even if the thrust of the first two, even three, volumes, critically assessing economics imperialism and economic history, is one of value subtracted through the interdisciplinarity deriving from mainstream economics.

Be all this as it may, introductory essay aside, the articles included in this volume are slightly revised, enhanced even, but remain much the same as their originals. This has created some problems, especially of repetition across the articles of some key elements, not least as each contribution is still required to be able to stand alone rather than taking the option of cutting core material

---

2 See Fitoussi (2022) for the suggestion that current mainstream economics sees itself as a successor to Keynesianism, as opposed to being more akin to its ante-diluvian predecessor – the better to be able to present itself as later and superior rather than a regression to the past.

and referring to other chapters. Such is the imperative of contemporary publishing with the feature of downloading parts of books and reading selectively. But, as it turns out, the repetition is not heavy duty and might help reinforce the most salient aspects for someone hardy enough to wade through more than a single chapter.

Last, and by no means least, I cannot begin to thank enough those who have supported me throughout my career, particularly co-authors and collaborators but ranging beyond this to family and friends. Appreciation must also go to David Fasenfest and Brill for making the venture possible, and for encouraging and supporting its coming to fruition.

References

Fine, B. (2019) "Post-Truth: an Alumni Economist's Perspective", *International Review of Applied Economics*, vol 33, no 4, pp. 542–67, shortened version of, SOAS Department of Economics Working Paper No. 219, 2019. https://www.soas.ac.uk/economics/research/workingpapers/file139489.pdf.

Fine, B. and D. Milonakis (2009) *From Economics Imperialism to Freakonomics: the Shifting Boundaries between Economics and Other Social Sciences*, London: Routledge.

Fitoussi, J.-P. (2022) "The New Speak and Economic Theory or How We Are Being Talked to", Sciences Po Economics, Discussion Paper, no 2022–02.

Milonakis, D. and B. Fine (2009) *From Political Economy to Economics: Method, the Social and the Historical in the Evolution of Economic Theory*, London: Routledge.

CHAPTER 1

Economics Imperialism as Intellectual Revolution

1   The Personal Background

In the mid-1990s, the coming together of a number of factors inspired my interest in what has subsequently become a major focus of research, economics imperialism (although some confusedly, and inappropriately, refer to economic imperialism) by which is meant the colonisation of the subject matter of other disciplines or (heterodox economics) by mainstream economics.[1] The long journey of economics imperialism scholarship to the present is outlined in what follows in this chapter, although also in the first two chapters of the next volume, with the details of my own participation marked by the chapters that follow across this and two further volumes. Section 2 of this chapter specifies how my account of economics imperialism was first conveyed as a 'revolution' in economic thought more than twenty-five years ago. It identifies what was already present, and continued, in my work in specifying economics imperialism as well as what was absent in this original contribution whether by omission or of necessity by virtue of later, unanticipated developments. Section 3 locates economics imperialism's early practitioners and implications prior to a second phase based on market imperfections as opposed to market perfection as a template for the non-economic. Following some (early) discussion of reactions to the hypothesis of economics imperialism, Section 4 suggests that, whilst critical commentary on economics imperialism peaked early in the second decade of the new millennium, the forward momentum of economics imperialism was sustained and was even accelerated by a third phase based on core economic principles plus whatever took the fancy through plunder from other social sciences. One of the main concerns of the next volume is to offer an explanation of why economics imperialism should be so strong and yet so little remarked after an initial period of both promotion and criticism. This explains my reference to a "watershed", not in economics imperialism itself which has proceeded and expanded apace to the present day, but the shift to lack of reference to it by its proponents and (potential) critics alike.

But why did I get motivated by the idea of economics imperialism initially? First was my move to the School of Oriental and African Studies, SOAS,

---

1   This chapter is newly drafted for this volume.

from Birkbeck College (each of the University of London and adjacent to one another) in 1992.[2] This plunged me into the world of development economics and, inevitably, for the more rounded approach to which I was inclined, to development studies. It also pushed me, more than willingly, to becoming (even) more interdisciplinary.

Second, from before the move to SOAS, I had been undertaking major research on consumption in general (beginning with consumer durables and then food in particular). These fields of study also pushed interdisciplinarity – did durables allow for female labour market participation and the demise of the male bread-winner syndrome, leading to attention to the social science and history of consumption and of labour markets – and why were we literally eating ourselves to early illnesses and deaths (health studies, sociology and social psychology, and politics and media and cultural studies not far away).[3]

Third, within economics itself, the monetarist reaction to Keynesianism, spearheaded by Milton Friedman, had given rise to the even more extreme New Classical Economics, led by Robert Lucas, in which markets were perceived to work perfectly and the state was inevitably thwarted (and at most/worst distorting) in its interventions by the responses of rational and, consequently, neutralising, individuals optimising on the basis of available information and their own given preferences. Crucially, this subordinated macroeconomics to microeconomics, the latter itself heavily reduced and problematic, reversing the previous relative status of the two leading fields of the discipline that had prevailed since the Keynesian revolution. As it were, 'how could micro serve macro' had become 'micro is macro'. The result was to reinforce the role of an increasingly reduced microeconomics and microeconomists as such, even where macroeconomic questions and implications were involved and especially where they were not.[4]

Fourth, and in particular, the leading role of Chicago in the new macro monetarism equally elevated the prominence of its longstanding, what we would now call neoliberal, microeconomics – and microeconomists, with Gary Becker to the fore (following in the footsteps of George Stigler who has been to Chicago microeconomics what Milton Friedman has been to its macro). Becker was a headbanging microeconomist – in my work on consumption, it was unsurprising to find him seeing addiction as simply reflecting an individual preference for short-term satisfaction over long-term pain, just as crime is

---

2 For a fuller autobiography of my life as an economist, see Fine (2001a, 2012 and 2019b).
3 See Bayliss and Fine (2021) for a retrospective on consumption through the system of provision approach.
4 On developments in micro and macro, see Fine (2016) and Fine and Dimakou (2016).

an individual cost-benefit analysis of rewards against penalties (Fine 1995).[5] But, significantly, he had a longstanding record of putative interdisciplinarity, holding a joint Chair in sociology and collaborating with leading rational choice sociologist, James Coleman. Indeed, Becker was a leading pioneer of what I came to call the old or first phase of economics imperialism. Reduce all economic and social phenomena to microeconomics – the optimising behaviour of individuals.

Fifth, the neoliberal economists, even if on the ascendancy, did not have it all their own way, not even within the mainstream (for which divergence from the new conventional neoliberal wisdoms very rapidly became to be seen as heterodox, especially by its own proponents even though it was less radical both analytically and policy-wise than perspectives from within the erstwhile Keynesian era). Indeed, the new orthodoxy was challenged by those who claimed individual markets do not work perfectly, and so neither does the macroeconomy. To the fore here was Joe Stiglitz who, as Chief Economist at the World Bank, became famous for launching the post Washington Consensus. Joe is, first and foremost, a mathematical economist – I had first met him in the early 1970s, as a student, at a scarcely attended mathematical economics seminar. He was at his most comfortable within the world of his models, which continue to inform, if not underpin, his thinking. But from this foundation, he has branched out in the scope of what he covers and the comfort with which he deploys his analytics in more informal discourses and policy implications.[6]

Sixth, and most significantly, many of these previous factors came together – consumption, labour markets, micro, macro, Becker, Stiglitz, development (World Bank and shift to post Washington Consensus), and interdisciplinarity – as I became aware of the rise of "social capital" as a category in use across the social sciences. Its leading proponent, Robert Putnam whom I subsequently dubbed the Ronald McDonald of social science, became the single most cited author across the social sciences in the 1990s. Bringing down social capital itself became an obsession of mine, variously pursued with vigour over

---

5   For Becker on crime, see Fleury (2020). Becker is seen as piggybacking on a broader movement for the redefinition of crime as a standalone problem of individual pathologies to be managed as opposed to a product of society's dysfunctions and lack of social provision and opportunities.

6   For more on Stiglitz and development economics more generally, and the role of the World Bank, see forthcoming volume on development. For Stiglitz as public intellectual, the most striking aspect of which is the inverse relationship between his prominence and his policy influence in practice, see Fridell (2011). The contrast with, say, Gary Becker and Richard Posner for example, let alone Milton Friedman, is striking (Fleury and Marciano 2013). See also Fine (2006) and Fine and Van Waeyenberge (2006).

twenty years or more.[7] As a result, social capital offered a leading, if blunt, edge in my understanding of economics imperialism as care had to be taken not to generalise from its origins and evolution to other topics and interdisciplinary relations. Unsurprisingly, in my contributions on economics imperialism, social capital has a stronger presence than is otherwise justified. But it did raise one particular initiating puzzle for me in getting to grips with economics imperialism – how could Becker and the radical sociologist, Pierre Bourdieu be deploying the same concept, social capital, and with what implications?[8]

The final factor, seventh, concerns my teaching, something I have always seen as substantially overlapping with research rather than to be got out of the way to provide space for research.[9] In particular, at SOAS, I took over responsibility for teaching all of the theory courses, essentially micro, macro and growth, for its development MScs (half of each degree), something entirely new to me in a developmental context. My approach, as always and apart from offering alternatives, was to cover the mainstream not only critically but also by locating it analytically, historically and contextually (including interdisciplinarity and policy) within the evolution of economic theory.

In other words, I was concerned to unravel what the hell was going on in economics in the, by then, well-established world of neoliberalism. Was it business as usual or not? How did theory reflect intellectual, ideological and material developments. At most, history of economic thought as a field within the discipline offered very few answers, as it had become more or less marginalised, so much so that, subsequently, its practitioners institutionally removed themselves – lock, stock and barrel – to the history of science in order to get a hearing and some status. Indeed, from the perspective of those with a critical attitude to the mainstream, and an inclination to offer alternatives, it was so bad and so obviously so (in methodology, methods, interdisciplinarity, conceptualisation, realism, even its own technical assumptions, etc) that it simply needed to be discarded. Much the same has been especially true of those entering the economic domain from other social sciences whose understanding of the nature of economics has tended to be simplistic, if not false,

---

7 See especially my two books (Fine 2001b and 2010 and, most recently, Fine 2023).
8 I never met either Becker or Bourdieu. But Bourdieu's son published a French edition of *Marx's Capital* (Fine and Saad Filho 2016).
9 Apart from *Marx's Capital*, the first edition of which was published in 1975, with Fine and Saad Filho (2016), the sixth edition – arising out of teaching a course on theories of distribution across the history of economic thought (across Marx and others) – my next two books reflect these aspects of teaching as research, *Economic Theory and Ideology* and *Theories of the Capitalist Economy* (Fine 1980 and 1982b).

misrepresenting it in its weakest versions, and as unchanging, in order to be able to move on to some sort of political economy or otherwise.[10]

2 The Revolution Displayed

This is the context within which I made my first explicit contribution to the study of economics imperialism (Fine 1997). This is reproduced as Chapter 4 of this volume. But it is preceded, oddly at first sight, by two chapters, concerned with and around rent theory, which date from more than a decade before economics imperialism, as such, first came to my attention (Fine 1982a and 1983). Why do these two chapters appear here at all?

The answer is primarily because they offer insights into the nature and history of economics imperialism and can be seen to cover unwitting contributions to economics imperialism before it was acknowledged as such. This is explained in detail in their preambles. But, in a nutshell, the marginalist revolution was responsible for taking the historical and the social out of economics or, more exactly, political economy. Understandably, this was neither immediate nor without resistance and discomfort in terms of both the consequences and the inertia of continuing traditions.

One of the latter concerned the role of land and rent (agriculture as well as mining). The problem with marginalism is that it treats all factors of production in exactly the same way so that analytically the distinctions between land and other factor inputs, capital and labour in particular, are more or less discarded. This is so across both their economic and social/political roles and their attachments to economics and social classes, equally reduced relative to classical political economy by methodological individualism. As a result, the forward march of marginalism entailed discarding these aspects along the way and, especially, distribution theory – rent, profits and wages are just prices.

With the benefits of hindsight, it can now be seen that the marginalist revolution as a process paved the way for the bringing back in of the social and historical, both by subject matter and by colonising other disciplines by virtue of having taken out the social and historical and consolidated its separation from other disciplines. But it also served as a sort of economics imperialism

---

10 The nature of, and the weaknesses in, the mainstream are selectively covered in a forthcoming volume. Subsequently, with Dimitris Milonakis, a major effort was made to situate mainstream economics in its own evolution and, especially, in its relationship to other social sciences. Milonakis and Fine (2009) and Fine and Milonakis (2009). These won the Myrdal and Deutscher Prizes, respectively.

in reverse since so much was being taken out rather than, as later, being put back in. In a way, a snapshot of early marginalism looks in many ways like, and anticipates, its future both promoting marginalist principles and their implications whilst seeking to hold onto what these suggest should be discarded. Consequently, Chapter 2 reveals these conundrums in the context of historical debates over rent theory (as applied to agriculture) as rent theory as marginalism was being extended beyond land to every factor of production; and Chapter 3 does something similar for a debate over rents of mining and whether a royalty as such is distinctive from a rent.

These two chapters on landed property, then, set a different context for economics imperialism than my own personal engagement with the history of economic thought except, at the time, I was unwittingly unravelling something in the prehistory of economics imperialism. Significantly, my first witting contribution appears in *Capital & Class*, the journal of the Conference of Socialist Economists, in which I had previously long played an active role, under a section entitled *Polemic*. So, it was very clear in the minds of the editors of the journal and my own, that the hypothesis of economics imperialism was novel and controversial, given the common presumption was, as to some degree already indicated, that economics is unchanging and, especially, is marred by its lack of engagement with other social sciences (not least because it is irreducibly asocial and ahistorical in its conceptualisations).

Subsequently, after the passage of just a few decades, I suspect that the fact of economics imperialism is no longer controversial in the sense that everyone can see it everywhere if they care to look, including both mainstream economists for its potential, and their heterodox critics for its legion deficiencies. But this presents a paradox and, personally, a bitter intellectual disappointment, insofar as critical attention to economics imperialism has been extremely muted, as discussed at length in the second volume in detail.

For the moment, though, consider what is and what is not present in my first foray into economics imperialism (Fine 1997). First, to the fore, is what was termed fortress economics, a term, also disappointingly not taken up by others, to symbolise the sacrosanct elements of the mainstream.[11] Subsequently,

---

11   Whilst recognising that there can be sound reasons for carefully distinguishing mainstream, neoclassical and orthodox economics, I will use the terms interchangeably. The reader may also have noticed, what has often been pointed out to me, that I love lists, possibly as a result of my training, more or less exclusively from the age of fourteen to twenty, in mathematics. Students tend to like them as an aid to learning but others do not, especially if of a literary bent.

this has been renamed, with no increase in popularity and prominence than fortress, as TA² to represent the intersection between the mainstream's technical apparatus and technical architecture, TA1 and TA2, respectively. Across these we have production and utility functions, individual optimising, and the focus on the efficiency properties of equilibrium.[12]

Second, in order, again unsuccessfully, to signal the significance of the extent and speed at which economics imperialism was proceeding, reference is made to a "revolution" in economics. Whilst Keynesian and monetarist revolutions would have been closer to mind, the marginalist revolution of the 1870s is taken as critical point of departure. Specifically, it is seen to have reduced mainstream economics relative to the political economy of the classics and Marx, taking out the social and historical, and confining the discipline of economics to the study of supply and demand, quantity and price, in the context of a supposed market without underpinnings in broader structures, relations, processes and agencies. Methods have also tended to be confined to axiomatic, mathematical modelling in what Mirowski (1989 and 1992) has termed physics envy. In later specifications of economics imperialism (Fine 2002, 2008 and 2019a), the marginalist revolution and its aftermath would be characterised as an "implosion", to garner the properties and implications of the fortress, from which a subsequent "explosion" could be launched across the social sciences by virtue of its application and modification through bringing back into economics what had been left out in order to establish its TA².

Third, two broad ways of colonising other disciplines are pinpointed. One, the intensive, is by addressing and transforming the subject matter within the discipline of economics itself, and the other, the extensive, is through exerting influence within other disciplines (cliometrics for the latter for example, and human capital straddling both avenues). Examples were given in this first article but these have now expanded and consolidated out of all earlier proportions, if unevenly and in different ways across topics and disciplines in light of the subject matter and how and to what extent topics and disciplines are amenable and open to economics imperialism given continuing traditions across the social sciences (as well as broader material and ideological factors).

Fourth, whilst the fortress/TA² has remained sacrosanct, it has been subject only later to what has been termed "suspension" in which it is complemented by adding other explanatory factors from across the social sciences (Fine 2008

---

12   The TA² terminology was proposed by my PhD student, Humam Al-Jazaeri (2009), in his study of technical change and mainstream deficiencies in how it is understood.

and 2009).[13] This has intensified the depth and breadth of economics imperialism, in part by making it more palatable to other disciplines – look, we take your concerns seriously and do not exclusively reduce them to our core concerns. Initially, though, as reflected in this first contribution on economics imperialism, and for a decade or more subsequently, economics imperialism seemed to be confined to the consequences of single-minded individuals committed to, or in the context of, TA^2, if in the context of market imperfections.

Fifth, the distinction is drawn between the Becker-type, old economics imperialism and the potentially more invasive, new form based on responses to asymmetric information in particular and market imperfections in general. Again, palatability to non-economists is strengthened, if in the weak form of squaring the circle of incorporating the social, the collective, the institutional, the non-market or apparently non-rational, optimising behaviour on the basis of rational pursuit of self-interest in the context of market imperfections. More significantly, the distinction between market-perfect and market-imperfect forms of economics imperialism would later become the basis for periodising economics imperialism into its old and new forms. Subsequently, the current form of economics imperialism has involved the "suspension" of TA^2 (or, more exactly, its being retained and rejected at one and the same time by being combined with other, generally, incompatible considerations – are individuals rational or not for example and, if both, where are the boundaries drawn and made analytically consistent). As the "revolution" in economics, in its designs on other disciplines and non-economic subject matter, gathered pace, market imperfections (and the prominence of Stiglitz, in particular) came to the fore through the passage from the old to the new economics imperialism.

Sixth is noted the conundrum for heterodox economists of whether, how and how much to compromise with the mainstream in order to engage with it and gain a foothold for alternatives. This is both a matter of substantive content and strategy in teaching, research and professional status and advancement. Given the nature of the mainstream's institutionalised intolerance of alternatives – through control of jobs, curricula and journals – whatever the motives and postures of individuals, dissent will always tend to be self-selecting in terms of compromising with, and even becoming incorporated within, the mainstream.

---

13 To some degree Stilwell (2023, p. 191) captures the notion of suspension through suggesting, "the neoclassical origins have continued to operate rather like a gravitational force", with colonised disciplines, fields and concepts orbiting accordingly.

Finally, there is some discussion of the poverty of the mainstream, the nature and weakness of heterodox economics, the material conditions that have promoted economics imperialism, and the extent of dissatisfaction by students with economics, more through flight than through dissent. Significantly, the notion that economics imperialism, or economics more generally, is a simple reflection of material conditions or of vested interests (this is what capitalism and capitalists need now in light of its prospects or crises) is firmly rejected, not as an influence altogether but one that is tempered, even dominated by, internal logical developments within the discipline itself. After all, if you are after policy advice rather than ideological support, your last port of call might well be the discipline of economics. For it is surely inconsistent to argue both that economics is not grounded in realities and that it can serve as a sound source of vested interest policy – although it can and does both set the terms in which policy is (mis)represented and squeeze out consideration of alternative ways of framing policy.

It is more important that these issues appear at all as opposed to the extent that the superficial commentaries at the time, in a polemic, were and remain relevant. At that time, heterodoxy was well past the influence of its sixties heyday and the millennial eruption of student discontent with the mainstream and the demand for pluralism, especially following the Global Financial Crisis (GFC) of 2007/8, was a distant prospect – not least as Keynesianism had given way to increasingly formalised and extreme versions of monetarism, with mainstream market imperfections economics primarily occupying the terrain of dissent. Perversely, though, the GFC fuelled both the demand for pluralism and student popularity for mainstream economics reflecting, respectively, dissatisfaction with what was being taught and acknowledgement that it might provide a more secure route to well-rewarded employment.

Consequently, a major motivation at that time for me was not so much that economics would rip across the social sciences but that it would remain uncontested at home, within its fortress – with the flight of more critical students to more realistic and compelling disciplines without the need to command testing technical material from within the discipline. Why go to all the trouble of studying for a degree that offered so much by way of lack of critical content and space for independent reasoning? As a result, the prospect was for there to be limited renewal of supply of those who could both command the mainstream and retain critical and alternative approaches.[14]

---

14   This was a major reason for setting up IIPPE, the International Initiative for Promoting Political Economy, iippe.org.

3   From Becker to Bourdieu via Kuhn and Coleman

In sum, in terms of a short, initial polemic, this first piece on economics imperialism can be considered to have got it pretty much correct, with some considerable insight into its nature, content and dynamic, upon which future contributions would build, in part in light of developments in and around the discipline, including heterodox economics.

The next two contributions are still marked by my own initial coming to terms with economics imperialism as a revolution in thought within and around economics as a discipline. Fine (1999a), reproduced as Chapter 5, goes into some detail into the conundrum raised earlier concerning the common use of the term "social capital" by Pierre Bourdieu and Gary Becker (and his sociology counterpart, James Coleman, at the University of Chicago). Remarkably, this seemed to allow for a dialogue of the deaf so flexible is conceptualisation around social capital, prompting a jointly organised conference with published proceedings (Bourdieu and Coleman (eds) 1991). Yet, this initiative is an anomaly, given the differences in methodology, conceptualisation, theory and methods involved, whether for social capital or otherwise. And, for economics or otherwise, there could be and was only one winner in the battle over what is social capital and how it should be used – mainstream social science, with beaten alternatives excluded or incorporated as a form of repressive tolerance.

Nonetheless, some explanation is offered for the conceptual overlap in use of social capital in terms of the way in which the fluidity of capital itself – across structures, relations, processes and agencies – gives rise to the illusion that more or less anything can be capital. In Becker's case, there is a "natural" starting point in treating capital as a thing, not least so that it can appear as a variable in a production function. As a result, with the exception of social capital which stands for everything else that cannot be explained by the personally-owned, the structures, relations and processes of capitalism are reduced by Becker to capital as a thing around which the individual agent optimises as if exchange were universally present. By contrast, Bourdieu is extremely sensitive to the differences in structures, relations, processes and agencies (and cultures) under and through which different activities proceed (and constructs a language of differentiated habituses and fields to accommodate them and to address the reproduction and exercise of power). However, despite this rich variegation, Bourdieu falls under the illusion that different activities, including the non-economic, do have some market-like equivalence with one another as forms of capital (the symbolic, cultural and educational for example).

In short, in addressing social capital, a leading example of economics imperialism is brought to the fore as are some of economics imperialism's more general features. Whilst human capital is a more longstanding and, even now, a more commonplace illustration of economics imperialism, and its evolution, than social capital, the latter's rise is part and parcel of the emergence of what Baron and Hannan (1994) had already dubbed a plethora of capitals. If economics wants to address some aspect of social life, call it a capital and away we go as there is a well-established TA² for dealing with capital (in a production function). As a result, economics imperialism can bring back in (something that was to become so frequently referenced in my work that I gave it an acronym, BBI) what was previously omitted and putatively become interdisciplinary.

What has more recently become a leading example of such capitalisation upon conceptualisation is the rise of natural capital to the fore even if it has longstanding traditions. How useful to reduce environmental relations to stocks (and flows) that can be unduly depleted as a result of market imperfections whether as externalities or vested interests attached to monopolisation. Like social capital, such use of natural capital has its origins both within economics and other disciplines. As a result, with these examples, there are complex and variable resolutions around how and to what extent economics exerts its influence over the other social sciences and, to some extent, vice-versa (although economics is not receptive to reciprocal influence other than as a source of plunder, see discussion on 'reverse imperialism' in the second volume). Contributions from within the other disciplines can even be hostile in their overt perceptions of economics (as insufficiently ecological and environmental for example) even as they fall under its sway.

Significantly, each of social capital and natural capital are single terms for a huge variety of different phenomena that fall under the rubrics of the 'social' and the 'natural' – with much overlap between the two and covering more or less everything. In case of social capital, with hundreds of potential variables, these can be readily fitted into multiple regressions and, thereby, implicitly derive a production function for social outcomes, with the estimated coefficients (in log form) being the elasticity of impact of the social variable on outcomes. For policy variables, you have a machine for assessing impacts against one another. In general, such formalities are not engaged in the social capital policy literature (although there was a study suggesting the building of mental institutions in locations where social capital is low) but there is a strong parallel with new growth theory. It too has hundreds of variables from Barro-type regressions, estimated coefficients for which there are potentially policy elasticities, and these have been deployed as such by the World Bank in its models for structural adjustment.[15]

Thus, each of social capital and new growth theory opens up the terrain of the social sciences to economics imperialism, given its heavy and increasing reliance upon statistical methods, in the lead of, and more heavily than, most other disciplines. In this light, Chapter 5 begins to offer an account of why economics imperialism was emerging at the time that it did. But it does so almost exclusively within the world of ideas – the longstanding illusions created by capital whether as a thing (with a marginal product and, ultimately, marginal utility for Becker) or as contextualised relations and activities with some capital-like equivalence between them (as for Bourdieu). Such reliance upon commodity (or, more exactly, capital) fetishism as Marx would have dubbed it, only goes so far. It leaves open why economics imperialism should have been so characteristic of the neoliberal period since the illusions of everything as capital are as longstanding as capitalism itself – although some explanation is offered by reference to the retreats from the excesses of postmodernism and the wish of the social sciences to "get real" in light of increasingly unavoidable material developments in contemporary capitalism, namely erosion and privatisation of public services, austerity, globalisation, ultimately financialisation, etc.

I return to this issue in Chapter 6, reproduced from Fine (2001c), but it is also primarily concerned with the world of ideas, specifically whether and in what ways should the changes taking place in, and around, economics (imperialism) be considered revolutionary. To do so, close attention is paid to the strengths and weaknesses of Thomas Kuhn's notion of scientific revolution, specifically in the context of social science in general and economics in particular, even though Kuhn was predominantly concerned with the natural sciences. Whilst the approach is deemed to be flawed for a variety of reasons,

---

15 For the new growth theory, see Fine and Dimakou (2016, p. 63) where, for the World Bank, it is reported, "Literally, in some studies, increase the number of telephone lines per population, and growth will go up by so much". Interestingly, in my own early, critical survey of new growth theory, the abstract points to anticipation of its role in economics imperialism in its newer phase, just as old growth theory reflects the old (treat production as if a simple function) (Fine 2000, p. 245): "A critical assessment is made of endogenous growth theory from the perspective of recent developments within economics as a discipline. These include its increasing mathematical formalisation, its focus upon microfoundations, the casual use of econometrics to test models, and the incorporation of factors that have traditionally been outside mainstream economics ... The generalisation from exogenous growth theory is, however, associated with even more extreme assumptions and analytical distance from the socioeconomic processes of growth itself".

especially in framing and explaining in terms of shifts from one paradigm of "normal" science to another – if, indeed, this is the way science, social or otherwise, proceeds – the application of some of its key aspects to economics imperialism are revealing. This is especially so in the extent to which it incorporates: a world vision (market perfections or not, with or without non-market factors); exemplars (leading applications, derived from TA² that serve as templates for other applications); and a community of scientists (the orthodoxy and their professional stranglehold on the discipline at the expense of alternatives from heterodoxy which is marginalised).

Across both Chapters 5 and 6, the decline and fall of the centrality of postmodernism across the social sciences (with the notable exception of economics, including heterodoxy to a major degree) is remarked, with two implications drawn. The first is that irrespective of being in, or depending upon, its first or second phase, contributions to economics imperialism necessarily tended to steer clear of the other disciplines or topics where the social construction of meaning is involved. This is hardly surprising for an approach that takes the nature of, or options for, production, consumption, individuals and technology as rigidly fixed, certainly as opposed to being open to innovative reinterpretation by agents/agencies themselves. Second, even though its non-overlap with postmodernism had eased relations with some of the social sciences through inhabiting parallel worlds, where there was engagement with economics imperialism, the more rounded and less superficial alternatives from the other social sciences involved – across methodology, methods, concepts and theories – rendered the possibility, if not certainty, of hostile reactions to economics imperialism.

In the context of the turn across the social sciences to understand the nature and dynamics of neoliberalism and globalisation, and a focus on pressing material realities, this offered some optimism in terms of contesting not only economics imperialism but also the subject matter of economics itself through the renewal of political economy. However, any such optimism needed to be set against what was an increasingly severe domination of economics as a discipline by the mainstream not least, in the UK for example, as a result of the impact of research assessment exercises (Lee 2007, Lee et al 2013 and Stockhammer et al 2021).[16] Such considerations, alongside the nature and dynamics of other disciplines, inevitably gave rise, and still gives rise, to

---

16   And the UK is a place where heterodoxy is relatively strong, if absolutely weak within economics as a discipline (see Aigner 2021).

what might today be termed the variegated impact of economics imperialism by topic and discipline.

4 The Revolution Betrayed by Way of Concluding Remarks

The final chapter in this volume, based on Fine (1999b) concerns my response to some early critical commentary from heterodoxy to the hypothesis of economics imperialism, starting with Thompson (1997 and 1999), the latter itself a response to myself which I address in the preamble to the chapter.

Thompson is sceptical of the scale and scope of economics imperialism. Against the evidence of the time, let alone from later work, the contributions from Thompson seem to be suggesting that I consider that economics imperialism will swamp the social sciences. This is not the case as I am already very clear that, although the number of cases is expanding with some being renewed – as old is displaced by new economics imperialism – outcomes are variegated by discipline and topic with considerable no go areas especially where critical deconstruction of the meanings of subjects/objects of analysis are present. Perversely, Thompson's interventions, and a much later commentary on both Thompson and myself by Nielsen and Morgan (2005), reflect an early anticipation of at least a lack of warmth for, even a denial of, economics imperialism, and certainly limited engagement against it despite my best efforts. The reasons for this have always puzzled and disappointed me. But detailed discussion of the issue, as mentioned, is postponed until the following volume on economics imperialism.

Nonetheless, as Chapter 7 was being drafted, I was already on a roll in terms of the number of citations I could make to my own work on economics imperialism, amounting to no less than nineteen, across different topics, disputes and disciplines.[17] For a time, it seemed as if my own contributions and mission to expose economics imperialism critically would gather participation and further momentum from others. Collaboration with Dimitris Milonakis, in particular, gave rise by 2009 to the two highly praised and previously mentioned prize-winning books, with the origins and incidence of economics imperialism as their focus. We also located new developments within (the new) economic history, the rise of cliometrics from 1957, in terms of economics imperialism

---

17   Ultimately, however obliquely, I have published almost eighty pieces that can considered to be on, or relevant for, economics imperialism, see the Appendix to this volume.

with a number of corresponding contributions, see the forthcoming volume on economic history (and economics imperialism).

However, these efforts to bring economics imperialism to the attention of heterodox economists, and to social scientists engaging in political economy, proved unsuccessful beyond what appeared to be a small window of opportunity that lasted for at most a decade or so, during the period when mainstream economics was explicitly promoting, and priding itself, on its economics imperialism in the crudest forms. As a result, I have described this period of (critical) attention to, and debate over, economics imperialism as leading to a watershed after which it gathered momentum in practice without being recognised and designated as such. This is, however, to anticipate the subject matter of the second volume on economics imperialism.

References

Aigner, E. (2021) "Global Dynamics and Country-Level Development in Academic Economics: an Explorative Cognitive-Bibliometric Study", Department of Socio-Economics, Institute for Multi-Level Governance & Development, Vienna University of Economics and Business, Social-Ecological Discussion Paper in Economics, no 7, https://www-sre.wu.ac.at/sre-disc/sre-disc-2021_07.pdf.

Al-Jazaeri, H. (2009) "Interrogating Technical Change through the History of Economic Thought in the Context of Latecomers' Industrial Development: the Case of the South Korean Microelectronics, Auto and Steel Industries", unpublished PhD thesis, University of London.

Arestis, P. and M. Sawyer (eds) (2001) *A Biographical Dictionary of Dissenting Economists*, Aldershot: Edward Elgar, second edition.

Baron, J. and M. Hannan (1994) "The Impact of Economics on Contemporary Sociology", *Journal of Economic Literature*, vol XXXII, no 3, pp. 1111–46, reproduced in Swedberg (ed.) (1996), pp. 530–66.

Bayliss, K. and B. Fine (2021) *A Guide to the Systems of Provision Approach: Who Gets What, How and Why*, Basingstoke: Palgrave MacMillan.

Bourdieu, P. and J. Coleman (eds) (1991) *Social Change for a Changing Society*, Boulder: Westview Press.

Damodaran, S., S. Gupta, S. Mitra and D. Sinha (eds) (2023) *Development, Transformations and the Human Condition: Volume in Honour of Professor Jayati Ghosh*, New Delhi: Routledge, forthcoming.

Decker, S., W. Elsner and S. Flechtner (eds) (2018) *Advancing Pluralism in Teaching Economics*, London: Routledge.

Fine, B. (1980) *Economic Theory and Ideology*, London: Edward Arnold.

Fine, B. (1982a) "Landed Property and the Distinction between Royalty and Rent", *Land Economics*, vol 58, no 3, pp. 338–350.

Fine, B. (1982b) *Theories of the Capitalist Economy*, London: Edward Arnold.

Fine, B. (1983) "The Historical Theory of Rent and Price Reconsidered", *Australian Economic Papers*, vol 22, no 40, pp. 132–143. See also Chapter 2.

Fine, B. (1995) "From Political Economy to Consumption", in Miller (ed.) (1995), pp. 127–163.

Fine, B. (1997) "The New Revolution in Economics", *Capital and Class*, no 61, Spring, pp. 143–48. See also Chapter 4.

Fine, B. (1999a) "From Becker to Bourdieu: Economics Confronts the Social Sciences", *International Papers in Political Economy*, vol 5, no 3, pp. 1–43. See also Chapter 5.

Fine, B. (1999b) "A Question of Economics: Is It Colonising the Social Sciences?", *Economy and Society*, vol 28, no 3, pp. 403–25. See also Chapter 7.

Fine, B. (2000) "Endogenous Growth Theory: a Critical Assessment", *Cambridge Journal of Economics*, vol 24, no 2, pp. 245–65, a shortened and amended version of identically titled, SOAS Working Paper, No 80, February 1998, pp. 1–49.

Fine, B. (2001a) "Ben Fine", in Arestis and Sawyer (eds) (2001), pp. 172–79.

Fine, B. (2001b) *Social Capital versus Social Theory: Political Economy and Social Science at the Turn of the Millennium*, London: Routledge.

Fine, B. (2001c) "Economics Imperialism as Kuhnian Revolution?", *International Papers in Political Economy*, vol 8, no 2, pp. 1–58. See also Chapter 6.

Fine, B. (2002) "'Economic Imperialism': a View from the Periphery", *Review of Radical Political Economics*, vol 34, no 2, pp. 187–201.

Fine, B. (2006) "Joseph Stiglitz", in Simon (ed.) (2006), pp. 247–52.

Fine, B. (2008) "Vicissitudes of Economics Imperialism", *Review of Social Economy*, vol 66, no 2, pp. 235–40.

Fine, B. (2009) "The Economics of Identity and the Identity of Economics?", *Cambridge Journal of Economics*, vol 33, no 2, pp. 175–91.

Fine, B. (2010) *Theories of Social Capital: Researchers Behaving Badly*, London: Pluto.

Fine, B. (2012) "Being Radical or Radical Being?", *Review of Radical Political Economics*, vol 44, no 1, pp. 100–106.

Fine, B. (2016) *Microeconomics: a Critical Companion*, London: Pluto.

Fine, B. (2019a) "Economics and Interdisciplinarity: One Step Forward, N Steps Back?" *Revista Crítica de Ciências Sociais*, no 119, pp. 131–48.

Fine, B. (2019b) "Post-Truth: an Alumni Economist's Perspective", *International Review of Applied Economics*, vol 33, no 4, pp. 542–67, shortened version of, SOAS Department of Economics Working Paper No. 219, 2019, https://www.soas.ac.uk/economics/research/workingpapers/file139489.pdf.

Fine, B. (2023) "Social Capital: The Indian Connection", in Damodaran et al (eds) (2023), forthcoming.

Fine, B. and O. Dimakou (2016) *Macroeconomics: a Critical Companion*, London: Pluto.
Fine, B. and D. Milonakis (2009) *From Economics Imperialism to Freakonomics: the Shifting Boundaries between Economics and Other Social Sciences*, London: Routledge.
Fine, B. and A. Saad Filho (2016) *Marx's 'Capital'*, London: Pluto, French (fifth) edition, Paris: Raisons d'Agir, 2013.
Fine, B. and E. Van Waeyenberge (2006) "Correcting Stiglitz: From Information to Power in the World of Development", in Leys and Panitch (eds) (2005), pp. 146–68.
Fleury, J.-B. (2020) "Crime", in Fontaine and Pooley (eds) (2020), pp. 258–89.
Fleury, J.-B. and A. Marciano (2013) "Becker and Posner: Freedom of Speech and Public Intellectualship", *History of Political Economy*, vol 45, no 5, Supplement, pp. 254–278.
Fridell, G. (2011) "Joseph Stiglitz: the Citizen-Bureaucrat and the Limits of Legitimate Dissent", *New Political Science*, vol 33, no 2, pp. 169–88.
Lee, F. (2007) "The Research Assessment Exercise, the State and the Dominance of Mainstream Economics in British Universities", *Cambridge Journal of Economics*, vol 31, no 2, pp. 309–25.
Lee, F., X. Pham and G. Gu (2013) "The UK Research Assessment Exercise and the Narrowing of UK Economics", *Cambridge Journal of Economics*, vol 37, no 4, pp. 693–717.
Leys, C. and L. Panitch (eds) (2005) *Telling the Truth, Socialist Register*, 2006, London: Merlin Press.
Milonakis, D. and B. Fine (2009) *From Political Economy to Economics: Method, the Social and the Historical in the Evolution of Economic Theory*, London: Routledge.
Mirowski, P. (1989) *More Heat than Light: Economics as Social Physics, Physics as Nature's Economics*, Cambridge: Cambridge University Press.
Mirowski, P. (1992) "Do Economists Suffer from Physics Envy?", *Finnish Economic Papers*, vol 5, no 1, pp. 61–68.
Nielsen, P. and J. Morgan (2005) "No New Revolution in Economics? Taking Thompson and Fine Forward", *Economy and Society*, vol 34, no 1, pp. 51–75.
Simon, D. (ed.) (2006) *Fifty Key Thinkers on Development*, London: Routledge, second edition, 2019.
Stilwell, F. (2023) "The Future for Political Economy: Towards Unity in Diversity?", *Review of Political Economy*, vol 35, no 1, pp. 189–210.
Stockhammer, E., Q. Dammerer and S. Kapur (2021) "The Research Excellence Framework 2014, Journal Ratings and the Marginalisation of Heterodox Economics", *Cambridge Journal of Economics*, vol 45, no 2, pp. 243–69.
Thompson, G. (1997) "Where Goes Economics and the Economies", *Economy and Society*, vol 26, no 4, pp. 599–610.
Thompson, G. (1999) "How Far Should We Be Afraid of Conventional Economics? A Response to Ben Fine", *Economy and Society*, vol 28, no 3, pp. 426–33.

CHAPTER 2

The Historical Approach to Rent and Price Theory Reconsidered

Postscript as Personal Preamble

> Hegel remarks somewhere that all great world-historic facts and personages appear, so to speak, twice. He forgot to add: the first time as tragedy, the second time as farce.
>
> MARX (1852)[1]

Lawson (2013)[2] proved a provocation to heterodox economics, and to orthodoxy if it cared to take notice, for suggesting there is no such thing today as neoclassical economics. There are two main pillars to his argument – one is that neoclassical economics, as it was first defined by Thorstein Veblen in the early years of the marginalist revolution, is certainly not what either the self-proclaimed neoclassical economists of today or their critics have in mind. This is because Veblen saw the marginalists at the time as caught upon a tension between relying upon both marginalist principles and broader considerations of an evolving economy and society. The second pillar, and what must be suspected to be the motivation for his piece, is to offer an alternative definition of the mainstream in terms of its (lack of) social ontology, not least in its being determinist and closed, and primarily dependent upon mathematical modelling.

As is apparent from other contributions, not least explicitly in the following volume on economics imperialism and the one on heterodoxy, I am in

---

1 The tragedy in this case is the impact upon interdisciplinarity of the marginalist revolution and the transition from political economy to economics, an implosion. The farce is the renewal of interdisciplinarity with the emergence of economics imperialism, an explosion, see below. Marx, after a two-sentence filling out of concrete examples from recent French history, offers two further stunning quote(able)s, each equally applicable to marginalism and economics imperialism: "Men make their own history, but they do not make it as they please; they do not make it under self-selected circumstances, but under circumstances existing already, given and transmitted from the past. The tradition of all dead generations weighs like a nightmare on the brains of the living".
2 See Lawson (2021) for a restatement.

profound disagreement with Lawson although there is much common ground including especially with regard to his ontological critique of the mainstream. However, I do not consider that mainstream economics can be defined by its ontology alone but needs to be specified much more fully, taking into account different aspects, not least what it studies, how, with what conceptualisations and techniques, and how it is taught and deployed. As I would parody, go into any classroom and you will find neoclassical economics is alive and well. Further, mainstream economics has evolved through three phases of economics imperialism, with the last being dependent upon both its core technical apparatus and architecture, TA^{2},[3] (together making up optimisation upon the basis of utility and production functions, leading to considerations of equilibrium and efficiency) together with the addition of whatever considerations take the fancy of the practising economist, giving rise to the augmentation if not "suspension" of TA^{2}. From Lawson's perspective, this means that the mainstream has no particular theoretical commitments as opposed to its social ontology which allows it to go wherever it chooses subject, presumably, to initiative and acceptance. By contrast, looking at the same developments in a different way, my position is that the third phase of economics imperialism involves departure from, or supplement of, but not abandonment of core analytical principles.

In this respect, the contemporary mainstream might be considered to be closer to the Veblenesque notion of neoclassical economics than is acknowledged, even if lacking appropriate ontological underpinnings. Indeed, Lawson's musings over the nature of the mainstream in the immediate aftermath of the marginalist revolution, through the prism of Veblen's interpretations of them, is not contested here. But they are seen through a different perspective and for a different reason.

The difference in perspective is provided by the hypothesis of economics imperialism. For, whilst this is based upon the bringing back in from the 1950s onwards of the social and the historical, these had previously to be taken out in order to establish TA^{2}. And, this taking out in order to be able to bring back in, was far from immediate, overnight as it were. It was a process that only began with the marginalist revolution of the 1870s, taking decades both to complete and to establish itself as the norm. To some extent, this will have been a result of disciplinary inertia – holding onto the residues of classical political economy, its concerns and methods. But it was also a holding on to what would

---

[3] See Chapter 1 in this volume, and many chapters in the second, forthcoming volume on economics imperialism.

otherwise be lost – the historical and social in general but the specifics of these in terms of the role and significance of classes, institutions, culture and traditions, etc. All of these had to be sacrificed to the dull analytical compulsion of the optimising individual and disembodied market supply and demand. It was against these losses that the Veblenesque neoclassicals were reacting by retaining what they could, even if inconsistently with marginalist principles.[4]

To define neoclassical economics in Veblenesque terms is, then, to do so in its dirty form, hardly appropriate for what it was to become in its pure form (general equilibrium and its analytical underpinnings) followed by a renewal of its dirty form with the bringing back in of what had been taken out. This is what offers the different reason for these considerations. For they suggest that the immediate post-marginalism period can be seen as not defining neoclassical economics (in Veblenesque terms, never to be sustained) but as a sort of process of economics imperialism in reverse (not to be confused with reverse economics imperialism, the putative appropriation of economics by other disciplines, on which see next volume on economics imperialism). For, take snapshots of the economics of this period and you will find greater or lesser, faster or slower discarding of the principles of political economy as those of marginalism are embraced, the taking out rather than the bringing back in, an implosion within economics as opposed to an explosion out of it, see especially following volume on economics imperialism.

This is illustrative of a much more general point about the history of economic thought and its relationship to mainstream economics in the wake of the marginalist revolution. The latter putatively reduces the economy to the market as if it, and its optimising individuals, were or could be disembedded from the social and the structural and, equally, from the sociological, the political, the legal, the cultural and the institutional. But the embedded nature of markets is more or less unavoidable, whatever the pretenses to the contrary, most notably in the way in which labour, financial and other markets work, let alone landed property, and in whose interests and with what language – with rents pointing to the presence of landed property, wages to the terms under which the capacity to work is bought and sold, and profit and interest to the terms under which capitalist and financial enterprises function. As a result, even before economics imperialism proper – the deliberate assault upon the social, etc, on the basis of purely economic principles – there is inevitably going to be

---

4 This is brought out by Pratten (2023) in Lawsonesque terms with a particular focus on Marshall and, to a lesser extent, John Neville Keynes, Maynard's father. The tensions in Marshall have long been acknowledged, not least by Marshall himself, but see also Milonakis and Fine (2009).

some degree of unwitting, accidental, ante-diluvian economics imperialism, as economists seek to address, what is for them, the non-economic (or political economy) aspects of the economy. In other words, economics imperialism is always at least latent even if its primitive excursions do not appear as such. Whether by lingering attachment to elements of classical political economy from the nineteenth century at the outset of marginalism, or arbitrary application of new (i.e. previously discarded) principles in its later trajectories in reaching beyond the dull intersections of supplies and demands, economics imperialism is liable to be present, even if unconsciously so, both before and after it is named as such.

This might warrant revisiting the history of mainstream economic thought from the marginalist revolution of the 1870s to the formalist revolution of the 1950s, and beyond, in light of the subsequent emergence and development of economics imperialism. What was being lost, how and with what consequences. At one level, unrecognised as such, Cambridge Capital Theory is a telling example. It brings out how distribution theory (the determination of profit cannot be from the marginal product of capital) faltered. But, in the interwar period, capital was understood in many different ways, especially in the context of the strength of US old institutional economics and the emergence of corporate and monopoly capitalism. By the same token, labour market and wage determination was understood in terms of the emergence of trade unions and increasingly formalised labour relations (over and above the tensions between work as a leisure/income/disutility choice).

These involve stories or pre-histories of economics imperialism that have yet to be told, at least explicitly, in these terms. But what follows in this and the following chapter is such a pre-history for the case of rent and royalty, respectively. And rent has a peculiar history of its own. Analytically, marginalism represented the triumph of Ricardian rent theory through its application across the economy as a whole according to marginalist principles, as was explicitly promoted by Jevons, a founder of marginalism. But, by the same token, this triumph of rent theory by extension to the whole economy had the perverse effect of extinguishing the availability of a specific theory of rent itself. It became a factor of production just like any other. And with the loss of rent, we equally have the loss of landed property and landlords as a class. Of these losses, the most keenly felt was that of distribution (as opposed to a price of land). The tensions between applying marginalist principles and yet retaining a theory of rent as an aspect of distribution is what is involved.

The preceding account provides a rationale for the inclusion of a piece, and another that follows, predating considerations of economics imperialism as such. It also appears to be confined to esoteric topics, the determination of rents and royalties. The topics came about for me because of my interest in the interwar coal industry and my conviction that it was heavily impeded in its restructuring for higher productivity – through consolidation into smaller numbers of larger mines in conjunction with mechanisation of extraction – by the role of privately owned landed property. To understand this theoretically, I undertook a review of rent theory. For reasons that should be apparent from the previous discussion, there was very little literature following the immediate aftermath of the marginalist revolution. There was even less on the nature of mineral royalties and whether they are or are not equivalent to a rent, as is covered in the next chapter.

These two chapters are of interest in their own right as histories of economic thought and, as histories of thought is how they were written. But their inclusion in this volume also locates them in the pre-history of economics imperialism. Paradoxically, as landed property became increasingly reduced to a source of revenue (price of use of land) with no effects, other than to determine revenue recipient, as opposed to embodying economic and social relations, so the British state began a long period of taking private land into public ownership in order to facilitate economic and social development, something that was thrown into reverse by Thatcherism (see Christophers 2018). Equally paradoxically, the theory of rent, or at least its nominal application, has also experienced a new lease of life most recently, with rents being seen everywhere and from within many different conceptual framings, ranging over everything from corruption to finance (and financialisation). It may not be economics imperialism, but it is rent imperialism, with both imperialisms sharing capacity for lack of conceptual coherence.

1   Introduction[5]

In this Chapter I examine certain economic theories of rent in order to discover the particular ways in which landed property has been understood. Associated with each rent theory is a particular specification of the way in which landed property intervenes in the operation of the economy. We will conclude that an adequate rent theory can only be established by taking into

---

5   Based upon Fine (1983). This paper was written whilst the author was in receipt of Social Science Research Grant HR5724/ 1 to study the effect of royalties on the UK inter-war coal industry. I am grateful to an anonymous referee for comments. Revisions were made whilst the author was in receipt of a grant from The Nuffield Foundation to study the British coal royalty system.

account the specific effects of landed property. Where effects have been taken into account, it is often only implicitly or by 'proxy'. As a result, rent theory has been as underdeveloped as the associated and neglected examination of landed property itself. For neoclassical economics, rent theory either dissolves in general equilibrium theory or is restored by the restrictions involved in moving to partial equilibrium. In the case of Ricardo, rent theory is based upon distinguishing the process of value formation in agriculture and industry. For Smith, the generation of rent under capitalism is treated by reference to Physiocratic notions which have greater relevance for feudal society. In each case, a theory of rent only emerges on the basis of a more or less chaotic understanding of the role of landed property.

The chapter also has a second purpose. It is to demonstrate that different schools of economic theory cannot be reduced to special cases of a more general theory which is itself usually taken to be neoclassical economics. There are differences in the conceptual content of different schools of thought. By viewing Smith's theory through the prism of neoclassical economics, for example, the concepts unique to Smith become stripped of their distinguishing features and merely serve to reproduce those of the prism. Although this is a general proposition about the history of economic thought, it is illustrated here by reference to rent theory.

To this end, I mount a criticism of a paper by Buchanan (1929) written some fifty years ago. The reason for doing so does not lie in any particular hostility to this author or to his contribution. On the contrary, Buchanan's article will be seen to be a remarkable synthesis of a number of contradictory themes concerning rent theory and it is this which enables it to serve so well as a focus for analysing the theories of rent that have both preceded and followed it.

Buchanan sets himself two tasks. First, he states the basis within the prevailing neoclassical economics for a dispute over whether rent is price determined or price determining so that he may resolve the conflict involved. He does so by drawing the distinction between two problems. For one, there is a single product so that the last unit of capital applied pays no rent, determining price and consequently the differential rents on all other units of capital and their associated lands. For the other problem, there are competing demands between products for land usage so that a rent enters into the price of a commodity as the opportunity cost of the land's use for an alternative product. Buchanan prides himself on being the first person to point out "that the two problems involve different hypotheses and different conclusions", p. 134.[6] Accordingly,

---

6   Buchanan could not have searched extensively for predecessors. Carlton (1906), for example, reviews contemporary debates over rent theory in terms of the use of the margin of

Buchanan reckons the dispute over rent theory is a false one since "the essential difference in the two questions is that in one the land was supposed to have an alternative use, while in the other it had none", p. 123. Consequently, he can close his article with the conclusion that, "The theories ... are not antagonistic, but complementary; they arise from the application of the same *principle* to *two different questions* and constitute together something like a complete theory of the subject", p. 155, original emphasis. The principle involved for Buchanan is the neoclassical theory prevailing at his time of writing and so we can agree with his conclusion to the extent that we accept the immature version of general equilibrium theory utilised and to the extent that we accept general equilibrium theory at all as the basis for analysing economic relations in general and rent theory in particular.

The second task that Buchanan sets himself, justifying his claim to "the historical approach" is to consider various theories of rent in the light of these two problems. For him, the history of rent theory is the treatment of these two problems, p. 124:

> Some writers have discussed the question from one point of view at one time and from another at another time. Other writers have confused the two points of view but have allowed one of them to dominate their discussion. In still other cases a writer has treated the matter exclusively from one point of view. The first of these comments applies to Smith and J.S. Mill, the second to the Ricardians and the third to Jevons.

Within this framework, Buchanan's historical approach to rent theory is to assess the extent to which various writers tackle the problems with the solutions that are suggested by "the equilibrium theory of value and distribution" to which he subscribes himself. This is a popular but misguided method of approach to the history of economic thought, or indeed to the history of any discipline. The doctrines of the past should not be seen as an evolutionary path to those of the present. Different theories utilise different concepts and theoretical frameworks as well as posing different questions, ones which may not be posed let alone be answerable within another theory.[7] Buchanan's historical approach is to impose one theory upon others as if all were using the same concepts and posing the same problems.

---

transference to alternative land use (marginal rent) as opposed to the extension to inferior lands (differential rent). See also Hollander (1895).

7 The reader may be reminded here of the Kuhnian concept of "paradigm". The author [at, and reflecting, the time] prefers the concept of "problematic" (see Althusser and Balibar 1970).

The way in which he does this is instructive. Necessarily, it involves the reduction of the differences between theories on all matters relating to rent to the difference between allowing alternative land use or not. Correspondingly, where rent does enter into the price of a commodity, a writer must be considering the existence of competing land use or be making a mistake or suffering from confusion.[8] Where rent does not enter into the price of a commodity, it must be the price of the only commodity being produced on the land as far as the particular author under consideration is concerned. The basic problem for Buchanan, of the distinction between theory with alternative land use and without an alternative, is mirrored by the distinction between exchange and distribution, "since the question of rent and price properly lies in two main fields, namely exchange and distribution".[9] Exchange theory, that is relative prices, corresponds to the existence of alternative land uses from which distribution theory is derived since rents (and wages and profits for that matter) are simply the prices of lands (and labour and capital). On the other hand, in the case of a single commodity, exchange theory necessarily evaporates leaving a residue consisting of distribution theory. Consequently, Buchanan should not have argued that the question of rent and price properly lies in the two main fields of exchange and distribution, but that it lies in the one or the other in exact correspondence to the existence of alternative land use or not. This view is borne out by Buchanan's treatment of the historical elements in the distribution theories of rent. They are characterised by considerations of social classes, necessarily of landlords, and are thereby associated with Physiocracy. Thus, the single product theory of rent becomes the single product/rent is price determined/class relations of distribution/Physiocracy theory of rent. All of these characteristics come together, or not at all, since they are derivative of the single land use assumption. For Buchanan, "there is much in common between

---

8 Thus "Mill was an accomplished logician, and it is unbelievable that he, a life-long supporter of the Ricardian position, would publish in the same chapters in which he upheld that theory another theory which, *on the same hypotheses*, upheld the opposite. We have shown that the hypotheses were different, and it appears clear that Mill recognised them to be so", p. 147, original emphasis. Here Buchanan presumes that apart from the universal validity of his own economic theory, there is a universal logic of which Mill is a past master. Hence Mill must be in agreement with Buchanan. In fact, Mill is caught in a contradictory confusion brought about by his straddling the fence dividing classical political economy from marginalism, a process of the mixing of theories that is characteristic of Buchanan.
9 It is not clear why production, however conceived, is excluded by Buchanan from being an element of rent and price theory. For him it would enter merely as the technical conditions of production relating land as an input to one or more outputs, rather than as the social conditions governing access to land as a means of production.

the point of view with which they [Ricardians] approached the subject and the point of view of the Physiocrats, which also dominated Smith's second treatment [single land use]. *Their discussions were dominated by the point of view of distribution between social classes*", p. 139, original emphasis.

Thus, in summary, for Buchanan there are two complementary theories of rent, and each theorist can draw on the one, the other or both without inconsistency although possibly making for confusion. In the following sections we shall show that Buchanan's approach leads to profound errors of interpretation of various theories of rent. In the next Section I am predominantly concerned with Smith's theory, and in the section following that the marginalist theory that preceded Buchanan, but which has also been reconstructed as the modern theory of consumer surplus. In Section 4, I consider other neoclassical contributions to rent theory and the final section contains concluding remarks.

2   Adam Smith's Theory of Rent

The Physiocratic theory of rent is not predominantly concerned, despite Buchanan, with the distribution of a single product between classes.[10] Rather, it sees the agricultural surplus, which is appropriated in the form of rent, as the means of employing non-agricultural labour (such as, but not exclusively manufacturers). Thus, the size of the agricultural surplus, when set against the level of subsistence, does determine distributional relations, but more important it determines the potential non-agricultural population that can be sustained.

Now, as Buchanan observes, Smith is commonly considered inconsistent in his treatment of rent and price. He stated both that rent was and that it was not an element determining the price of commodities. For Buchanan this inconsistency is explained away by the dichotomy between the two rent questions. When rent was price determined for Smith, he was theorising Ricardian single land usage, but when rent was price determining, he was concerned with alternative land usage. It is with this latter interpretation that we disagree. In our view, Smith's theory of rent in so far as it is price determining, with rent as one of the elements in his components theory of price, is an integration of Physiocratic notions into the analysis of capitalism. As such it is anomalous because Physiocratic theory does not depend upon the co-existence of wages

---

10   Buchanan's framing leads to a simple one product, distributional concept of economic relations between classes. That neoclassical theory only treats classes in the context of a single product is one way of viewing the Cambridge capital critique that exposes its own limitations in constructing a theory of class.

and profits with the rent component, since it is concerned with the production that can be sustained by the agricultural surplus. As Meek has shown in his work, it is for Physiocracy more a case of agriculture versus manufacture, with little distinction being made between worker and capitalist and therefore between wages and profits. Nevertheless, the rewards to manufacture can be interpreted as if they were divided between profits and wages as component parts of price and then the Physiocratic notion of rent is also incorporated into an analysis of capitalism but its effect on prices is not determined by marginal principles of alternative land usage. In short, Smith's use of rent as a price determining component is quite independent of the possibility of alternative land usage. However, it is certainly not true that Smith's rent theory relies exclusively upon these Physiocratic notions. He also employs Ricardian-type concepts of differential rent, but these were in addition to, and never at the expense of, the Physiocratic theory. It should be observed that my view has become diametrically opposed to Buchanan's. Where for him Smith's rent as a component part is derived from alternative land usage, for us it arises from single land usage, what is the class (Physiocratic) theory of rent for Buchanan.

To justify my interpretation of Smith and the criticism of Buchanan I begin with Chapter XI of Book I of the Wealth of Nations, entitled "Of the Rent of Land". Here Smith certainly begins with the often-quoted observation that rent is price determined. "High or low wages and profit are the causes of high or low price; high or low rent is the effect of it", p. 249. For Buchanan, this can be safely interpreted as the case of single land use and he passes over the next "two 'parts' which have little bearing upon our problem", p. 131. In fact, these parts will be found to be crucial, but first note that the causal relation between rent and price quoted above is not for Smith as simple as it seems. For it is discussed in the context of the suggestion that some commodities always pay a rent, and some do so only sometimes. Thus, whether there is rent at all or not depends upon the product and not upon the price. Once it is determined that a product always bears a rent then it can be determined whether it is high or low according to the product's price. This view of Smith's would be consistent with Buchanan's if the irreducible rent of products that always bear one were determined by the opportunity cost of alternative land usage. This cannot be so. For the necessary rent is one paid for the product that always affords a rent, whereas other commodities may not afford rent and therefore cannot set a standard of rent through competition for alternative land usage.

If Buchanan's interpretation of Smith cannot be correct, it remains to demonstrate the Physiocratic element of Smith's theory as I have understood it. This is relatively easy, if we do not ignore the parts that Buchanan correctly observes have "little bearing upon our [i.e. his] problem". Part I of Chapter XI is entitled "Of the produce of Land which always affords Rent". It is concerned with food, that is with subsistence, since "land in its original rude state can afford the materials of clothing and lodging to a much greater number of people than it can feed", p. 266. Whether the common food be corn, beef or potatoes, "land in almost any situation, produces a greater quantity of food than what is sufficient to maintain all the labour necessary for bringing it to market, in the most liberal way in which that labour is ever maintained. The surplus, too, is always more than sufficient to replace the stock which employed that labour, together with its profits. Something, therefore, always remains for a rent to the landlord", p. 250.[11] In Smith's theory, then, rent is first determined by absolute fertility in the production of labourer's food, p. 263:[12]

> A rice field produces a much greater quantity of food than the most fertile corn field ... Though its cultivation ... requires more labour, a much greater surplus remains after maintaining all that labour. In those rice countries, therefore, where rice is the common and favourite vegetable food of the people, and where the cultivators are chiefly maintained with it, a greater share of this greater surplus should belong to the landlord than in corn countries.

However, because rice is produced in bogs, its land has no alternative use, but the principles of rent determination have remained the same as for corn even though alternative land use cannot serve as the basis for calculating other rents, p. 264:

> A good rice field ... is unfit for corn, or pasture, or vineyard, or, indeed, for any other vegetable produce that is very useful to men; and the lands which are fit for those purposes are not fit for rice. Even in the rice countries, therefore, the rent of rice lands cannot regulate the rent of the other cultivated land, which can never be turned to that produce.

---

11   The other component parts for Smith are profits and wages, with the costs of raw materials supposedly taken care of by their prices being divided down into their constituent elements of profits, wages and rents.
12   See also p. 278, "It is otherwise in estates above grounds (as opposed to mines for precious metals or stones). The value both of their produce and of their rent is in proportion to their absolute, and not to their relative fertility ... The value of the most barren lands is not diminished by the neighbourhood of the most fertile".

Buchanan cannot possibly be right in his interpretation of Smith's rent theory, since the Physiocratic element correctly understood is present whether there is alternative land use or not.

I conclude this section with some further comment on Smith's rent theory and contrast his theory with Ricardianism with which it was followed. In Part II of Chapter XI, Smith (1971) considers those products that may but do not necessarily afford rent. Essentially, he applies Ricardian principles of differential rent with some confusion, but he does not do so exclusively. His confusion concerns his establishing which coal mine, for example, determines the price of output as opposed to the process by which that mine itself establishes the price. Competition, particularly when superior mines are brought into production, tends to eliminate the inferior mines so that for Smith the most fertile mine establishes price rather than the least fertile as demanded by the Ricardian principles. Compounding this confusion is Smith's reluctance to rely upon the Ricardian principles exclusively, since he is concerned with property rights on the land. Some mines (in Scotland) may "afford some profit to the undertaker of the work, but no rent to the landlord. They can be wrought advantageously by nobody but the landlord ... [who] will allow nobody else to work them without paying some rent, and nobody can afford to pay any", p. 270. "At a coal-mine for which the landlord can get no rent, but which he must either work himself or let it alone altogether, the price of coals must generally be nearly about this price", p. 272. Yet, on the very same page, Smith asserts that "the most fertile coalmine, too, regulates the price of coals at all the other mines in its neighbourhood". Leaving aside this latter statement, whose source is a confusion identified above, the question is why Smith does not argue that the price of coal is exactly at the level determined by the no rent land, as Ricardo (1971, p. 327) interprets him to do so and would have him do so:

> After Adam Smith has declared that there are some mines which can only be worked by the owners ... We should expect that he would admit that it was these particular mines which regulated the price of production from all mines.

The answer is that Smith is concerned with property rights; the landlord will not let another onto the land without paying a rent so that, if the landlord does not work the land, it is left unworked, or a rent is paid pushing up the price by the amount of that rent. This last possibility is not openly admitted by Smith since he has already confusedly expected the most fertile land to regulate the price. However, this regulated price includes a rent payment determined at the outside by the price of wood which is preferable to coal as a fuel and whose cultivation is substitutable for corn or pasture and whose rent is thereby determined according to the Physiocratic principle, Smith (1971, p. 271). Thus, determination of price by the most fertile mine is consistent with rent on the least fertile, a rent that has to be paid to use the land.

The purpose of extending our interpretation of Smith to allow for his rent on all land, even in the absence of the Physiocratic element in the production of food, is to show that non-Ricardian rent arises even in the absence of that element. But another element takes its place, that of the capitalist independent of the constraint of landed property, for this is precisely what constitutes the landlord acting as his own proprietor. For another capitalist to take his place, a rent must be paid even if the land would otherwise lie idle. In this case, just as in the Physiocratic element of Smith's theory of rent, price must include rent as a component part quite apart from Buchanan's considerations of alternative land usage. This allows to be seen the complexity of Smith's rent theory and, because of its diverse elements, the source of its confusions. Smith is seeking to understand rent in the context of a capitalist economy. In doing so, he draws directly upon an understanding of capitalism itself, for example in constructing price from the addition of wages, profits and rents. However, he also utilises an understanding drawn from other modes of production or from underdeveloped capitalism as is suggested by the use of the Physiocratic notions.[13] Further he confronts a capitalism in which landlords work their own land with one in which they do not. The result is not so much confusion, as an important divergence from Ricardian rent theory. For, it is because Smith draws upon different modes of organising production, that capital is confronted in his theory by landed property. Capitalists must pay a rent to use land and this is the source of Smith's rent as a determining component part of price. His element of Physiocracy applied to capitalism insists that this absolute rent must exist.

In complete contrast, Ricardo and the Ricardians expunge the Physiocratic element from their theory. For them, rent arises out of the (relative) natural conditions of fertility and situation, independently of landownership. The latter simply determines who receives the rent. Here there is complete disagreement with Buchanan, whose own rent theory is independent of landownership. For he argues that the Ricardians confuse Physiocracy with alternative land usage, simply because they consider rent as a class revenue when analysing alternative land use, whereas I would argue Physiocracy is absent

---

13 Similarly, Smith draws for his measure of value as labour commanded from Physiocracy and his theory of labour embodied from the rude society (in which there would be no need for exchange) (see Fine 1980). Smith draws upon many different notions of what constitutes a capitalist (see Meek 1956).

from Ricardianism and also from Mill's theory which is seen by Buchanan as treating his two questions separately in an unconfused way. Following Ricardo then, rent theory, whether allowing alternative land usage or not, has been constructed more with an absence of the effects of landownership as such.[14]

3   Marginalist Rent Theory

I cannot elaborate here all of those characteristics which together formed the basis for the marginalist revolution and led to the break with classical political economy. Instead, I focus upon those elements that were essential in defining marginalist rent theory. We begin by observing that marginalism depended upon the generalisation of Ricardian differential rent theory to the economy as a whole and by focusing upon the intensive rather than the extensive margin. This process of generalisation from agriculture to industry is recognised by Mill (1929, p. 477) who remarks that:

> any difference in favour of certain producers, or in favour of production in certain circumstances, being the source of a gain, which, although not called rent unless paid periodically by one person to another, is governed by laws entirely the same with it. The price paid for a differential advantage in producing a commodity cannot enter into the general cost of production of the commodity.

The result of such an approach is to determine prices at the margin and to explain differential circumstances in terms of diminishing returns and the substitution of one factor of production for another. In addition, the marginalists applied the same principles to consumption and were ultimately concerned with the economy as a whole only in so far as it produced individual utility efficiently. The net result is well known. A more or less well worked out general equilibrium is theorised in which prices are determined by the interaction of supply and demand in each market, these in turn being based on initial endowments, technical possibilities and subjective preferences. Factor incomes such as wages, profits and rents are themselves derivative from these prices.

---

14   The main exception is to be found in Marx's theory of rent, although modern interpretations of his theory tend to replace the effects of landownership by Ricardian notions of differential and monopoly rent. For a different interpretation of Marx's theory from this, see Ball (1977) and Fine (1979).

One crucial logical implication of the marginalist system is that the different sources of factor income are conceptually distinguishable only insofar as the conditions governing supply and demand are differentiated. This is why Hobson (1891) refers to "the law of the three rents",[15] and Clark (1891) sees "distribution as determined by a law of rent". For Walras (1964),[16] rent is a "part of the expenses of production at every moment of time exactly as every other outlay is",[17] and Jevons (1871)[18] argues that "so far as cost of production regulates the value of commodities, wages must enter into the calculation on exactly the same footing as rent". In addition, the factor incomes are determined simultaneously, with their ultimate effect to be measured in terms of the individual utility generated. This involves what Fetter (1901) termed "the passing of the old rent concept" which relied upon the Ricardian notion of a differential surplus measured exclusively in terms of the conditions of supply that satisfy a given demand. The passage of the old concept has reached its perfection only in modern times, for reasons that will be discussed in the next section. The modern theory of consumer surplus has formalised the conclusions implicit in the early marginalist theory by taking "rent as a measure of welfare change" and by abandoning producers' surplus altogether as being incompatible with the measurement of the economic surplus associated with utility gains in general equilibrium (see Mishan 1959 and 1968).

Buchanan, however, interprets the early marginalists differently. He recognises that "the essence of that theory is that *no expenses determine* prices, but that prices of production and rewards of productive agents are *mutually* determining", p. 140. But in utilising his theory of alternative land use, Buchanan focuses exclusively upon the supply of alternative crops. Thus, land is treated equally to other factors of production only in terms of substitution in supply rather than in demand as a means of providing utility. This creates the illusion that a theory of rent has been constructed (just as marginal products of capital or labour would create the impression that profits or wages had been uniquely explained). Consequently, the marginalists, particularly Jevons, are interpreted as if they provide a theory of rent whereas we have argued that the effect of

---

15 Where no page numbers given for quotes, unless otherwise indicated, they indicate the titles of the pieces cited.
16 I was unable to track down page number for this quote.
17 See Larmour (1979) who argues that, for Walras, land is therefore capital. He also observes that the generalisation of the Ricardian margin in agriculture to industry has the effect of undermining a theoretical distinction between the two.
18 I was unable to track down page number for this quote but see p. xliv at, https://oll.libertyfund.org/title/jevons-the-theory-of-political-economy.

marginalism is to eradicate the distinction that can be drawn between rent and other sources of factor income. Buchanan leaves the false impression that marginalism has a theory of rent which is produced by the consideration of alternative land usage. This is, however, no more a special theory of rent than the alternative uses of capital and labour constitute separate theories of profit and wages.

4 Compromise in Neoclassical Rent Theory

In his article, Buchanan did not seek simply to resolve a conflict between classical and neoclassical rent theory. By introducing his two problems and their solutions he sought to close a debate that had taken place within neoclassical economics itself. The early marginalists had generalised Ricardian rent notions to the economy as a whole thereby undermining the possibility of a theory specifically of rent. This is the logical conclusion to which general equilibrium is forced and it explains in part the almost total disappearance of rent as a current subject of economic theory. Contemporary economists, however, were dissatisfied with this result for two reasons. Firstly, rent was recognised to be a uniquely defined factor income and, secondly, it had a special relationship to land. Whereas Buchanan was content to embrace all the modern propositions pretending that a theory of rent remained as a result of alternative land usage, others were less happy to do so.

Marshall, in particular, clung to the notion of Ricardian rent and managed to do so by two devices. The first involved specifying the special conditions of land supply which various authors have usually characterised as indestructibility and fixed supply. By contrast, capital could be specified uniquely in terms of its productivity over time and dependence upon abstinence (waiting), and labour was defined in terms of its disutility and sacrifice of leisure. For Marshall (1893, p. 76) utilising the concept of producer surplus ("a convenient name for the genus of which the rent of land is the leading species") the question of time was crucial for the distinction between rent and quasi-rent because land could not be expanded in supply whereas capital could do so and, thereby, eliminate quasi-rent. Unfortunately, this special property of land as a means to generate a special factor income depended upon Marshall's second device, the use of partial equilibrium analysis. Clearly, the measurement of the producer surplus depends upon the rest of the economy being exogenously fixed or the presupposition of a one good world. Otherwise rent as a factor income can only be derived from the set of equilibrium prices.

Thus, Marshall failed to produce a theory of (rent within) general equilibrium theory. Neoclassical theory has compromised over this situation by abandoning general equilibrium whenever a theory of rent is required and otherwise adopting a theory of consumer surplus, even occasionally recognising its schizophrenia. Thus Brown (1941, p. 835) in response to Boulding (1941), but see also Boulding (1945), asks "Is the expression 'economic rent' now to do the duty for every sense in which we may say there is a 'surplus'. If so, what can the economist who believes the distinction between income from landownership and other income to be important do about the matter?" This concern with rent as a factor income in the theory of distribution has recurred from time to time, most notably following Mishan's (1968) criticism of the notion of producer surplus and the recognition that there were historically two theories of rent was rediscovered without reference to Buchanan.[19] Essentially Mishan has rediscovered the early marginalist position in which final utility is the ultimate measure of economic activity and the laws of distribution are all equivalent to the one rent theory. His opponents have rediscovered the marginalists who reacted against this euthanasia for rent theory as a specific source of revenue tied to the land. At times the arguments may be more technically sophisticated, but the conundrums remain the same and unresolved. As already observed, those theories that produce a distinct notion of rent are incompatible with general equilibrium theory either presuming a one good world or that the opportunity cost of alternative land use is already determined. Only if it recognises a distinct role for landed property can economic theory construct a notion of rent that distinguishes it from other factor incomes. Otherwise, by hopping from partial to general equilibrium or from a one- to a many-good world, it can only create the illusion of having explained rent as a distinct source of income.

5   Concluding Remarks

Two sets of conclusions can be drawn from the preceding analysis. The first concerns the theory of rent itself. I have shown that an economic theory contains a theory of rent as a factor income distinct from the revenues drawn by other factors only in so far as it constructs a theory of landed property. Thus, for Smith, a theory of an absolute rent was constructed as a component part of price by imposing notions constructed from pre-capitalist or underdeveloped

---

19   See Mishan (1959, 1968 and 1969) and Wessel (1967 and 1969) and also the debate in the *Southern Economic Journal* in the early 1970s. It became usual to refer back to Ricardo and Pareto as the sources of Buchanan's two rent theories.

capitalist economy (Physiocratic element) upon capitalism.[20] The same result followed when Smith compared and contrasted capitalism in which there was and was not independent landownership. Ricardian theory expunges the Physiocratic element and produces a theory that treats landownership as if it has no effect. It thereby abolishes the existence of an absolute, price determining rent just as Smith permits it by confronting capital with landed property in the form of a landlord appropriating the absolute surplus. As Marx (1969, p. 331) observes in response to Ricardo's quoted suggestion that, "In America ... no one maintains that the principles which regulate rent, are different in that country and in Europe", original emphasis:

> Indeed, those principles are substantially "different". Where *no landed property* exists – actual or legal – no absolute rent can exist. It is absolute rent, not differential rent, which is the adequate expression of landed property. To say that the *same* principles regulate rent, where landed property exists and where it does not exist, means that the *economic form of landed property* is independent of whether landed property exists or not.

Nevertheless, Ricardo can sustain a theory of rent but only at the expense of treating value determination in agriculture (at the margin) differently from value determination in industry[21] and by relying upon the partial equilibrium of a single land use. Marginalism, in its general equilibrium theory, perfects Ricardo's abolition of the effect of landed property and can only restore a theory of rent in the framework of partial equilibrium and in general by allowing some physical attribute of land to stand as a proxy for the social relations of ownership. Thus, for Marshall (1893, p. 79):

> this account of the relations between rent and value is independent of the incidents of land tenure. For modern analysis regards these incidents as holding but a secondary role in the fundamental problems of economics.

He then proceeds to use the role played by time to distinguish between the quasi-rent of a capital good and the rent of land, with the movement to equilibrium

---

20   It should be observed that Physiocracy is a theory which itself is based upon understandings drawn from different modes of production and their stages of development, encompassing elements from feudal, petty commodity and underdeveloped capitalist production.
21   See Ball (1977).

ultimately fixing the latter whilst eroding the former. Unfortunately, it is in that final equilibrium that the special effect of landed property in producing rent disappears. Accordingly, subsequent theories of rent produce insights into the role of landed property only in so far as they depart from equilibrium analysis or construct effects from special forms of landed property (which force the economy to depart from competitive equilibrium).[22]

I can also draw further broad conclusions from this paper about the history of economic thought. I have found that theories contain inconsistencies which are not necessarily logical in origin, although they can be. Marginalism constructs a theory of rent on a partial basis that evaporates when generalised whereas Smith does produce a theory of rent but only at the expense of combining understandings drawn from different economic organisations of society. Elsewhere,[23] I have shown that these are general characteristics of economic theory, that understandings of the economy are drawn from categories specific to different modes of organising the economy and these hybrids contain inconsistencies that often give a theory its specific insights, so that only Smith's Physiocracy-cum-capitalism produces absolute rent and only partial equilibrium a specific neoclassical rent. In addition, the elimination of inconsistencies, whilst desirable in principle, does not guarantee a positive advance, since it may also eliminate particular insights which are produced by the inconsistencies (such as general equilibrium's abolition of rent theory). This leads us to the general conclusion that it is the study of economic relations that should be our goal rather than the perfection of the logic of our models. Hopefully this venture into the history of rent theory has borne this out.

References

Althusser, L. and E. Balibar (1970) *Reading Capital*, London: New Left Books.

---

22   See, for example, Cheung (1968) who analyses sharecropping, Pribram (1940) who examines the effects of an exogenously given business cycle upon rents, and also many contributions to location theory which is forced to depart in many instances from the assumptions necessary for competitive equilibrium because of the uniqueness of space. That neoclassical and Ricardian rent theory are aloof from the effects of landed property also leads them to be conservative in land policy. For them, changes in the system of landed property have no effect and so are unnecessary. Thus, the rent problems associated with resource extraction tend to be seen to be practical rather than theoretical. For a discussion in the context of land and the British coal industry, see Fine (1982).
23   See Fine (1980, Chapter 7).

Ball, M. (1977) "Differential Rent and the Role of Landed Property", *International Journal of Urban and Regional Research*, vol 1, no 3, pp. 380–403.

Boulding, K. (1941) *Economic Analysis*, New York: Harper.

Boulding, K. (1945) "The Concept of Economic Surplus", *American Economic Review*, vol 35, no 4, pp. 851–69.

Brown, H. (1941) "Economic Rent: in What Sense a Surplus?", *American Economic Review*, vol 31, no 4, pp. 833–35.

Buchanan, D. (1929) "The Historical Approach to Rent and Price Theory", *Economica*, vol 9, no 26, pp. 123–155.

Carlton, F. (1906) "The Relation of Marginal Rents to Price", *Quarterly Journal of Economics*, vol 20, no 4, pp. 596–607.

Cheung, S. (1968) "Private Property Rights and Sharecropping", *Journal of Political Economy*, vol 76, no 6, pp. 1107–122.

Christophers, B. (2018) *The New Enclosure: the Appropriation of Public Land in Neoliberal Britain*, London: Verso.

Clark, J. (1891) "Distribution as Determined by a Law of Rent", *Quarterly Journal of Economics*, vol 5, no 3, pp. 289–318.

Fetter, F. (1901) "The Passing of the Old Rent Concept", *Quarterly Journal of Economics*, vol 15, no 3, pp. 416–55.

Fine, B. (1979) "On Marx's Theory of Agricultural Rent", *Economy and Society*, vol 8, no 3, pp. 241–79.

Fine, B. (1980) *Economic Theory and Ideology*, London: Edward Arnold.

Fine, B. (1982) "Landed Property and the Distinction between Royalty and Rent", *Land Economics*, vol 58, no 3, pp. 338–350.

Fine, B. (1983) "The Historical Theory of Rent and Price Reconsidered", *Australian Economic Papers*, vol 22, no 40, pp. 132–143.

Hobson, J. (1891) "The Law of the Three Rents", *Quarterly Journal of Economics*, vol 5, no 1, pp. 263–288.

Hollander, J. (1895) "The Concept of Marginal Rent", *Quarterly Journal of Economics*, vol 9, no. 2, pp. 175–87.

Jevons, W. (1970/1871) *The Theory of Political Economy*, London: Pelican.

Larmour, P. (1979) "The Concept of Rent in 19th Century Economic Thought", Resources Paper no 36, University of British Columbia.

Lawson, T. (2013) "What Is This 'School' Called Neoclassical Economics?", *Cambridge Journal of Economics*, vol 37, no 5, pp. 947–983.

Lawson, T. (2021) "Whatever Happened to Neoclassical Economics?", *Revue de Philosophie Economique*, vol 22, no 1, pp. 39–84.

Marshall, A. (1893) "On Rent", *Economic Journal*, vol 3, no 9, pp. 74–90.

Marx, K. (1969) *Theories of Surplus Value, Part II*, London: Lawrence and Wishart.

Marx, K. (1852) *18th Brumaire of Louis Bonaparte*, https://www.marxists.org/archive/marx/works/1852/18th-brumaire/ch01.htm.

Meek, R. (1956) *Studies in the Labour Theory of Value*, London: Lawrence and Wishart.

Mill, J.S. (1929/1848) *Principles of Political Economy*, London: Longmans, Green and Co.

Milonakis, D. and B. Fine (2009) *From Political Economy to Economics: Method, the Social and the Historical in the Evolution of Economic Theory*, London: Routledge.

Mishan, E. (1959) "Rent as a Measure of Welfare Change", *American Economic Review*, vol 49, no 3, pp. 386–94.

Mishan, E. (1968) "What Is Producers Surplus?", *American Economic Review*, vol 58, no, 5, pp. 1269–82.

Mishan, E. (1969) "Rent and Producers Surplus. Reply", *American Economic Review*, vol 59, no 4, Part 1, pp. 635–37.

Pratten, S. (2023) "Veblen, Marshall and Neoclassical Economics", *Journal of Classical Sociology*, vol 23, no 1, pp. 63–88.

Pribram, K. (1940) "Residual, Differential and Absolute Urban Ground Rents and their Cyclical Fluctuations", *Econometrica*, vol 8, no 1, pp. 62–78.

Ricardo, D. (1971/1817) *Principles of Political Economy and Taxation*, London: Pelican.

Smith, A. (1971/1775) *The Wealth of Nations: an Inquiry into the Nature and Causes of the Wealth of Nations*, London: Pelican.

Walras, L. (1964/1874) *Elements of Pure Economics. A Translation of the Edition Définitive, 1926*, Homewood, Illinois: Richard D. Irwin.

Wessel, R. (1967) "A Note on Economic Rent", *American Economic Review*, vol 57, no 5, pp. 1221–26.

Wessel, R. (1969) "What Is Producers Surplus? – Comment", *American Economic Review*, vol 59, no 3, Part 1, pp. 634–35.

CHAPTER 3

Landed Property and the Distinction between Royalty and Rent

Postscript as Personal Preamble

Before revisions for this collection, this piece was published under same title in *Land Economics* (Fine 1982) the leading US journal for the subject matter suggested by its title. Research into the UK royalty system had been funded by the UK's SSRC (now ESRC) under Grant HR5724/1, the Central Research Fund of the University of London and by the Nuffield Foundation. My interest in the British interwar coal industry had been prompted by a wish to examine the historical origins of post-war state interventionism with coal as a leading case study.[1] It unexpectedly led to close attentions to the role of landed property, not least as coal-bearing land, and the right to access it, was generally owned separately from the capitalists who owned the mines themselves. The referee's report from *Land Economics* rejected my submission on the grounds that I favoured nationalisation and was a supporter of the Labour Party (with the latter, to a large degree, untrue and certainly unmentioned within, and irrelevant to, my paper). I was sufficiently outraged that, against my common practice in response to ridiculous reviews of treating them like inclement weather, I complained to the editor who both took my side and published the paper on its merits.

My expertise in the area of royalties led to my being invited by an intercontinental phone call to give evidence before the US Congressional Commission on Fair Market Values Policy for Federal Coal Leasing, 1983. Perversely, if under Reagan, it was set up to get fair value for the sale of public land to promote coalmining (rather than using state ownership for this purpose as happened in the UK if only after 1938). The Commission attracted unfavourable publicity when, https://www.washingtonpost.com/archive/politics/1983/09/22/watts-off-the-cuff-remark-sparks-storm-of-criticism/133520cc-9b53-49f4-83fa-a1ec532669ba/:

---

1 This was itself prompted by conjunctural studies of the role of the state in the contemporary British economy, especially as an agent of domestic and international economic restructuring. See Fine and Harris (1975 and 1976) and the book to which it led, Fine and Harris (1985), including studies of the British coal industry, co-authored with Kathy O'Donnell and Martha Prevezer (Fine et al 1985a and b).

> Interior Secretary James G. Watt yesterday characterized the commission reviewing his embattled coal-leasing program by saying, "We have every kind of mix you can have. I have a black, I have a woman, two Jews and a cripple. And we have talent".

I felt obliged to respond to the request by informing that the mix would be further enriched by the addition of evidence from a member of the British Communist Party, for which a visa for visiting the USA was more or less impossible. Although reassured that this would make no difference to the Commission's invitation, I never received any further communication.

Even so, in numbers of other ways, pursuing the royalty/rent distinction led to profound effects on the directions taken by my research and beyond. My interest in rent and landed property took on a life of its own, not least within and enriching my contributions to, and from the perspective of, Marxist political economy, see forthcoming volume on Marxist political economy and Fine (1979, 1980b and c, 1985 and 2019). My interest in coal led to my being invited by the ANC to help formulate economic policy for a post-apartheid South Africa, prompting a longstanding research and policy initiative. Corresponding contributions to the political economy of South Africa is also the theme of a forthcoming volume. It also led to intense engagement with the National Union of Mineworkers, with research and presentation of evidence around: pit closures (Fine 1990a); nuclear power (Sizewell B, strongly supported by the managers of the UK's state-owned electricity who switched to being its opponents upon privatisation), evidence presented under Sweet (1984); and the act of parliament required to approve a new coal-importing port (in which I was cross-examined by Anne Widdecombe who posed as favouring the closure of UK pits to save the health of miners) (see HoC 1989). There was also a (successful) equal pay claim for NUM female employees in canteens and cleaning, the latter itself prompting an interest in labour markets (Fine 1990c and 1998).[2]

Last, interest in South Africa inevitably gave rise to attention to other minerals, not least diamonds. And the role of oil in the world economy added a third case study with coal to allow for a comparative analysis of early mineral

---

2 I have posted Kathy O'Donnell's (1990) evidence also. We had worked closely together on this case and were planning to write up an article on its substance and the processes and lessons involved (it is very, very hard to win and that it was won is a testimony to the NUM's persistence, despite putatively being a bastion of white, male, macho trade unionism). Tragically, Kathy died of cancer before we could prepare a joint contribution.

development, giving rise to one of my favourite articles (because of the rare, bordering unique, use of pictures) (Fine 1994).[3]

Be all this as it may, an obvious question is why this piece is reproduced in this first volume on economics imperialism, or in what way at all is it related to (my work on) economics imperialism, given it was published in 1983 long before I was consciously aware of economics imperialism alongside many others apart from those aggressively promoting it (in its first phase) from the University of Chicago, see forthcoming volume on economics imperialism. The answer is exactly the same as for the preceding chapter where a fuller answer is to be found. In a nutshell here for completeness, economics imperialism involves the extension of a narrow set of mainstream principles to other disciplines and topics. It begins in earnest from the 1950s onwards. But it can only do so because the historical and the social, and much of the subject matter of the other social sciences, had been taken out of economics from nineteenth century political economy by the marginalist revolution.

In a sense, the taking out, as opposed to the bringing back in, of the social and historical represents a process of economics imperialism in reverse (not to be confused with reverse economics imperialism, the appropriation of, or influence on, economics by other social sciences on which see next volume on economics imperialism). Economists or political economists of the period between the marginal revolution and the emergence of economics imperialism were caught to a greater or lesser degree between promoting the principles of marginalism and retaining those of political economy. As a result, debates reflected corresponding tensions between acknowledging the social and the historical and drawing upon methodological individualism of a special type (utility maximisation) in the context of a disembodied market grinding out more or less efficient equilibria between supply and demand. Where is the social and historical for the latter, quite apart from class distribution in general and rent in particular, and wages, profits and interest more generally?

What is shown in the previous chapter is that debate over rent theory, in the context of (being unable to square the circle of applying marginalist principles and retaining a specific theory of landed property) was fudged by wavering between general and partial equilibrium. This remains so in finessing the even finer royalty/rent distinction which also became debated in terms of the

---

3 The other major exception derives from my work with Ellen Leopold which benefits from her aesthetic sensibilities, especially where it comes to the study of clothing, Fine and Leopold (1993) although I also added a photo of huge Father Xmas taken by Weegee, played by Joe Pesci in the film, The Public Eye.

relative merits of partial and general equilibrium with limited, if not absence of, implications for practical or policy purposes. Strikingly, the royalty question became embroiled in the single most serious industrial dispute in British history, the General Strike of 1926. As a result, the royalty/rent dispute that is covered here is like the dog that did not bark – now what light exactly can be shed on the General Strike by the relative merits of general and partial equilibrium?

Unsurprisingly, at the time, the debates of the economists were effectively ignored, and policy was made on what was presumed to be pragmatic and/or empirical grounds. Whilst there are some resonances with the current status of economics – especially relatively recently in the wake of the Global Financial Crisis of 2007/8 when even the late Queen wondered where the economists were at – the situation of economics imperialism is much more mixed. It certainly should not be presumed that there is a direct line between economic theory and policymaking, but, especially in the context of economics imperialism and neoliberal policymaking, the ideas of economists can play a crucial role in promoting, but not determining, certain, select policies and modes of policymaking and squeezing out others. In the case of the royalty/rent distinction, the debate overlooked the role of landed property as an (obstructive) influence other than as a recipient of revenue and was at least complicit with delay in nationalising the royalties for the duration of the interwar period (if ahead of nationalisation of the industry itself after the second world war, see below and forthcoming volume on economic history and economics imperialism). In the make-belief world of economics following the marginalist revolution, there was no way for royalties or rent (however the distinction was understood), and for many subsequent scholars of economic history, to acknowledge the profound impact of private landed property on the restructuring of British coal mining into larger, more mechanised production.

1   Introduction

The purpose of this chapter is to examine a debate that took place among economists at the turn of the nineteenth to the twentieth century on whether or not a mineral royalty constitutes a rent. Before examining the debate itself, I investigate why the debate should have taken place at all. This investigation is in two parts. The first part, treated in Section 2, attempts to discover why there should have been any interest in royalties at all. I suggest that towards the end of the nineteenth century, the system of landed property in Britain began to impede the organisation of the coal industry so that the system of private royalty ownership came under question but was not yet at that time to be found to be seriously wanting. Accordingly, with an interest having been stimulated into the nature of royalties, which was considered to be of limited relevance for practical purposes, so a debate over the royalty/rent distinction could be engaged for other, extraneous theoretical purposes. This is the focus for the second part of my investigation in Section 3, where I argue that at the turn of the century there was disagreement amongst economists over the merits of partial and general equilibrium analysis irrespective of royalties, rents or the British coal industry. The royalties controversy provided the terrain for a battle in this debate. In Section 4, I review the debate itself and show how positions taken correspond to broader theoretical positions in relation to partial and general equilibrium analysis. Finally, in Section 5, I draw some concluding remarks concerning the relevance of the debate for how we might best approach rent and landed property.

2 The Historical Background

The source of interest on the economics of royalties was clearly derived from the British coal industry, even if the debate itself made little reference to Britain or the specific mineral, coal. The British industry experienced an enormous expansion over the fifty years preceding the first world war.[4] From 1850 to 1913, employment increased from 250,000 to over a million. Output increased from sixty million to almost three hundred million tons. Nevertheless, the industry was not without difficulties. It was characterised by pronounced cyclical movements around its trend of expansion. From the last decades of the nineteenth century, it began to suffer from stagnation and even to decline in productivity. From as early as 1863, one of the founding fathers of marginalism, W. S. Jevons, in *The Coal Question*, had anticipated this decline.[5] He saw coal replacing agriculture as the source of the Ricardian extensive margin through the exchange of manufactured exports for food imports, with the inevitable diminishing returns from less fertile mines leading to a stationary state. Finally, the industry also had to contend with the rising competition from the development of coal industries in other nations.

In the climate generated by the Great Depression of 1873, concern for the British economy became expressed in the setting up of Royal Commissions.

---

4   For a discussion of the industry over this period, see Taylor (1968). For my own account, see Fine (1990a).
5   The title of Jevons' classic contribution was recycled for my own book, Fine (1990a) into which many of the other of the works cited here were eventually incorporated.

One of these, the Royal Commission on Mining Royalties of 1890,[6] is of interest for the royalty/rent conundrum. It had the task of investigating the extent to which the separation of the ownership of land and its minerals from the ownership of the working capital of mines impeded the progress of industry. It set about this task in two ways. The first involved an empirical examination of how the royalty system worked, and it was carried out in great detail. The Commission discovered that there were varieties of ways in which royalties were paid (acreage, tonnage, rental) with fixed, dead, certain or minimum rents, sliding scales according to the price of coal and varying lengths and conditions of leases. No major objections were made to the royalty system by mine owners. Nevertheless, difficulties were recognised for transporting the coal, as this might involve a wayleave royalty for carrying coal through worked-out land, as well as the need to gain access to railway lines to transport it. Otherwise, there were perhaps no more complaints than one might have expected in the negotiation of complex leases.

The second method employed by the Commission to investigate what they called the "economic operation of the royalty system" was theoretical rather than empirical and cursory rather than detailed. The concern was with the effect that royalties had on the price of coal and manufactures produced with it and, consequently, the effect of royalties on foreign competitiveness. The conclusions can be summarised as follows. There is a difference between a royalty and a rent because one involves the removal of a mineral while the other, in principle, leaves the land unchanged, the level of royalties evening out profitability differences between different mining conditions. Consequently, the only addition that royalties make to price is given by the minimum royalty charged, other royalties being price-determined rather than price-determining.

I will return to these arguments later in Section 3. For the moment, it is important to point out that the economic assumptions, on which they are based, have not been linked to the earlier mentioned empirical analysis of the royalty system. What the economic theory presumes is that capital can flow

---

6   Sorry to say that citation standards at the time, or where, this article was published were considerably impoverished relative to those of today. Given the trouble it would take to meet contemporary standards for sources and for quotes, I have only made a token effort to do so. I had large swathes of hand-written notes from dusty volumes – no electronic sources nor note-taking at the time of the research. And large data sets and computer programmes were punched on, and loaded by, cards. Unfortunately, although kept for many years, these records were recently thrown away.

freely onto the land and between lands so that royalties drop out, technically determined by differing mining conditions quite independently of the system and complexities of landownership involved.

These remarks are borne out by the Commission's consideration of alternative systems of royalty ownership. Again, their empirical analysis was substantial, as a survey was made of the royalty systems prevailing in many other countries. What was found without exception in Europe is that the royalties had been taken into state ownership a hundred years or so before. The reasons for this were made clear by representatives from various countries who were questioned by the Commission. The prevailing patterns of landownership were so subdivided that, for a reasonably sized mine to be established, terms would have to be arranged with many separate landowners. Thus, "it is unanimously admitted that the fertile results follow the absolute distinction that exists between surface property and the working right of mines. In a country where property is so minutely subdivided as it is in France, the reasonable and active working of mines would be impossible on any other system (than state ownership)" and, for Germany, "in many industrial districts of the country the ownership of the surface is so divided that it would be impossible to carry on deep mining under any other principles" and:

> Besides, in many cases a strata of minerals extends underneath the property of several landowners, and it would be almost impossible to work different mines scattered on the larger or smaller plots belonging to different owners, and to this would come the additional difficulty of arriving at an agreement between the owners with regard to the working of mines ... it has been arranged in Austria-Hungary to make them (minerals) entirely independent from the landowner ... This system has specially promoted the establishment of mines.

The same story is also told for Spain, Portugal, Italy, and Luxembourg; landownership is so fragmented that minerals had been taken into state ownership to promote the development of mining. Without this, capital could not flow freely onto and between lands. By contrast, for Great Britain this problem scarcely seems to have been considered by the Commission who simply, and revealingly, observe that, "where a large mineral field is the property of *one* individual no difficulty arises in respect to its full development", emphasis added.

The reason for this is not difficult to discern. In Britain, the pattern of landownership was not fragmented, ownership was highly concentrated and much the same was true of royalty ownership.[7] Rather than small landowners obstructing mining through the charges that would be made for the small quantities of coal that they owned, it was more a case of large landowners encouraging a number of mine owners to extract as much coal as possible and this explains the occurrence of fixed rents to be paid irrespective of the quantity of coal removed but against which royalties were set. It is this pattern of large, landed property that made nationalisation of the royalties unnecessary in Britain.

The same is also true of those countries such as India, Australia, America, and Canada, where English law prevailed but large concessions and often the coincidence of land and mine ownership had been created. In other words, it is not the state or private ownership of royalties as such that was important but the extent to which large enough coal holdings could be leased to form mines of adequate size. Indeed, in many of the European countries, mineral rights were no sooner taken into state ownership than they were sold as concessions to private individuals. These concessions could then be traded and amalgamated. Further regulation of this to prevent concessionaries obstructing the development of mining through outrageous charges does not seem to have been a major problem. Where it was, state regulation was still possible and this could also be used to guard against monopoly of supply. Thus, "the tendency in Belgium is towards the amalgamation of several neighbouring concessions, these being often of small extent", and:

---

7 For an analysis of the ownership of land in Britain covering many sources, see Catalano and Massey (1979). See also Christophers (2018) for an update in light of the privatisation of state-owned land in the UK since Thatcher, reversing previous trends of increasing state ownership. In 1925 the Samuel Commission found that there were 3,789 royalty owners, of which the most fortunate 100 alone received 51% of revenue and the top ten over 12%. The royalties were eventually nationalised in 1938 for which data were collected upon compensation paid – and available from the ESRC as a valuable resource for local histories, and information on (coal) land ownership. See Brunskill et al (1985) for an account, with particular attention to Scotland. The two biggest owners were the Church and H. M. King, a mysterious person until it twigged, and with which the Crown's holdings could be amalgamated. It is unimaginably hard to investigate overall patterns of landownership in the UK (although Scotland is slightly easier), with the first, and last, national survey (apart from Norman Conquest Domesday) dating from the so-called New Domesday Survey of 1873, for which see Bateman (1883) for meticulous compilation. It was set up to appease agitation for nationalisation of land but had the opposite effect so concentrated was ownership found to be. I made a valiant effort to link the coal royalty data to broader ownership of land but gave up, even for Scotland, although see McEwan (1981) whom I tried to emulate through personal correspondence with managers of Scottish estates (factors), one of whom advised me of his disregard for the agitational McEwan. Following Catalano and Massey, Christophers is particularly to be congratulated for his unique efforts albeit focusing on privatisation of state-owned land.

It is a common practice for concessionaires to sell or let their concessions to companies who undertake the working of the mines ... There is absolutely no guard against companies enlarging their holdings through purchase of other undertakings: in fact this is proceeding very rapidly in all the German coal fields without check.

Further, "in the north of France at least, concessions are commonly united and are generally worked by companies" and "in Austria-Hungary, concessions can be and are freely sold".

In light of this evidence, the Commission felt justified in concluding on empirical grounds that the system of private royalties had presented no substantial impediment to the development of the British coal industry. It preferred to draw that conclusion, however, on theoretical grounds by considering the effects of alternative royalty systems. If the royalties were taken into state ownership, then apart from the minimum royalty, the state could simply charge the same as private landowners and there would be little change. If the royalties were abolished, production would be concentrated on better mines given competition, and this would dislocate the trade of the worst mines by lowering price. Whatever the merits of this argument, the Commission's conclusions are drawn, paradoxically, by refusing to consider alternative systems of royalty ownership. For nationalisation of the royalties, they presume that the private system is reproduced so that what happens is independent of the system of landownership. Their treatment of the abolition of the royalties is made in the absence of a consideration of the system by which the right to mine a piece, or combined pieces, of land would be determined. Their conclusions are in any case an aberration from their normal line of argument. If a royalty owner worked his own minerals (an individual abolition of the royalty), the equivalent would accrue to him rather than to another. Were royalties to be reduced by a landowner, then the reduction would simply produce a transfer of the royalty to the lessee. A general reduction in royalties (in the absence of suggesting a method for doing this) would ultimately benefit the mine owner or consumer, although this was seen again merely as a passing on of the royalty revenue. In other words, whether the royalties remained private, were nationalised, or abolished, there would be very little effect on the industry so things might as well remain unchanged and subject to individual initiative.

The best way to summarise the Commission's deliberations is as follows. On the basis of their empirical investigations they came to the view that the royalty system in Britain posed no problem for the development of the coal industry because capital could flow easily onto the coal lands.[8] They elevated these empirical observations to a theoretical truism; as long as capital could flow freely onto the land, any royalty system would have little or no effect on the industry. The system of royalty ownership and the mobility of capital are treated independently with the latter being determinant. The size and effects of royalties are separated from the system of landownership, this merely determining the beneficiaries of the royalty revenues, which are themselves predetermined by the mobility of capital across different mining conditions.

The opinion of the Commission in 1890 on the royalties in Britain was fated to be the last that could be so favourable to non-intervention. Mine sizes were expanding as the fixed costs of deeper and more difficult conditions increased and as extraction followed the extending seams, potentially into neighbouring properties. Prophetic evidence of this is to be found in the Commission's investigations as increasingly mining becomes dependent upon relations between more than one landowner, significantly in arranging transport and wayleaves rather than necessary multiple leases to access the coal itself. As mine size expands relative to a given pattern and distribution of landownership, so the same obstacle that plagued the European industry in its infancy and necessitated state ownership of royalties, comes to the British industry in its (very late, centuries-old) adolescence.

The associated difficulties matured extremely rapidly so that by 1919 the Coal Industry (Sankey) Commission Report found mine owners' representatives unanimously supported nationalisation of the royalties. The reasons for this are to be found reported elsewhere. For the Acquisition and Valuation of Land Committee of the Ministry of Reconstruction discovered an intensification of the problems investigated by the Commission of 1890 together with difficulties in extending mines across boundaries of surface ownership.[9] By 1925 the Samuel Report found that on average each mine required five leases

---

8 In part, the Commission believed that the industry's record spoke for itself, and this alone proved that there was nothing wrong with the royalty system. Unfortunately, the same record of success did not exist for iron ore extraction, which suffered from severe international competition at this time. However, this empirical evidence was forgotten when drawing conclusions on mineral royalties as a whole. An exception to the Commission's conclusions was also to be found in Ireland's peculiar system of landed property, but this was also ignored.

9 A major source of lost coal was the barriers that were erected to the boundaries between mines in conformity with the pattern of surface leases. These would be more substantial for mines whose boundaries do not lie within a stretch of land owned by a single individual, for which the removal of the barriers is less easily negotiated. Thus, the problem of lost barriers would tend to increase with the expansion of the industry through mine size across land held by different landlords.

and reorganisation of the industry depended upon nationalisation of the royalties.[10] In the meantime, in a wave of legislation in the early 1920s that reduced the rights of private landowners, the position of the mine owners had been improved by the possibilities of the granting of compulsory powers. This, as well as the fear of royalty nationalisation as the thin edge of the wedge of nationalisation of the mines themselves, turned the mine owners against royalty nationalisation.

As a result, royalty nationalisation was delayed until 1938, before the second world war which intervened prior to the nationalisation of the industry itself. I have argued elsewhere that this long delay in nationalising the royalties impeded not only the rational organisation of the industry in mine layout but also the mechanisation of mining.[11] This is, however, not strictly relevant to our purpose here. As seen above for the Mineral Commission, a separation was made between the empirical or institutional conditions in which the royalty system operated and the theory of royalty determination. This distinction was universally maintained. Consequently, the dispute over royalty nationalisation in the interwar period was official and practical rather than academic; did the royalty system work to impede or promote the rational (re)organisation of the industry? For this, the distinction between royalty and rent is a rarefied luxury.

Now we can explain the timing of the debate over the distinction between royalty and rent. Towards the end of the nineteenth century, the private system of royalty ownership in Britain was beginning to produce problems of reorganisation for the coal industry, but they were not severe enough to prevent taking a complacent attitude toward the system. Consequently, debate over the royalty system did not concern the practical organisation of mining in relation to landed property. Instead, controversy could be elevated to a theoretical plane independent of the system of landed property, as has been seen for the Mineral Commission.[12] Thus, while the debate over royalty and rent was produced by

---

10 Samuel's interest in royalties concerned the apparently futile attempt to find ways to reduce the price of coal other than to cut wages, ultimately provoking the General Strike of 1926.
11 Apart from Fine (1990a), see Fine (1978, 1985, 1990b and 1993), Evans and Fine (1980a and 1980b), and Fine et al (1985). Unfortunately, the historiography of the interwar industry was for a time dominated by those who denied the benefits of larger, mechanised mines. Ultimately, my work on this issue to the contrary (and in line with common sense) was described by a referee as the last word on the question.
12 There is a striking analogy here, with Marx's (1969) analysis of Ricardo's theory of rent for agriculture. Marx suggests that the assumptions behind Ricardo's theory correspond to the conditions of British agriculture and were accordingly peculiar to European economists for whom the system of landed property could not be ignored nor the free flow of capital onto land be assumed, p. 237: "Both of them (Ricardo and Anderson), however,

a specific conjuncture in the development of the British coal industry – when the royalty system was producing problems that were not too severe – the debate itself had little or nothing to contribute to solving the problem that had produced it when they later became more severe. It had another purpose, and it is to this that I turn in the next section.

3   The Theoretical Background

In the previous section, I have shown that an interest in the economics of royalties arose in conditions where the practical problems of the royalty system were considered negligible. Consequently, the debate over royalties could pose its own theoretical problems and turn a blind eye to the system of royalty ownership itself in practice. Conversely, during the interwar period when the system of royalty ownership increasingly became a burden on the industry, the problems became practical and concerned with the intervention into the system of landownership for which the theoretical assumptions of the free flow of capital were irrelevant along with the royalty/rent debate. In short, the royalty/rent debate is located around the turn of the century, and rather than being concerned with mining as such, it was used as an instrument in the debate over economic theory. Before considering the debate itself in the following section, I first suggest what the debate was really about by examining the economic theory of the time in which it took place.

For those of us trained with the modern concepts and techniques of mathematical economics, the passage from the marginalist revolution of the 1870s to the present day might be seen as the uncontroversial evolution towards the perfections of, and framing through, general equilibrium theory. This is not what happened. While economists such as Walras and Jevons had an idea of the simultaneity involved in general equilibrium determination, the principles of marginalism after the 1870s were initially applied within a partial equilibrium framework. This is most notable in the work of Alfred Marshall. At the same time, economic theory was informed by the principles of general equilibrium theory but in an uncertain way that lacked the confidence of today's practitioners.[13]

---

start out from the viewpoint which, on the continent, seems so strange: 1. that there is no landed property to shackle any desired investment of capital in land; 2. that expansion takes place from better land to worse ... 3. that a sufficient amount of capital is always available for investment in agriculture".

13   See relevant contributions in this and the next volume on economics imperialism, as well as those in the forthcoming volume on the mainstream.

The reason for this is not to be found exclusively nor necessarily predominately in the newness or difficulty of the mode of thinking – in the use of mathematical techniques, for example. For there was a conceptual problem involved which made economists at the turn of the century hesitate from embracing general equilibrium theory even though the logic of their analysis inevitably drove them into its arms. One major result of general equilibrium theory is to eliminate the causative significance between different factor inputs as the source of revenues. Revenues are essentially derived from factor prices, and each of these prices is determined simultaneously and by exactly the same principles. Consequently, distinctions made at the level of revenues such as wages, profits, and rents can only be maintained by distinctions drawn over the conditions of supply and demand which are specific to labour, capital, and land. Rent, for example, is then explained in terms of land in fixed and indestructible supply. A royalty might then be reserved as the term to characterise the remuneration due to a factor in fixed but destructible supply. It becomes simply a question of names and not principles of determination, for these remain the same whether rent, royalty, wages, or profits are under scrutiny.

Some economists, though, were understandably conscious of, and uneasy about, the conceptual loss involved in moving to general equilibrium, over and above the loss of non-economic factors. As this was itself based on generalising, through marginalism, the Ricardian principles of rent determination to the economy as a whole,[14] it is not surprising that the problem was most acutely felt in rent theory itself. It gave rise to a debate over whether rent was price-determined or not.[15] Now, for general equilibrium theory the debate is ridiculous since all prices, including that of land, are determined simultaneously. But it is this which precisely eliminates the specificity of land as a source of revenue (apart from its hypothesised fixed supply) as is made clear by Jevons: "so far as costs of production regulates the values of commodities, wages must enter into the calculation on exactly the same footing as rent".[16] Logically, those who shied away from these implications of general equilibrium theory could do so

---

14   Thus, we have Hobson's (1891) "The Law of the Three Rents" to explain wages, profits, and rents.
15   This debate was surveyed by Buchanan (1929) who attempted to confine all schools of rent theory within the debate among marginalist economists. See Fine (1980b) for a criticism of Buchanan on this score and a more detailed consideration of the debate over rent theory than the one presented here.
16   The quote from Jevons is remarkably succinct. It says that wages and rents are equally causative but only as far as cost of production is concerned.

within the marginalist framework only by using partial equilibrium analysis. In a one good world, rent would be price-determined according to the differential productivity of better over the marginal (no rent) land in use, and a particular role could be assigned to land in causing differential productivity and hence rent as in Ricardian theory.

Because the conceptual specificity of rent required partial equilibrium in the marginalist school, the debate over the rent theory was a debate over the relative merits of partial and general equilibrium and, to that extent, a "dialogue of the deaf".[17] Each antagonist could be right about their different concepts of rent. The debate was, however, complicated by the different types of partial equilibrium that were utilised. One assumes a one-good world while another essentially does not do so but focuses on a single good by taking prices of other goods to be fixed. For purposes of economic models there is little to choose between these partial analyses since other prices will enter as exogenous technical constraints but conceptually the existence of other goods with their own prices is closer to general equilibrium as multi-sector than is a one-good model.

I draw this section to a close by bringing out its significance for the debate over the distinction between a royalty and a rent. We can observe immediately that the debate could only concern those who wished to distinguish rent from profit or wages. For those, who would not draw the distinctions between rent, profit and wages (other than as names to different sources of revenues or prices of factors), would have little to add by including royalties in their list of revenues to be distinguished or not. Because the debate does concern those who distinguish rent conceptually, but within a marginalist theory, it has to be conducted at the level of partial equilibrium. Those who distinguish rent from other factor incomes through the use of partial equilibrium implicitly recognise, in contrast to general equilibrium theory, that the access of capital to land differs from its access to industry in general. Pursuing this one stage further, those who distinguish a royalty from a rent recognise that access of

---

17   Wessel (1967) implicitly agrees with our assessment of the link between a price-determined rent and a partial equilibrium analysis; he also recognizes that the concept of general equilibrium was not an immediate and universal result of marginalism: "In reality, of course, economists have long known that rent is neither price determining nor price determined since neither rent nor price is a basic determinant of the system … We know from Cassell's (1932) simple general equilibrium model that these forces are the conditions of supply of the agents, the technical coefficients, and the preference patterns of consumers".

capital to mining or extraction differs from its access to land for agricultural purposes. But it only makes sense to have a debate over this with those who at least accept that rent is distinguishable as a revenue from wages and profits, that is, with those working within partial equilibrium in so far as we are confined to the marginalist school.

4   The Debate

The debate over whether or not a royalty is a rent did not concern what is to be called a royalty; this was recognised to be the payment for the right to remove a mineral in fixed supply. The debate was concerned with whether or not a royalty is caused in the same way as a rent, and this is why it is an irrelevant debate for the simultaneity of a general equilibrium theory, which is unable to assign a unique causative significance to individual factor inputs and their associated revenues. I begin the review of the debate with Ricardo since, in his theory, rent was determined in a manner distinct from that of wages and profits, and he stumbled upon the future debate in content if not in name. Consequently, the embryo of the later dispute between those who did and those who did not identify a royalty with a rent is to be found in Ricardo (1971). He is concerned with the principles of determination and not with the names of various factor incomes. Ricardo's desired solution is to determine the rent of mines in exactly the same way as the rent of (farm) land (pp. 108–9). This is done by reference to the differential productivities of the original and indestructible properties of the land. But because Ricardo's theory depends upon indestructibility, it is inappropriate for mineral extraction – a problem he appears to have neglected. He does refer to timber removal but in the context of the timber itself having a value determined by its costs of reproduction (pp. 91–2). Later he also removes the condition of original powers but in order to allow improvements, no matter what their origin, to be incorporated into the indestructible properties (p. 268). What is clear is that Ricardo's rent theory raises the problem of the value of destructible conditions (such as the presence of minerals) only to exclude it.

Nevertheless, Ricardo's approach can be judged to suggest two solutions to the pattern of the rents of mines, each solution requiring a partial equilibrium framework. Mines may be treated as land in general, as if they satisfied indestructibility and as if we have a one-good world in which rents are price-determined equalling the residual between cost on better and on the worst mine in use. Alternatively, when destructibility is recognised, the value of the mineral is predetermined and enters into the price of the extracted commodity as a royalty, distinct from rent that is price-determined and reflects the differential fertility of the first case. Ricardo himself, however, only predetermines the value of the mineral (in this case timber) by allowing it to be reproduced with an associated value so that indestructibility is restored.

The property these solutions share is that they depend upon a partial equilibrium analysis. For the first solution, the question of whether there is a distinction between the royalty of a mine and the rent of land must be answered in the negative for a one-good world. For the second solution, there remains the question of predetermining the value of the mineral, a problem that ultimately creates circularity in the simultaneity of general equilibrium since it will affect the subsequent costs of extraction as well as depending ultimately upon final demand. The debate over rent and royalty, for which Ricardo was the precursor, led to the adoption by protagonists of one or the other of the solutions outlined above. The view of the Royal Commission on Minerals, which was presented earlier, can now be seen in the following terms. A royalty is distinguished from a rent on the basis of the destructibility/indestructibility distinction. Consequently, a royalty is made up of two parts, one reflecting differential mining conditions and corresponding to the normal Ricardian idea of rent determination, the other corresponding to a minimum royalty which reflects the value of the mineral extracted. Sorley (1889), Orchard (1922), Flux (1923), and Marshall (1959) supported this position that a royalty was distinct from a rent. For Sorley, who appears to have been the brains behind the Commission's theory, a minimum royalty entered the price of coal as the price of the mineral to be extracted together with a compensation for the loss of beauty to the land. Here we see demand considerations associated with utility entering quite openly as causative factors. Marshall (1959, p. 364) argues that:

> A royalty is not a rent, though often so called. For, except when mines, quarries, etc., are practically inexhaustible, the excess of their income over their direct outgoings has to be regarded, in part at least, as the price got by the sale of stored-up goods, stored up by nature indeed, but now treated as private property; and therefore, the marginal supply price of minerals includes a royalty in addition to the marginal expenses of working the mine ... the royalty itself on a ton of coal, when accurately adjusted, represents the diminution in the value of the mine, regarded as a source of wealth in the future, which is caused by taking the ton out of nature's storehouse.

Thus, for Marshall, the royalty represented the price of the mineral in the ground to which the expenses of working the marginal mine had to be added to determine the price of the extracted mineral.[18]

The preceding authors are relatively close to general equilibrium because they rely upon a partial equilibrium in which there is another good, the unextracted mineral, even if its price is predetermined. Consequently, to use Marshall's terminology, the remuneration to the landowner includes a producer surplus for differences in extraction costs, plus a royalty determined exogenously by supply of, and demand for, the extracted mineral.[19] The royalty is itself not caused in principle by anything which distinguishes it from any other price or revenue, it is merely distinguished by being fixed in supply and destructible.

In contrast to this distinction drawn between royalty and rent, Gray (1914) and Taussig (1939) argue that a royalty and a rent are indistinguishable. Taussig in his rent theory adopts a model that essentially assumes a one-good world. Thus, "rent forms no part of the expenses of production; that is, it forms no part of those expenses of production which affect price", p. 96. This thinking is carried over into the consideration of mines for which the value of an unextracted mineral and its cost of extraction are indistinguishable. For him, the last mine in use will pay neither rent nor royalty, at least in theory, since it is on the margin of use and so the existence of an independent royalty distinct from a rent is denied, p. 140. Gray essentially puts forward the same argument, adding that only in accounting terms can the loss in the value of a mine due to the extracted minerals be attributed to a royalty.[20] For these authors, there can be no value of the mineral independent of the costs of extraction, and so in a sense they rely upon general equilibrium considerations. On the other hand, they do so in a partial equilibrium in which rent/royalty can be reduced to differences in costs of extraction, essentially a one-good world, in which the

---

18 Steele (1967) has argued that Marshall is hinting at a mineral replacement cost to restore the destructible powers of the soil (e.g., by exploration) in his reference to the excess of receipts over production costs only being due to royalties "in part". This is clearly wrong (the other part of the surplus referred to is the difference in costs of extraction relative to the margin) and reflects the imposition of an interpretation based on the modern preoccupation with the renewal of exhaustible resources onto Marshall's analysis.

19 It is significant, and long well-known, that for general equilibrium theory, producer surplus has to be abandoned as a concept since it changes within sector, where it is determined/measured, according to cross-sector interactions. See Mishan (1968).

20 Gray also introduces the innovation of discounting the mineral according to date of extraction, a procedure taken up by Hotelling (1931) and modern theories of optimal exhaustible resource usage.

exhaustibility of the resource is secondary to the costs of extraction.[21] They allow producer surplus alone. Marshall et al rely more upon the physical differentiation between mines and land in general on the basis of destructibility/indestructibility, for the former of which a price or royalty must be paid.

What emerges from the debate in our analysis is a paradox. Earlier, we argued that the debate itself was conducted by those who withdrew from the conceptual implications of general equilibrium theory, its inability to distinguish the causative roles of land, labour, and capital in creating the revenues of rent, wages, and profits. Yet within the debate itself those, such as Marshall, who were closer to general equilibrium, did distinguish a royalty from rent since a royalty was seen as a predetermined price and therefore as a condition of access to mining land. In contrast, those further away from general equilibrium, such as Taussig, argued for the identity of a royalty with a rent since their partial equilibrium was based on a single-good world. This paradox is then somewhat richer. For the closer the partial approaches general equilibrium, the richer the conceptual content of the theory, even though the ultimate destination of general equilibrium itself contains the minimum of conceptual wealth in this context, failing even to distinguish rent, wages, and profits. Conceptual consistency and conceptual richness are often uncomfortable and unfamiliar bedfellows.[22]

5   Concluding Remarks

For general equilibrium theory, the distinction between royalty and rent is purely semantic and much the same is true for the distinctions between wages, profits, and rents since all are simultaneously determined by the same principles according to the more or less free flow of resources through the market to equate supply and demand. Those who use partial equilibrium to specify a distinct theory of rent are able to debate whether a royalty is a rent or not, and the debate is not simply semantics. Those who argue that a royalty is not a rent are in essence adopting a position that distinguishes the way in which capital flows into mining from the way in which it flows into agriculture (just as rent

---

21   Taussig, for example, denies the difference between royalty and rent on the basis of sand and clay being available in abundant quantity.

22   I have attempted to show this for rent theory in Fine (1980a and 1982b) and for different schools of economic thought in Fine (1980b). Note also that the conceptual problems of partial equilibrium are to be found in other areas as evidenced, for example, by the need for the Cambridge capital critique.

payments distinguish agriculture from industry). Those who identify a royalty with a rent within the debate do so by suggesting that capital flows into mining in a way comparable to its flow into agriculture. At least the debate raises the question of the role of landed property in the access of capital into the mining sector, even if an unsatisfactory way, as argued below. It is worth being reminded that the form taken by landed property is important as is symbolised by the very term "royalty". As Nef (1932, p. 318) observes:

> In Great Britain, the meaning of the word has undergone, in fact, a curious inversion. An attribute of sovereignty in feudal times, when sovereignty was decentralised, the regale has been absorbed, not by the sovereign state, as in France and most other continental countries, but by the landowners. Thus a word originally applied to the rights of the sovereign as against the subject, is now applied to the rights of the subject, as against the sovereign.

Nef goes on to observe that it was the concentration of mineral rights in private hands in Britain that allowed the privately owned coal royalty system to promote the development of mining, whereas in France and elsewhere the highly dispersed pattern of landownership necessitated state ownership. This applies, however, only as far as the end of the nineteenth century when the expanding size of mines in Britain increasingly brought the private system of royalty ownership into disrepute until royalties were finally nationalised in 1938.

Yet, since Ricardo, the effects of landownership have played a negligible role in economic theory. Rents (and the same is true of royalties) are determined independently of the system of landed property which merely determines who shall be the recipients of the rental income when it is distinguished as such. As a result, rent theory has a tendency to be neutral and, consequently, both unhelpful and conservative over changes in systems of landownerships since it sees them as having little if any effect other than the destabilising redistribution of income that could best be delivered, if at all, through other mechanisms. The impetus toward changes in systems of landownerships then tends to come from what are perceived to be institutional and practical difficulties which can be empirically rather than theoretically comprehended.

To some extent, these remarks are borne out by consideration of Dasgupta and Heal (1979). This book is exemplary in setting out in formal mathematical terms the propositions associated with the economics of exhaustible resources. In doing so, it unwittingly makes clear the extent to which there has been little or no progress in understanding the role of landed property in economic development. The same confusions over royalty and rent are reproduced in so far as a royalty is seen "as the competitive value of a pool of oil or a deposit of coal" (p. 159). But is this an accounting identity as for Gray or a condition of access to the land, as for Marshall; price-determined or price-determining? An answer can be given in terms of the partial equilibrium model employed – a one-good world in which the costs of extraction are indistinguishable from the value of the unextracted resource or a many-good world in which the price of the unextracted resource is given externally but implicitly through the demand function for the extracted resource. But these models can tell us nothing about the actual conditions of landed property. Elsewhere, proxies for the intervention of landed property are introduced, and these are to be welcomed, but they have no specific connection to landed property as they vary from the market for externalities, through the definition and enforcement of property rights, to the imperfections of monopoly, forward markets, expectations, and information.

It is time, however, that neoclassical economists learned that it is not legitimate to explain economic phenomena in terms of a divergence from the conditions of perfect competition and that they begin to examine those "imperfect" conditions themselves since imperfect they always are. What are the conditions of access of capital to the land and how do they differ from those of capital's access to industry in general? This involves economic and non-economic factors and cannot be successfully accommodated by grafting the economics of divergence from perfect competition onto the economics of land use and calling this rent theory or the economic theory of exhaustible resources.

Elsewhere I have shown how a theory of rent can be constructed to take account of the intervention of landed property. For agriculture, it is seen to have the effect of obstructing intensive cultivation of the land.[23] For coal mining I have shown that the existence of private royalties obstructed nationalisation and mechanisation of the British industry in the interwar period.[24] Thus, a prerequisite for the development of a theory of mining and the revenues that it generates is an examination of the empirical form of landed property that it confronts and how these are integrated into the production, financing, distribution and sale of the products from the land concerned.[25] Thus, the question

---

23 See Fine (1979) and, most recently, Fine (2019), each reproduced in the forthcoming volume on Marxist political economy. See also Catalano and Massey (1979) and Christophers (2018) for extensive discussion of the relative merits of public and private ownership of land in Britain.

24 See references cited earlier.

25 Nor should the physical characterization of mining as the extraction of an exhaustible resource be adopted without question. See Fine (1992) for some comparative account of diamonds, coal and oil. Interestingly both Marshall (1923) and Marx (1971) agree that

of whether a royalty is a rent or not is a misleading one except in so far as it raises the questions of the access of capital to mineral-bearing as opposed to agricultural land. Both royalty and rent are derived from something else, the particular intervention that landed property makes in relation to the economy and its development.[26]

Perversely, whilst the marginalist revolution had made everything rent-like (at the margin), thereby dropping the role of landed property and rent itself from a central position in the shift from political economy to politics, currently the position of rent has been restored as something that is more or less universally applicable. This is so across a whole range of different approaches and applications whether it be the (corrupt) rent-seeking of the mainstream or the post-workerist postures of Negri and Hardt (for whom profits are now rents). For myself, the category of rent should be reserved for the rewards of owning land in order to relate it both to historically-evolved conditions of access to land and to how such ownership is structured in relation to the accumulation of capital through economic and social reproduction more generally – how (surplus) value is produced and circulated. These two aspects of rent will not be shared by, and so should remain distinct from, the "rents" derived from monopoly, technology, or whatever – just as whether a royalty is or is not a rent is a road to nowhere.

References

Ball, M., V. Bentivegna, M. Edwards and M. Folin (eds) (1985) *Land Rent, Housing and Urban Planning: a European Perspective*, London: Croom Helm.

Bateman, J. (1883). *The Great Landowners of Great Britain and Ireland [Originally, The Acre-Ocracy of England]. A List of All Owners of Three Thousand Acres and Upwards, Worth £3,000 a Year; Also, One Thousand Three Hundred Owners of Two Thousand*

---

mining is akin to a transport industry. The former does so because of the process of underground haulage, whereas the latter argues that it is the relative absence of produced raw materials (constant capital) that renders extraction and transport similar. More generally, and in other words, rents and royalties associated with minerals are contingent upon the global commodity/value chains (or production networks) to which they are attached and, vice-versa, GCC/GVC/GPN need to take account of their differentiated relationships to landed property.

26   Thus, it is necessary to reject the notion that a royalty per unit output can be treated as if it were a tax on output. Taxes are derived from relations involving the state and so are determined by, and have different effects than, a unit royalty as the form of relation between mining and landowning.

Acres and Upwards, in England, Scotland, Ireland, & Wales, Their Acreage and Income from Land Culled from The Modern Domesday Book; also Their Colleges, Clubs, and Services. Corrected in the Vast Majority of Cases by the Owners Themselves (fourth edition, revised and corrected throughout), London: Harrison, 1971 edition, with a new introduction by David Spring, Leicester/New York: Leicester University Press/ Humanities Press.

Brunskill, I., B. Fine and M. Prevezer (1985) "The Ownership of Coal Royalties in Scotland", *Scottish Economic and Social History*, vol 5, no 1, pp. 78–89.

Buchanan, D. (1929) "The Historical Approach to Rent and Price Theory", *Economica*, no 26 (June), pp. 123–55.

Catalano, C. and D. Massey (1979) *Capital and Land*, London: Edward Arnold.

Christophers, B. (2018) *The New Enclosure: the Appropriation of Public Land in Neoliberal Britain*, London: Verso.

Dasgupta, P. and G. Heal (1979) *The Economics of Exhaustible Resources*, Cambridge: Cambridge University Press.

Evans, T. and B. Fine (1980a) "The Diffusion of Mechanical Cutting in the British Inter-war Coal Industry", Birkbeck Discussion Paper, no 75, University of London.

Evans, T. and B. Fine (1980b) "Economies of Scale in the British Inter-war Coal Industry", Birkbeck Discussion Paper, no 76, University of London.

Fine, B. (1978). "Royalties and the UK Inter-war Coal Industry", Birkbeck Discussion Paper, no 62, University of London.

Fine, B. (1979) "On Marx's Theory of Agricultural Rent", *Economy and Society*, vol 8, no 3, pp. 241–79.

Fine, B. (1980a) *Economic Theory and Ideology*, London: Edward Arnold.

Fine, B. (1980b) "The Historical Approach to Rent and Price Theory Reconsidered", Birkbeck Discussion Paper No. 69, University of London, published in *Australian Economic Papers*, vol. 22, no 4, 1983, pp. 132–43. See also Chapter 2.

Fine, B. (1980c) "On Marx's Theory of Agricultural Rent: a Rejoinder", *Economy and Society*, vol 9, no 3, pp. 327–331.

Fine, B. (1982) "Landed Property and the Distinction between Royalty and Rent", *Land Economics*, vol 58, no 3, pp. 338–350.

Fine, B. (1985) "Land, Capital and the British Coal Industry Prior to World War II", in Ball et al (eds) (1985).

Fine, B. (1990a) *The Coal Question: Political Economy and Industrial Change from the Nineteenth Century to the Present Day*, London: Routledge, 1990, reprinted as Routledge Revival, 2013.

Fine, B. (1990b) "Featherbedding Cartel or Economies of Scale: the Case of the British Interwar Coal Industry", *Economic History Review*, vol XLIII, no 3, pp. 438–49.

Fine, B. (1990c) "Gender Discrimination and Bargaining Structures in the Coal Industry: Evidence on Behalf of the NUM to the Equal Pay Tribunal", Case No: 31708/85/LS, available at https://eprints.soas.ac.uk/38044/.

Fine, B. (1993) "Is Small Beautiful? Mine Size in the British Inter-War Coal Industry", *Economic History Review*, vol XLVI, no 1, pp. 160–62.

Fine, B. (1994) "Coal, Diamonds and Oil: Towards a Comparative Theory of Mining", *Review of Political Economy*, vol 6, no 3, pp. 279–302.

Fine, B. (1998) *Labour Market Theory: a Constructive Reassessment*, London: Routledge, reprinted in paperback, 2010.

Fine, B. (2019) "Marx's Rent Theory Revisited? Landed Property, Nature and Value", *Economy and Society*, vol 48, no 3, pp. 450–61.

Fine, B. and L. Harris (1975) "The British Economy since March 1974", *Bulletin of Conference of Socialist Economists*, vol 4, no 3, issue 12, pp. 43–62.

Fine, B. and L. Harris (1976) "The British Economy from May 1975 to January 1976", *Bulletin of Conference of Socialist Economists*, vol 5, no 2, issue 14, pp. 1–24.

Fine, B. and L. Harris (1985) *The Peculiarities of the British Economy*, London: Wishart.

Fine, B. and E. Leopold (1993) *The World of Consumption*, London: Routledge.

Fine, B., K. O'Donnell and M. Prevezer (1985a) "Coal Before Nationalisation", in Fine and Harris (1985), pp. 285–319.

Fine, B., K. O'Donnell and M. Prevezer (1985b) "Coal After Nationalisation", in Fine and Harris (1985), pp. 167–202.

Flux, A. (1923) *Economic Principles*, London: Methuen.

Gaffney, M. (ed.) (1967) *Extractive Resources and Taxation*, Madison: University of Wisconsin Press.

Gray, L. (1914) "Rent under the Assumption of Exhaustibility", *Quarterly Journal of Economics*, vol 28, no 3, pp. 466–89.

Hobson, J. A. (1891) "The Law of the Three Rents", *Quarterly Journal of Economics*, vol 5, no 3, pp. 263–88.

HoC (1989) *Special Report from the Committee on the Associated British Ports (No. 2) Bill*, March 9th, London: HMSO.

Hotelling, H. (1931) "The Economics of Exhaustible Resources", *Journal of Political Economy*, vol 39, no 2, pp. 137–75.

Jevons, W. S. (1865) *The Coal Question: an Inquiry Concerning the Progress of the Nation, and the Probable Exhaustion of Our Coal Mines*, London: MacMillan.

Marshall, A. (1959) *Principles of Economics*, eighth edition, London: Macmillan.

Marshall, A. (1923) *Industry and Trade*, fourth edition, London: Macmillan.

Marx, K. (1969) *Theories of Surplus Value, Part II*, London: Lawrence and Wishart.

Marx, K. (1971) *Capital, Volume III*, Moscow: Progress Publishers.

McEwen, J. (1981) *Who Owns Scotland: a Study in Land Ownership*, Edinburgh: Polygon.

Ministry of Reconstruction (1919) Committee on the Acquisition and Valuation of Land for Public Purposes, First Report, January, 1918, National Archives, Kew, Reference: T 1/12308/15534.

Mishan, E. (1968) "What Is Producers' Surplus?", *American Economic Review*, vol 58, no 5, pp. 1269–82.

Nef, J. (1932) *The Rise of the British Coal Industry 1550–1700*, London: Routledge and Kegan Paul.

O'Donnell, K. (1990) "Canteen Workers' Wages and Collective Bargaining Arrangements in British Coal", Evidence on Behalf of the NUM to the Equal Pay Tribunal, Case No: 31708/85/LS, available at https://eprints.soas.ac.uk/id/eprint/38021.

Orchard, J. (1922) "The Rent of Mineral Lands", *Quarterly Journal of Economics*, vol 36, no 2, pp. 290–318.

Ricardo, D. (1971) *Principles of Political Economy and Taxation*, London: Penguin Books, Pelican.

Samuel Report (1926) *Report of the Royal Commission on the Coal Industry*, Cmd 2600, three volumes, London: HMSO.

Sankey Report (1919) *Reports of the Royal Commission on the Coal Industry, with Minutes of Evidence*, Cmd 359–61, London: HMSO.

Sorley, W. (1889) "Mining Royalties and Their Effects on the Iron and Coal Trades", *Journal of the Royal Statistical Society*, vol 52, no 1, pp. 60–98.

Steele, H. (1967) "Natural Resource Taxation: Resource Allocations and Distribution Implications", Gaffney (ed.) (1967), pp. 233–65.

Sweet, C. (1984) "Sizewell B Inquiry. Statements of Case, Proofs of Evidence and Addenda. Town and Country Planning Association", The National Archives, Kew – Department of Energy, Reference: EG2/262.

Taussig, F. (1939) *Principles of Economics, Volume II*, New York: Macmillan.

Taylor, A. (1968) "The Coal Industry", in D. Aldcroft (ed.) *The Development of British Industries and Foreign Competition*, Toronto: University of Toronto Press, pp. 37–70.

Wessel, R. (1967) "A Note on Economic Rent", *American Economic Review*, vol 57, no 5, pp. 1221–26.

CHAPTER 4

The New Revolution in Economics

Postscript as Personal Preamble

Before revisions for this collection, this piece was published under same title in *Capital and Class*, no 61, Spring, 1997, pp. 143–48. *Capital and Class* had become the new name for the Bulletin of the Conference of Socialist Economists, CSE. The CSE had been inspired by the renewal of interest in Marxist political economy in the 1960s, and the fierce debates that resulted around and over both whether Marx is valid or not in his value theory and its applicability to contemporary capitalism. And, if right, what is the correct interpretation of Marx's value theory.[1] CSE was organised around conferences, working groups and workshops (and this provided a nostalgic model for the International Initiative on Promoting Political Economy, iippe.org, founded in 2006, for which I became Chair).

I was an active participant and organiser in CSE. Together with Laurence Harris, we provided a couple of analyses of developments in and around the British economy (Fine and Harris 1975 and 1976). These empirical analyses dovetailed with our theoretical contributions, in which we emphasised the role of the state in both (domestic and international) industrial restructuring and the role of finance – as opposed to the more standard analyses around (conflict over) levels of effective demand and distribution between capital and labour. I even published three pieces in issue 12 of the Bulletin (Fine 1975a and b) and recall printing copies on a Gestetner from stencils (so much has technology moved on).

The first issue of the Bulletin appeared in Winter 1971.[2] As indicated, we did everything ourselves as a membership organisation. But, ultimately, reliance upon our own resources proved too demanding. With the change in name to *Capital and Class*, C&C, came its handing over to a professional printer in 1977, rather than a gestetner, and then to a publisher. The CSE moved closer towards being a normal academic association with a journal plus add ons. The focus of

---

1 Ultimately leading to my contribution through Fine and Harris (1979) – its title, *Rereading Capital*, reflecting the Althusserian moment – although debates have rumbled on, see forthcoming volume on Marxist political economy.
2 Go to https://journals.sagepub.com/page/cnc/collections/bulletin for a full archive for which I also have dusty hard copies.

CSE also drifted away from Marxist political economy as such to offer a more rounded approach to topics associated with capital and class.

Some twenty years from its founding, along with lingering loyalties, this all motivated the submission to C&C of my first explicit piece on economics imperialism, wishing to engage an audience beyond economics/political economy. The more substantive factors behind my positing a "revolution in economics" in light of economics imperialism are covered in the Introduction to this volume. The piece itself appeared under the following rubric at the beginning of the article, with POLEMIC in large, capitalised type:

> In this section Capital & Class carries contributions which address contemporary themes of concern to the left. It is our intention that contributions provoke controversy, challenge taken-for-granted assumptions and raise themes and issues of concern to readers of Capital & Class in an unusual manner.

I suspect that no other contribution was made to the section, in either past or future issues, and I appeared to fail to provoke interest let alone controversy. Looking back at it now, more than twenty-five years since it was drafted, I am both pleased and surprised how much it covers, not least for a short polemic, in terms of the issues involved. In general, my positions on these have remained much the same, with some updating as economics imperialism has moved forward, especially to its current phase, and these have been discussed in greater depth and breadth in continuing contributions as well as those appearing in the next volume on economics imperialism. The one major omission was the failure to anticipate the shifting rhythm of opposition to the orthodoxy which, especially following the Global Financial Crisis of 2007/8, is currently in an upswing compared to the doldrums at the time of writing even if mainstream hegemony and intolerance remains as strong as ever within its intellectual and institutional fortresses. The contribution now follows.

1   POLEMIC

The purpose of this polemic is to suggest that a profound change is underway in orthodox economics – one that in retrospect may appear to be as significant as the marginalist revolution that was substantially completed a century previously. At that time, the marginalist revolution marked the transition from classical political economy to the neoclassical orthodoxy which is now so well-known and pervasive. Indeed, the current revolution in economic thinking can be understood as reversing the direction that was taken in establishing neoclassical economics although, as will be seen, it has not involved a simple retracing of the steps to re-establish something akin to a modern day classical political economy.

In a nutshell, my argument is that the marginalist revolution established economics as a discipline by substantially limiting its scope of application. It did so on the basis of a particular methodology and by isolating itself from other social sciences. It retreated into and consolidated what I shall term "fortress economics". This is probably the least controversial part of my argument in its characterisation of the current orthodoxy. What is more challenging is the proposition that the fortress is now being used as the basis on which to expand the scope of application of the orthodoxy – to occupy the analytical terrain which was previously abandoned to establish the discipline, and which has previously been the preserve of other social sciences. In other words, the current revolution in orthodox economics is one in which it is "colonising" the other social sciences whether this be by incorporating them into its own fortress or through the analytical influence that it exerts over them. This process of colonisation is to be seen across a wide range of issues, more normally limited to other disciplines or lying outside the domain of the orthodoxy. It can be seen in the assault upon development economics, in segmented labour market theory, in human capital theory, in the treatment of trade unions, and in the new political economy of the right and its theory of the state and rent seeking, etc.

Contrast this with Alfred Marshall's *Principles of Economics*, where the "political" was taken out of "political economy". This is symbolic of a more general change wrought by the marginalist revolution. The economy became examined independently of social relations other than those attached immediately to the market. It became a study of prices and quantities, more or less harmoniously coordinated through the market system – the science of supply and demand. This allowed the discipline to develop its own peculiar methods, certainly from the perspective of other social sciences. Its concepts, such as production functions and utility, have been ahistorical and asocial even if applied to the capitalist era. The economy has been perceived as a model along engineering lines, susceptible to analysis in purely mathematical terms.

The separation of the economy from society has involved the excision of social relations and structures, with the embracing of methodological individualism in which macro outcomes are perceived to be the consequence of the aggregated behaviour of atomised and optimising agents. The orthodoxy has also been organised around the central concept of equilibrium; it has developed a particular relationship to verification in the use of empirical material in the form of econometrics.

No doubt, there are other features of the orthodoxy which are worthy of mention. Here, though, two points need to be emphasised. First, these characteristics have set economics aside from the other social sciences both in terms of methodology and assumptions which are and have generally been perceived to be absurd, and also in terms of precluding any prospect of a genuine interdisciplinary rapport between economics and other disciplines. Of course, those practising within orthodox neoclassical economics have increasingly taken their methodology and assumptions to be axiomatic and self-evident. This has only served to reinforce its isolation from other disciplines. Second, further consolidating the alien character of economics from the perspective of other disciplines, the century following the marginalist revolution has seen the strengthening of the technical and conceptual apparatus with and through which the discipline of economics has developed. The intensity and sophistication of this endeavour stands in sharp contrast to the scope of its application. Its crowning achievement has been general equilibrium theory which remains the focal point, even if by way of departure (of the economy from the ideal), for the vast majority of orthodox economics.[3]

Of course, there has always been radical opposition to these developments, some from within the orthodoxy itself in terms of deploying models in which methodological individualism is at most implicit. The 1960s and 1970s, from which the CSE itself emerged, however, represents the hiatus for economic heterodoxy. It is important to recognise, then, that fortress economics remains as strong as ever, continues to thrive through intensive development and is now even less challenged from alternative approaches from within the discipline than ever before. Quite apart from the opposition that might be posed by Marxist political economy, the age of heterodox economics is over and died with the likes of Schumpeter, Galbraith and others who used to be treated with respect in passing but who are now more or less ignored. Whatever is happening in orthodox economics, it is not at the expense of, and as a challenge to, its longstanding and increasingly hegemonic analytical citadels.

---

3 As will be apparent from other chapters, the notion of general equilibrium as an organising framework has faded considerably since this piece was first drafted (although always available as some sort of rationalisation along the lines of there but for imperfections goes the real world). For the mainstream, general equilibrium has become at most one amongst many other ways of looking at the economy whether as a whole or in part although its constituent parts do remain unimaginably important as technical and conceptual resources upon which the mainstream can draw.

By the same token, the rhythm of the orthodoxy's change is both uneven and not rigidly demarcated sequentially even if the broad trends are relatively clear. Certain branches of economics have resisted incorporation into the fortress, especially those which, at least initially, appeared to be resistant to model-building and the conventional methodology, with its individualistic focus and aversion to the social however conceived. Most notable here has been development economics, not least because it has been concerned with broad change, including social and economic structure, over relatively long periods of time. The same immunity or resistance has until recently been characteristic of many of those specialisms which used to go under the rubric of 'applied' – public sector, industrial, labour, and urban and regional economics, for example.

These required a sensitivity to institutions and to a descriptive discourse for which models were not always considered appropriate. At the opposite extreme, what I take to be the new revolution in economics, already has early antecedents, ventured upon whilst the fortress was still in the process of being consolidated. This is especially so where the market was excluded by necessity, as in the theory of the internal organisation of the firm based in Coasian terms on efficiency in expenditure of transaction costs.

More generally, there have been two ways in which orthodox economics has extended its sphere of application. The first, and more readily and earlier adopted, is the treatment of the social as if it were an individual. Little analytical innovation is required here other than to extend the scope of well-worn principles to new applications. For example, Heckscher-Ohlin international trade theory simply treats the nation as though it were an individual with given preferences, production possibilities and factor endowments. At the forefront of such applications have been economists like Gary Becker. For him, the principles of neoclassical economics are universally valid and are not to be confined to market relations. He sets himself the task of explaining as much as possible on the basis of individual optimisation usually with given preferences and production possibilities. Thus, educational choices are explained in terms of human capital theory; the division of labour within and between the home and the market place by reference to the new household economics; the demographic transition is tied to optimisation even across generations as the cost of child bearing rises; racism is understood as a taste for discrimination. And so the list could run on. It even now includes a theory of drug or other forms of addiction as arising out of the rational choice of today's pleasures when set against the discounted pain of tomorrow.

The colonising trend of neoclassical economics, then, is to be observed as progressing intensively. The areas within economics from which it was previously immune have been increasingly occupied by methodological individualism. This is most marked in the emergence of specialist journals which, other than in their names and terminology, are more or less indistinguishable from one another, especially in the extent to which they rely upon model building based on optimisation. Such journals have challenged, if not always completely displaced, the more traditional treatments of fields such as public sector and development economics. Further, whether in specialist journals or otherwise, the treatment of trade unions, for example, is readily incorporated by treating them as if each was an individual with preferences over employment-wage trade-offs. Similarly, economic policy can be understood in terms of the state as an individual with preferences over potential outcomes in terms of trade-offs between macroeconomic targets such as employment, inflation, balance of payments, etc. At the same time, economics has clearly been extended on the same basis to areas of application where it was not previously thought appropriate as in the economics of crime as a cost-benefit analysis and defence economics as a calculus of costs and threats.

In this way, economics has colonised intensively through extensions from within its own fortress with little or no understanding of the subject matter from the perspective of other disciplines. This does not mean that the latter are unaffected as is illustrated by the neoclassical theory of human capital and of the family. But the extent of colonisation is limited by the continuing dependence on methodological individualism, although this can be implicit, as terms like human capital and rent-seeking, for example, insidiously move into popular parlance without displaying their methodological and analytical origins.

The second and more intellectually challenging way in which economics has extended its scope is by accepting and directly addressing the weakness with which it has so reasonably been accused by other social sciences. This is that it has, on the basis of methodological individualism, no way of confronting the obvious empirical existence of institutions and collective behaviour – in other words, the social and its historical evolution. This conundrum has been resolved by developing theories of social or collective agencies and structures on the basis of individual optimisation. The issue is posed of under what conditions does it make sense for individuals to act in unison or in common or to form such uniformity. The new political economy, for example, constructs a theory of collective interests in terms of setting the rewards to be gained against the costs of achieving, distributing and policing them. Another example is provided by the new institutional economics. In this and other areas, radical political economy and economists have often been seduced into a compromise with methodological individualism. More narrowly, on the orthodoxy's traditional terrain, economics has deployed the absence of full, or the presence of, asymmetric, information as the basis on which markets are structured. It is in this extensive development from fortress economics that a more genuine colonisation of other disciplines accrues from a conceptual point of view since it is not based on methodological individualism to the exclusion of social structures. The result, however, is not necessarily a more successful colonisation in this extensive form, since it depends upon how its assaults are responded to by the disciplines under threat. In this respect, whether the assault from the fortress is intensive or extensive is probably of secondary importance compared to whether it is met with incorporation, resistance and/or tolerance alongside other continuing and evolving intellectual traditions.

In the light of the above discussion, five questions present themselves. First, is the hypothesis of colonisation correct? The term may not be the most appropriate for a variety of reasons, some of which will emerge below. But is economics currently experiencing a revolution which will appear as dramatic one hundred years hence as the marginalist revolution does today? Or are the examples I have chosen temporary, limited and counterbalanced by retreats back into fortress economics?

Second, if the hypothesis is correct, how is it being realised across the various subdisciplines within economics and in its relationship to the other social sciences that it seeks to colonise? The rhythm of colonisation will be uneven and the specific conceptual content of the process will vary according to how the issues concerned are broached. Nor is this simply an intellectual exercise and conflict. For the triumph of economics over other disciplines in certain areas, if such it is, in part reflects the balance in material conflicts, most notably if misleadingly expressed in terms of the triumph of the market over the state.

Third, the discussion so far has essentially been economics-centric. How has the territory previously occupied by the other social sciences been colonised by economics. What is the view from the fortress? But matters will appear differently from the perspective of the colonised. What has been their response? In some cases, after initial resistance, the concepts deployed by economists have become the stock terminology across the social sciences as a whole – as in the general acceptability of 'human capital' as an organising concept. Industrial relations have become riddled with individualistic models of trade union behaviour – in analysing whether to join or not and what they do. The new household economics has been both incorporated and resisted. Cliometrics, or neoclassical economic history, has been well-established but not apparently at the expense of other branches or methods within social and economic history. A telling illustration is provided by the bourgeoisification of Marxism, ultimately in the form of analytical Marxism – a special case of a more general trend for radical economics to be some amalgam of neoclassical economics and some more or less arbitrary social structure or constraint. Again, the list could be extended. It seems, though, that the process is both varied and uneven, reflecting differences in the issues broached and the continuing traditions and dynamics of the colonised disciplines or subject matter.

Fourth, why is this happening and why now? One answer, which I would judge to be incorrect and to reflect wishful thinking, is that the neoclassical orthodoxy is in crisis on its traditional analytical patch, and so is seeking pastures new on which to sustain itself. As already argued, fortress economics is as strong as ever and is not suffering at the expense of colonisation. Indeed, the two have a positive synergy irrespective of the longstanding recognition of the weaknesses of methodological individualism. By contrast, it is almost certainly the weaknesses of heterodox alternatives that have vacated the space for the orthodoxy to expand its scope without intellectual embarrassment.

This no doubt is connected causally to the ideological triumphalism of the market over the past twenty years. As policy stances have again and again emphasised the virtues of extending market forces to as many areas of activity as possible, it is hardly surprising that this should induce the economics of the market to tread where previously methodological individualism had been unable to obtain a foothold. In addition, the teaching of economics has become more widespread on the conservative basis of given technical principles, and an expanding teaching staff has been coerced to jump through performance hoops that require quick and acceptable returns on the research front.

This has encouraged an increasing scope for orthodoxy within the discipline and the creation of journals to accommodate it. The final question, even if only token answers have been provided to the others, is what to do about it? Should political economy abandon the attempt to contest the field of economics altogether and retreat to more favourable terrain in or around other disciplines? This is a matter both for teaching and for research. It seems unnecessarily defeatist to concede the field of economics to the economists. Yet, it is hard to persuade students that their increasingly hard-earned technical expertise within the orthodoxy is of limited worth, especially when the time and recognition, let alone the teaching materials, for alternatives are heavily constrained. Students and staff alike are increasingly limited by available career opportunities, especially as standards within economics are becoming internationalised and uniform.

Nor does the option of reading the classics, not least Marx, appear as a viable alternative, invaluable though it would be, since it fails to engage with the orthodoxy and defeat it. On the research front, how are we to keep the traditions of political economy alive and defend its presence within other disciplines when it is so obviously not at home within economics? These questions are easier to answer in intellectual principle than they are in academic practice.

The prospects seem far from rosy, especially in the current intellectual climate which contrasts so strongly with that of a generation ago when radical political economy was on the offensive, neoclassical orthodoxy on the defensive and interest in Marxist economics was so powerfully represented through, for example, the emergence of the CSE and Capital & Class, and the debates in and around them. But, despite the intellectual swing, there are contradictions in the current situation and, hence, positive features and opportunities. Orthodox economics, with it esoteric and alien content and its increasingly demanding technical requirements, is proving extremely unpopular with students both in terms of the problems that it addresses and how it addresses them. The very same processes that consolidate the fortress leave it bereft of widespread support. Even those students who are commercially rather than critically minded, prefer accountancy, finance, and business studies, with only a token course or two taken in economics. It remains to be seen whether such antipathy to economics can be galvanised into a critical alternative and whether it can best be launched from within economics or as a reaction against it from outside.

References

All added for this volume; none, nor footnotes, in the original Polemic.

Fine, B. (1975a) "The Circulation of Capital, Ideology and Crisis", *Bulletin of Conference of Socialist Economists*, vol 4, no 3, Issue, 12, pp. 82–96.

Fine, B. (1975b) "A Note on Productive and Unproductive Labour", *Bulletin of the Conference of Socialist Economists*, vol 4, no 3, Issue, 12, pp. 99–103.

Fine, B. and L. Harris (1975) "The British Economy since March 1974", co-author L. Harris, *Bulletin of the Conference of Socialist Economists*, vol 4, no 3, issue, 12, pp. 43–62.

Fine, B. and L. Harris (1976) "The British Economy from May 1975 to January 1976", *Bulletin of Conference of the Socialist Economists*, vol 5, no 2, issue 14, pp. 1–24.

Fine, B. and L. Harris (1979) *Rereading Capital*, London: Macmillan.

CHAPTER 5

From Bourdieu to Becker: Economics Confronts the Social Sciences

Postscript as Personal Preamble

In the second half of the 1990s, a number of themes in my research came together. One is the subject of this volume, and two that follow, on economics imperialism. The other two fell under this umbrella but, in my work and more generally, took on lives of their own – social capital and the shift from the Washington Consensus to the post Washington Consensus. This contribution brings these themes together for the first time. It does so by seeing both social capital and development economics as examples of economics imperialism but each with its own distinctive origins and dynamics.

Social capital came to economics as a gift from the social sciences and it might be thought to have been repaid with vengeance, not least as it became seen as the missing ingredient in explaining economic success (and everything else for that matter). Whilst social capital came in main part, directly and indirectly, to mainstream economics via rational choice sociologist, James Coleman, it was picked up by his Chicago colleague, Gary Becker, in a desperate attempt to extend his so-called economic approach to the social as opposed to its being confined to the personal. In doing so, it anticipated in the simplest of forms what was to make economics imperialism, and social capital within it, much more wide-ranging by its being seen as the means by which to correct market imperfections.

As a result, it was an ideal concept for explaining (lack of) development drawing upon what might be termed the Stiglitz moment as he occupied the role of Chief Economist at the World Bank and promoted his own version of market (information) imperfection economics. In the event, Stiglitz himself rarely ever use the notion of social capital but he created the space for it to prosper at the World Bank.[1] Like a rag doll, social capital was picked up and played with at the World Bank and then precipitously abandoned once it had

---

1 For a late exception, see Haldar and Stiglitz (2016) and Fine (2023) for a critique with full referencing for the propositions that follow. But see also Stiglitz (1999, p. 59), which opens by placing social capital within his own version of market imperfections: "Social capital ... can be interpreted ... as a social means of coping with moral hazard and incentive problems".

served its purpose. According to the World Bank's own 'social capitalists', social capital had been deployed to cultivate economists into taking the social seriously. On the contrary, it had allowed them to appropriate the concept whilst their economics remain internally unchallenged. The Washington Consensus is dead, long live the (post) Washington Consensus, especially in the world of scholarship.

This contribution is also notable for introducing some further elements in the study of economics imperialism of wider relevance. In seeking to explain why economics imperialism should have been prospering at this time, and in the forms that it did, emphasis was placed not only on developments within economics (from market perfection to imperfection, and old to new economics imperialism, from Becker to Stiglitz). In addition, across the other social sciences, the retreat from the excesses of postmodernism is observed as well as the wish to get to grips with the realities of neoliberalism, globalisation, and the like. To do so, reliance has been placed upon what might be called capital (as opposed to commodity) fetishism, as this piece carefully explains how the fluidity of capital as an economic category as it passes through its various forms and structures, induces the notion that anything can be capital as long as it positively contributes to economic and social outcomes.

This is certainly true of Coleman whose social capital was a crude restatement of his theory of social exchange (and drawn from an extraordinarily reactionary notion of social capital proposed by James Buchanan, that bemoaned that privileged white, middle-class American life was under threat).[2] But, inspiring strange bedfellows, the same fetishism, if in entirely different ways and with entirely different substance, is displayed by Pierre Bourdieu, the progressive French sociologist who is concerned with the material and cultural ways in which class is reproduced and hierarchies sustained. In effect, this set the two limits between which social capital could vary – twixt the connected individual and the exercise of hierarchical power. If only Bourdieu, and the latter, had prevailed, rather than becoming a radical tinge and fringe to the literature, I would not have spent the best part of two decades seeking to bring social capital down.[3]

Otherwise, where this contribution remains weak is in not incorporating more fully the influence of material as opposed to intellectual explanations for economics imperialism in general and social capital in general. There are

---

2 A similar conclusion can be drawn from the account of Fleury and Marciano (2017) of Buchanan's shifting views on education, and towards an authoritarian vein within libertarianism – what are we to do if there is abuse of educational opportunities and liberties?.
3 See especially Fine (2001 and 2010a) and, most recently, Fine (2023).

at most hints of what was to come in terms of understanding the nature of neoliberalism as a new stage of capitalism, contingent upon financialisation (a term scarcely yet in use) and the passage of neoliberalism through three separate stages (shock, Third Way, and overt interventionism despite ideology to the contrary) corresponding to a large degree, respectively, to the three phases of economics imperialism (old, new and newer, with the latter contingent on supplementing market imperfection economics with whatever social variables to suit). Further, but by no means least, Robert Putnam, the eminence grise of social capital – or the Ronald McDonald of social science as I dub him in Fine (2010a) – is only mentioned in passing alongside the contributions that rocketed him into being the most cited author across the social sciences in the 1990s (from a late social capital start within the decade), Putnam (2000) being just around the corner albeit developed massively from Putnam (1995).

I never met Putnam, nor Bourdieu and Coleman although Bourdieu's son published the French edition of the fifth English edition of *Marx's Capital* (Fine and Saad Filho 2010). Whilst Putnam was to become the poster boy of the second phase of neoliberalism (most obviously the poor can help themselves by helping one another rather than organising to contest the causes of poverty), Coleman was a product of its first phase – with relations with James Buchanan (public choice theory) and Gary Becker (representative of old economics imperialism par excellence), both Nobel Prize Winners in Economics, and members of the Mont Pèlerin Society, the institutionalised intellectual fountainhead for neoliberalism. I have not been able to find out if Coleman was a member but Deepak Lal, James S. Coleman Professor of International Development Studies, University of California, Los Angeles, California, USA, has been its President, nuff said.[4]

1   **Introduction**[5]

Interdisciplinary research is prospering as never before. This is even so for economics which is traditionally the least amenable to collaboration with other

---

4 On the Mont Pèlerin Society, MPS, see Mirowski and Plehwe (2015). Coincidentally, Lal was on the staff at Oxford University in the early 1970s and innocently offered me a job as a research assistant for fieldwork in Africa (at the very beginnings of the rent-seeking, corruption trope of which I was then unaware). But I never heard from him again. For details of the MPS as intellectual fountainhead for promoting neoliberalism, see https://www.desmog.com/mont-pelerin-society/.

5 Based upon Fine (1999a). Thanks to Costas Lapavitsas and others for comments on earlier drafts.

disciplines. From within the perspective of its own orthodoxy, economics is scientific in view of its mathematical formalism in model-building and its heavy reliance upon statistical testing. By contrast, for other disciplines, the methodology, methods and assumptions of economics have generally been perceived as both alien and unacceptable.[6]

It is time to stand back and take stock of the shifting relationship between economics and the other social sciences. Elsewhere, I have argued that it is potentially experiencing a revolutionary change, with economics colonising the other disciplines as never before.[7] This is most marked in case of rational choice theory through which the "economic approach" is extended to all areas of life. In other words, social theory is reconstructed, and reduced to, the aggregated behaviour of otherwise isolated optimising individuals.

Such colonisation is longstanding and is well represented in the work of Gary Becker. He is strongly associated with human capital theory, the new household economics, the economics of crime, the new political economy, the economics of addiction, etc.[8] What is relatively new, however, is that internal developments within economics have provided new techniques by which it can colonise social theory. In particular, mainstream economics now has models in which it putatively explains the formation of social or economic structures, institutions and customs on the continuing basis of individual optimisation. Where there is imperfect or asymmetric information, or transaction costs around exchanges, a rationale can be constructed for otherwise isolated individuals to impose structures or coordinate with one another on a voluntary basis. Significantly, this has given rise to the notion of *social* capital within the work of Becker. He sees it as a generalisation of *personal* capital (freely chosen experiences) which is itself a generalised form of *human* capital (which is confined to education and skills, derived by choice or otherwise).

Human capital has, over a number of decades, found its way into the lexicon of social theory even though it was deeply criticised when first mooted.[9] Social capital has sprung to prominence and widespread use much more quickly. This reflects a number of factors. First, social capital has not simply, nor even primarily, passed from economics to the other social sciences, it has also been

---

[6] For a critical assessment of mainstream economics, appropriate to the themes developed here, see Fine (1995b and 1997b).

[7] See other volumes on economics imperialism, and, cited in the original (Fine 1997a and 1998b and c).

[8] See especially Becker (1996) and a remarkable collection of essays by his followers (Tommasi and Iurelli (eds) 1995), which provides an overview of, and references to, Becker's work.

[9] See Fine (1998a).

given life from within these other disciplines. Second, the intellectual climate of the current period is one of uneven retreat from the excesses of postmodernism and its subjective construction of the social as meaning. Consequently, there is a wish to return to scrutiny of material realities and, where the economy is concerned, the notion of social capital provides a convenient tool for this purpose.

Third, also in part as a consequence of postmodernism, social theory has found eclecticism to be more acceptable. Arguments and concepts can be picked up from different sources and combined together without regard to their separate, let alone their mutual, consistency. Indeed, the point is well-illustrated by the term social capital itself. As has been observed in recent surveys of the literature,[10] themselves a mark of the concept's rapid rise to adolescence, social capital is used ambiguously and chaotically. Equally important though, one of these surveys, rather than rejecting the notion altogether, suggests a more positive approach that can only intensify the problems involved (Woolcock 1998, p. 159):[11]

> Where do these criticisms of the idea of social capital ... leave us? Short of dismissing the term altogether, one possible resolution of these concerns may be that there are different types, levels or dimensions of social capital, different performance outcomes associated with different combinations of these dimensions, and different sets of conditions that support or weaken favorable combinations. Unraveling and resolving these issues requires a more dynamic than static understanding of social capital; it invites a more detailed examination of the intellectual history of social capital, and the search for lessons from empirical research that embrace a range of any such dimensions, levels, or conditions.

The initial purpose of this chapter is two-fold. First, it seeks to examine how select, if diverse, analytical traditions have been brought together around the

---

10   See Harriss and de Renzio (1997) and Woolcock (1998).
11   Note that Woolcock, from critic of social capital, was seduced into being its most ardent proponent through the World Bank, Fine (2001, 2010a and 2023) and Fine (2008) in debate with Bebbington (2004) and Bebbington et al (2004 and 2006). Less ardently, Harris and de Renzio (1997) do not reject the concept but seek to ensure that it incorporates a more radical content. See also Christoforou (2022). My own stance is that social capital is analytically and strategically compromised and so should be both criticised remorselessly and abandoned – not because it cannot be deployed progressively in principle but, by doing so in practice, its hegemonic negative side becomes legitimised by allowing for marginal dissent against an unaccepting and unyielding core and momentum of its own.

notion of social capital. Section 2 argues that the structure and movement of capital itself promotes ambiguity and illusion in the way in which it is perceived. Section 3 applies these insights to the work of Pierre Bourdieu and his understanding of social capital. Section 4 undertakes a similar, if more limited, exercise for James Coleman, a sociologist in the Becker mould. Whilst Bourdieu and Coleman lie at opposite and incompatible extremes of the spectrum in terms of sociological method and theory, their common use of the term social capital has allowed them to serve as authority for a wide range of applications that draws, at times explicitly, upon them both. Some of these, however, draw upon less extreme stances, such as network theory within sociology or collective solutions to market imperfections within economics.

The final section, before concluding, examines the wider use of social capital within other disciplines and sets this against the second and broader purpose of this contribution. This is to examine the extent to which, and how, economics is colonising the other social sciences through the example of social capital. In particular, reference is made to the rapidity with which it has been applied to problems of economic development.[12] Indeed, by reference to a phrase coined by the World Bank, social capital is seen as the developmental "missing link". This allows it to miss or disregard all other links, especially those around (economic) power and conflict, whilst relegating the role of the state (if not the market which is to be corrected by social capital) as a developmental agency.[13]

---

[12] But, worth emphasising, social capital has been more or less everywhere by topic and place. In Scandinavia, social capital and health has a buzz with the following supposed benefits (Fine 2010a, p. 22): "it will improve mental and self-reported health, health at work, life satisfaction and well-being, and children's health; and lower risk of violence, accidents, suicide, coronary heart disease, cancer, teen pregnancy and 'risky' and premarital sexual activity, fatalism, being overweight, chances of drug (ab)use (apart from cannabis!) and addiction (but enhance successful withdrawal), being a depressed mother of young children, low birth weight of children, excessive alcohol consumption, and so on".

[13] Note that my first contribution on social capital (Fine 1999b) suggested that it would be used by the World Bank to circumvent serious (re)consideration of the developmental state paradigm, as it had done entirely until it at least took the step with *The East Asian Miracle* (World Bank 1993) to set it aside. But, in the event, this deployment of social capital as an alternative to the developmental state proved unnecessary and the concept was simply ignored by the post Washington Consensus as it had been by its predecessor.

2   The Enigma and Fluidity of Capital

One crucial factor in the warmer reception with which other social sciences are prepared to confront economics has been the general analytical environment across them and, in particular, the intellectual climate created by the shift to postmodernism and its aftermath. The intellectual environment over the past two decades has been marked by the influence of postmodernism, although the incidence of its content, depth and rhythm have varied across the different disciplines. As a result, there has been a broad corresponding shift of the balance within methodology and theory across a number of interrelated components. First, subjectivity has advanced at the expense of objectivity, with an associated rise in the appeal of relativism. Second, the economy, especially production, has been perceived to be unduly privileged, leading to a focus upon the non-economic, especially consumption and culture. Third, interest in the so-called new social movements has tended to discredit, and shift attention away from, class analysis. Fourth, novel forms of discourse have arisen, not least in discourse theory itself, with new analytical formalisms in the study of symbolic representation, and in the critical deconstruction of meaning, etc.

Jean Baudrillard has been a leading figure in the postmodernist movement. In the context of consumption, Fine and Leopold (1993, Chapter 19) have argued that his particular flight of fancy, through the use of the notion of symbolic value, has been based on an exclusive pre-occupation with the redefinition of the meaning of the use value of commodities without reference to their material properties, the latter not understood simply as objects with physical properties but as embodying the material outcome of the activities around the production of exchange value.[14] The purpose here is to extend that argument by suggesting how the dependence of contemporary consumption upon the commodities produced under capitalist relations has paved the way for social sciences to be influenced to follow particular directions.

Initially, consider what might be termed the fluidity of capital. In terms of Marx's theory of the circuits of industrial capital, for example, the latter – irrespective of what is produced – successively moves through three different

---

14   See also Slater (1997, p. 158) who perceives Baudrillard as having reduced consumption to a matter of signs alone: "Barthes and Baudrillard … merely adopt Veblen's general idea that the only real function of goods is to signify status. They then generalize this to all classes and translate it into semiotic terms. Baudrillard takes this furthest, to the point of arguing that we no longer consume things but only signs". See also Bayliss et al (2018) and, most recently, see Bayliss and Fine (2021).

forms, those of money, productive and commodity capital. Associated with each of these forms, there is encouraged a particular corresponding understanding of capital – as finance, an instrument of production, or output that embodies a surplus over inputs. In each case, whatever the analytical meaning deployed, capital is understood not only in isolation from its other forms but also apart from the social relations upon which it is based.[15]

A particularly apt and striking example is provided by Becker's (1996) work. For all his attention to human and other types of *capital*, never once throughout his book is the presence of money acknowledged.[16] This is despite money being the primary instrument through which access is gained to consumption and utility. Yet, further, capitalism is unambiguously dependent upon the presence of labour power as a commodity which is exchanged against money (capital). Apart from being dependent upon a labour market, the latter is monetised under capitalism as one of its distinguishing features.[17]

The crucial point that follows is that the failure to recognise and specify the fluidity of capital appropriately leads, paradoxically, to an even greater fluidity in its definition. This is because any recurrence of any one of its forms in any context, rather than in a logical relation to its other forms, is potentially open to be misconstrued as capital. For Becker, for example, anything that can yield a stream of utility either directly or indirectly becomes a form of capital. Consequently, and not surprisingly, it is not only the distinctiveness associated with the presence of exchange relations that is extinguished as all human activity becomes one generalised form of exchange, but also capital becomes infinitely fluid in interpretation. As observed, for Becker, apart from physical capital, human capital is divided into the two broad types of capital, personal and social, which themselves lead to finer categories such as addictive, imagination, eating, cultural and musical capitals.

Nor is this the end of the matter. For, the movement of capital through its circuits does presuppose the presence of, and interaction with, the general economic and social conditions that are its prerequisites. Obviously, irrespective

---

15   See Fine (1975 and 1980) and Fine and Saad Filho (2016) and also Arthur (1998).
16   There is equally, in his work and that of his followers, a notable absence of consideration of unemployment and power. On the latter, if anticipating, note that for Coleman, it is simply the weight of interpersonal allocation to different person's interests (Swedberg (ed.) 1990, p. 56): "And that constitutes power, which in my system – if it were applied to economics – power and wealth are equivalent. But when you deal not just with economic resources but also with other resources (including things involving collective actions), then it can be better interpreted as "power" rather than as wealth. So that is a very fundamental difference that I have with the neoclassical economists".
17   See Campbell (1998).

of the extent of mutual determination, the general socioeconomic environment can be more or less conducive to the functioning of capital whether this be the scope and efficiency of the credit, educational or policing systems, for example, let alone the role of the state more generally. Consequently, the fluidity of capital in that it needs to move through its various forms, leads to a conflation between capital itself and the conditions that are necessary for, or beneficial to, it.[18]

The leading example is provided by time itself and the longstanding notion that derives from the marginalist revolution that capital is nothing other than the productivity of time. More generally, anything that can contribute to productivity or efficiency can be understood as capital, whether it be a physical factor – a country has more capital because of a better climate – or, equally significant, one that is socially constructed. The latter constitutes the basis on which Becker understands social capital, something which is ultimately conducive to individual utility through interaction with others other than through exchange or use of personal capital alone.

A third aspect in the fluidity of capital needs to be emphasised over and above its movement through various forms in definite socioeconomic conditions. Capital is also fluid in the tendency to extend its scope of operations to new activities. Variously known as commercialisation or commodification,[19] the boundaries between what is and what is not capitalist production is constantly shifting – most notably, for example, in contemporary patterns of privatisation as opposed to many earlier forms of public provision that removed profitability as an operative criterion of production. More generally, household consumption has become increasingly dependent upon commodities as opposed to domestic production.[20] Such fluidity in forms of provision

---

18   Although this point is not developed here, it is worth observing the affinities between social capital and Marx's notion of the potential indirectly productive impact of unproductive labour (to which can be added non-wage labour). Note, however, that Marx's account is attached to a systematic understanding of the differences between the different types of labour in their relation to capital.

19   In later work, such concepts have been unbundled into commodification as such, commodity form and commodity calculation. See Bayliss and Fine (2021) for example.

20   It should be emphasised that the fluidity of capital into new areas of activity is a complex and contradictory process as opposed to a simple case of shifting but frictional comparative advantage. The productivity increases associated with capitalism which tend to undermine alternative forms of production also have the effect of supporting them through making other sources of income and cheaper inputs available. See Fine (1992) and Fine et al (1996) for discussion in the context of domestic labour and food, respectively. See also Fine (2012) on this in relation to Rosa Luxemburg's underconsumptionism.

reinforces the ambiguity attached to the notion of capital that has been highlighted in the previous discussion.

The final way in which capital is fluid is in a sense the sum of the three other aspects and, as such, more than the individual parts. Just as because money can buy anything, so it can buy everything and is a general power to purchase, so capital is a general power to command, and serves as a symbol of class and of exploitation. In a word, capital becomes synonymous with capitalism, its functioning within the economy extrapolated more generally to society as a whole, and even to pre-capitalist societies.

In short, that capital is fluid in reality – in its own movement, the conditions to which it is attached, the boundaries within which it moves, and the broader powers that it confers and exerts – is conducive to highly fluid interpretations of what constitutes capital. Broadly, two contradictory intellectual and even popular responses are evident, usually in combination in some way with one another. On the one hand, capital can become understood as almost anything according to the different forms, conditions and scope of activity with which it is embroiled, as is evident in the notions of personal and social capital especially once they are disaggregated. On the other hand, capital becomes specific as one or other of its aspects is perceived to be decisive. For example, in neoclassical economics, capital is routinely understood as the quantity of physical (fixed) capital that gives rise to output through a technically fixed production function. In general, neither of these extremes is all that is involved since, however much recognised, at least the fluidity of capital through its various forms is an object of analysis. How do resources, or the various forms of capital, give rise to consequences such as generating output and utility.

Once recognising the fluidity of capital between its different forms, there is also a presumption of the presence of economic and social structures between which movement takes place, not least between production and exchange and between the economic and the non-economic.[21] The necessity for these structures, however, and, to some extent, the form that they take, is a consequence of the class relations, between capital and labour, which are reducible to neither the economic nor the non-economic. Without corresponding property, political and cultural relations, the economic relations could not be sustained. Nonetheless, the structures associated with capitalism induce analyses

---

21 For a discussion at greater length of the issues that follow, see Fine (1997c) where they are addressed in terms of their relationship to value theory and to more concrete study both theoretically and empirically. For a later take, see also Fine (2020), and also for the important view that economic is embedded within social reproduction, not the two alongside one another (Fine 2020).

in which the economic and the non-economic are initially separate from one another and need to be brought back together. In addition, there is a blossoming of structuralism in the sense that, wherever difference or inequality is to be found, it is theoretically embraced as a structure.[22]

Consequently, the social sciences are replete with the economic and non-economic examined separately from one another, with each subsequently extended to consider the other. This is apparent in the notion of social capital. However understood, capital and social are broadly associated with the economic and the non-economic, respectively. Having been artificially separated, they are brought back together in these all-encompassing terms. By contrast, capital is social from the outset in the economic relations that it encompasses. Any use of the term social capital is an implicit acceptance of the stance of mainstream economics, in which capital is first and foremost a set of endowments possessed by individuals rather than, for example, an exploitative (economic and social) relation between classes.

Bringing together the social and capital, however, has another effect. As will be seen, this gives rise to notions of development and, by implication, change. For individuals, social capital is attached to personal development through environment and nurture; for economies, it increases the growth rate. Such is the impoverished recognition of the much more demanding issues attached to economic and social reproduction, incorporating attention to the relations and structures associated with capitalism. At best, these are understood as a shifting composition of, and interaction between, economic and social capital – around equilibrium growth as far as economists are concerned and with limited historical perspective for non-economists.

Further, capital not only exhibits fluidity, relations, structures, and economic and social reproduction, its existence depends upon satisfying the imperatives of profitability. This gives rise to tendencies and counter-tendencies in the forms taken by productivity increase, proletarianisation, urbanisation, globalisation, commodification, etc. Such tendencies are readily overlooked in analyses based on social capital for the simple reason that they are taken as the consequences of the more or less functional integration of the social and capital. The uneven and contradictory outcomes of these underlying tendencies are understood as unnecessary effects if only the levels and composition of social capital had been more developmental. In short, just as *laissez-faire* ideologues believe that the economy is best left without control, so the theorists

---

22   Although such structures can straddle the economic and non-economic, as in notions of patriarchy for example. See Fine (1992).

of social capital believe that it is subject to control to the extent allowed by degree of knowledge and historical contingency.

This discussion paves the way for assessing how notions of social capital might arise. It is now also possible to shed further light on the analytical posture adopted by the most extreme forms of postmodernism. The subjective shift away from the material realities of exchange value into the virtual world of use value is, in addition, an abandonment of the world of capital in all of its fluid, structural, relational and tendential forms.[23] Before commenting on the consequences of this departure from the fluidity of capital to the fluidity of the imagination,[24] it is worth probing in a little more detail what has opened the availability of this point of analytical departure.

First, the flight from capital is of necessity a flight from the economy and, hence, from economics. Consequently, quite apart from its historically inhospitable environment as far as social theory is concerned, mainstream economics has commanded a near monopoly of its subject matter, especially with the declining influence of radical political economy over the past twenty years. In this respect, however, it is crucial to recognise, secondly, that mainstream economics, and much of the heterodoxy, does not have a theory of consumption as such.[25] To be more precise, consumption is treated as if it were production – with individuals maximising the utility they can produce under the constraints imposed by the price system.[26] At most, the economics of consumer theory is a theory of the demand for quantities of goods. The activities and especially the meanings associated with consumption are simply set aside.

---

23 As will be seen, in this light, Berman's (1982) discussion of modernity in terms of Marx's *Communist Manifesto* dictum, "All that is solid melts into air", needs to be modified for the transition from postmodernism – "all that is air solidifies as capital". It is tempting to associate postmodernism with shifting economic conditions as in Stanley (1996, p. 1) quoting from Harvey (1989): "While simultaneity in the shifting dimensions of time and space is no proof of necessary or causal connection, strong *a priori* grounds can be adduced for the proposition that there is a sole kind of necessary relation between the rise of postmodernist cultural forms, the emergence of more flexible modes of capital accumulation, and a new round of "time-space compression" in the organisation of capitalism". Care must also be taken in deducing intellectual from material developments.

24 See a number of the articles collected in Jameson (1998) for the notion that the commercialisation of the image, etc, in late capitalism gives rise to the ideal abstractions attached to postmodernism. Note also that, whilst Jameson is acknowledged to be a leading theorist of postmodernism and one who particularly engages with the economy, his analysis of the latter is primarily both superficial and disengaged.

25 For this argument in greater detail, see Fine and Leopold (1993, Chapter 4).

26 Symbolically, the technical apparatus of isoquants and production is identical to that of indifference curves and consumption.

Postmodernism has exploited this duality in economic theory – the appropriation of the economic but the abandonment of consumption. For it has abandoned the economic and appropriated consumption. The one exception that proves the rule is where postmodernism has confronted the economic, as in theories of post-Fordism, neo-Fordism or flexible specialisation. Here, we find that deference is paid to the economy alone at the expense of engaging with postmodernist notions of consumption at all except as fragmented, or niche demand. For, post-Fordist notions of consumption are confined to the unjustified and unspecified assertion that mass consumption of uniform goods has given way to the demand for fast changing, differentiated and customised products. This suffices to support a particular view of the modern era as one based on new forms of flexible production.[27]

The period of postmodernist pre-occupation with consumption and its paraphernalia in isolation from the economic is now past its peak. Yet, in the hands of Baudrillard, for example, it continues to exert an influence. These two points are ably illustrated by contributions such as the aptly named, *Forget Baudrillard*, in which Rojek and Turner (1993) point out that he is now viewed as a figure of unique importance, subtle and powerful, but equally ludicrous and maladroit.[28] More generally, whatever the enduring influence of postmodernism, it has set the terms for a transition in social theory, or parts of it, in which the economic (and material more generally) is to be reintroduced. To illustrate this point, reference will be made to the work of two sociologists at opposite ends of the methodological and theoretical spectrums, Bourdieu and Coleman. By doing so, it is not being suggested that they are themselves traversing some more general and well-defined transitional path converging on the conceptualisation and deployment of social capital – quite the opposite, each displays intellectual origins and traditional modes of analysis that

---

27 For critical expositions of post-Fordism, see Mavroudeas (1990), Brenner and Glick (1991), and Fine (1995a), for example. For an account of post-Fordist consumption which unwittingly reveals how limited it is, see Smith (1998). It is notable how much post-Fordism has now fallen out of favour across the social sciences.

28 See Bourdieu and Haacke (1995, p. 39) for an appropriate ridiculing: "You probably remember how, in January of 1991, the prophet of the simulacrum announced in *Liberation*: "There will be no Gulf War". A few months later, the great dissimulator offered us a collection of his analyses under the title *The Gulf War Did Not Take Place*. Such an escape from reality looks ... more and more like a mental disorder. But there is also an occasional sign which demonstrates that Baudrillard has, in fact, not left the world of real exchanges. When *Der Spiegel* asked him whether he would accept an invitation to visit the battlefield in Iraq, he answered: 'I make my living with the virtual'". See also Porter (1993) who associates Baudrillard with hysteria in the context of history and consumption.

defy situating them in relation to postmodernism, especially Coleman. Rather, the significance of each is in the influence exerted on the evolution of social science more generally irrespective of and, at times, despite their own particular intellectual histories.

3 Bourdieu's Distinction of Social Capital

As just indicated, the intention is not to give a full account nor even an overview of Bourdieu's work but to demonstrate how it has the potential to serve as a bridge between the social sciences and, in particular, to support colonisation by economics in the flight or transition from postmodernism in its extreme, non-economic form. An appropriate starting point is his use of the term capital. First, he divides it into a number of broad categories – economic, cultural and symbolic – with each of these open to disaggregation in the light of particular activities, as in academic, professional, literary, scientific, legal-economic, philosophical, political, informational, and educational capital. At times, economic capital is simply seen as resources (Bourdieu 1996a, p. 83/4) of which the ideal type would be those most readily convertible into money.[29] Cultural capital, which itself has three broad forms (embodied, objectified and institutionalized, Bourdieu 1986b, p. 243) is typically marked by socially but differentially recognised and constructed qualifications. Symbolic capital is represented by prestige, as in honour.

There is even a place for social capital which is seen as the extent of connections or networks (Bourdieu 1996a, p. 361 and 368; and 1986b, p. 248). A favoured example is provided by the family (Bourdieu 1996b, p. 292):

> Thus, a network of family relations can be the locus of an unofficial circulation of capital.

This can give rise to "an extraordinary concentration of symbolic capital" (Bourdieu 1996b, p. 79) not least in the marriage potential of children (Bourdieu 1996b, p. 280). Further, the family serves as a parallel for the social capital embodied within large-scale corporations (Bourdieu 1996b, p. 286), or in the presumed shift in power from industry to finance (Bourdieu 1996b, p. 327). In short, for Bourdieu (1987, p. 4):

---

29 See Bourdieu (1986b, p. 243) where economic capital is what is, "immediately and directly convertible into money", quoted in Calhoun (1993, p. 70), with the inevitable implication that other forms of capital are indirectly convertible.

In a social universe like French society, and no doubt in the American society of today, these fundamental social powers are, according to my empirical investigations, firstly, *economic* capital, in various kinds: secondly, *cultural* capital or better, informational capital, again in various kinds; and thirdly two forms of capital that are very strongly based on connections and group membership, and *symbolic* capital, which is perceived and recognized as legitimate.

Second, as the notion of capital is consciously and deliberately spread across what are not directly economic categories, so it takes on a more general analytical content, and is specifically attached to the notion of power. Thus, capital and power almost become synonymous, "whereby the different types of capital (or power, which amounts to the same thing)" (Bourdieu 1986b, p. 243).[30] As Postone et al (1993, p. 4) observe:

Bourdieu's notion of *capital*, which is neither Marxian nor formal economic, entails the capacity to exercise control over one's own future and that of others. As such, it is a form of power.

The concentration of such powers is seen to reside within the state, Bourdieu and Wacquant (1992, p. 114) in "a specific capital, *properly statist capital*", confirming the identification of capital and generalised power with one another.

Third, then, capital is not only power in general, it follows that it is power of any type in particular even if subject to classification as economic, cultural, social, symbolic or whatever. Moreover, capital in its economic form is freely used as a metaphor, and its language and notions are readily deployed.[31] The various types of capital can be understood as assets and accumulated or depreciated. They are subject to cycles, generate returns, are distributed, acquired and inherited. Equally, there is accumulation, preservation (or depreciation), and transformation of the different types of capital (Bourdieu 1987, p. 4):

Thus agents are distributed in the overall social space, in the first dimension according to the global *volume* of capital they possess, in the second dimension according to the *composition* of their capital, that is, according to the relative weight in their overall capital of the various forms of

---

30 See also Bourdieu (1994, pp. 111 and 127; and 1996b, p. 265) and Bourdieu and Wacquant (1992, p. 97).

31 See Lamont and Lareau (1988, p. 159).

capital, especially economic and cultural, and in the third dimension according to the evolution in time of the volume and composition of their capital, that is, according to their *trajectory* in social space.

Fourth, however, because power is relative and not absolute and resources in general are available to all, capital readily becomes identifiable with socioeconomic groups or even with *all* individuals.[32] This is despite Bourdieu's concern to elaborate a theory of classes on the basis of distinction by volume and composition in overall possession of the different forms of capital, especially Bourdieu (1987). For, there is the issue of the amount of social capital of an agent dependent upon, "the size of the network of connections he can effectively mobilize and on the volume of the capital ... possessed in his own right by each of those to whom he is connected" (Bourdieu 1986b, p. 249) with "position in the field of power (defined by the structure of a person's capital)" (Bourdieu 1996b, p. 162). Capital is distributed across all students (Bourdieu 1996b). Individuals invest time in accumulating cultural capital (Bourdieu 1986b, p. 253) as in self-improvement (Bourdieu 1986b, p. 244). The linguistic capital of blacks in the form of their own vernacular is devalued by their subordinate social position (Bourdieu and Wacquant 1992, p. 143).[33] Women are seen as inferior across modes of production because, "men are the *subjects* of matrimonial strategies through which they work to maintain or to increase their symbolic capital" (Bourdieu and Wacquant 1992, p. 173). Most clearly, the individualistic basis of Bourdieu's notion of capital emerges in comparison between those with different portfolios of endowments (Bourdieu and Wacquant 1992, p. 99):[34]

---

32 As in the symbolic capital of the bachelor on a dance floor and his capacity to dress, dance and present himself (Bourdieu and Wacquant 1992, p. 165).

33 Compare with Becker's reference to the problem of the source of hegemonic language (Swedberg (ed.) 1990, p. 41): "The speaker last night at the rational choice seminar spoke on why one specific language gets chosen as the official language in a multilingual situation. He said that he wasn't a rational choice person until he concluded that he could best explain the behavior he was investigating with the rationality assumption. And that is OK to me".

34 See also Robbins (1991, p. 154): "Bourdieu argues that the notion of 'cultural capital' which he had used at that time (1964) has been necessary to differentiate his position from those of both the educational psychologists and the 'human capital' economists. Although he does not explicitly say so (in 1979), however, it is clear that 'cultural capital' was not wholly satisfactory because it was individualistic". It is far from clear that such individualistic content has been both recognised and rectified in subsequent work.

> Two individuals endowed with an equivalent overall capital can differ ... in that one holds a lot of economic capital and little cultural capital while the other has little economic capital and large cultural assets.

More generally, there is perceived to be a hierarchy both of cultural and of economic capital which is symmetrically but inversely distributed (Bourdieu 1986a, p. 120 and 1996b, p. 158).

Fifth, the attachment of capital to metaphors, individuals, resources and power(s) is also conducive to transhistorical use. Thus, for example, aristocratic status deriving from pre-capitalist relations is perceived as a form of social capital (Bourdieu 1986b, p. 251):[35]

> The title of nobility is the form *par excellence* of the institutionalized social capital which guarantees a particular form of social relationship in a lasting way.

Bourdieu (1993, p. 272) himself acknowledges that his notion of capital is transcribed from pre-capitalist concerns, with symbolic capital originally derived to explain honour in such societies.[36] Bourdieu (1981, p. 314) also refers to capital to construct a general theory of the power that bureaucrats derive from within the institutions to which they are attached:

> Such agents perform their oblation all the more easily because they have less capital outside the institution and therefore less freedom *vis-à-vis* the institution and the specific capital and profits that it provides ... He is predisposed to defend the institution, with total conviction, against the heretical deviations of those whose externally acquired capital allows and inclines them to take liberties with internal beliefs and hierarchies.

---

35   See also Bourdieu (1981, p. 308) where the positions of the Sun King's courtiers are interpreted as, "their power over the objectified degrees of the specific capital – which the king controls and manipulates within the room for manoeuvre the game allows him".

36   See also Wacquant (1996). From a Marxist perspective, this is a remarkable inversion in that the categories of capitalism are explained by those attached to a 'lower' form of development. A striking illustration of the use of such theory in advance of the object of theory is in the case study provided by Kolankiewicz (1996). He deploys the notion of social capital (education, connections, etc) to anticipate who will become capitalists in the Polish transition to capitalism. It is, "interpreted as various networks brought into play by the absence of conventional capital", p. 429.

Sixth, Bourdieu is concerned with the relationship between the various types of capital, in part as being in conflict with one another, as fractions or within and between agents, but also in terms of how one can be converted into another (Bourdieu 1986a, pp. 132 and 137; and 1986b, pp. 243 and 252).[37] The motivation for this concern is various – how does the artist or aesthetic appreciation retain autonomy (cultural capital) whilst dependent upon material resources (economic capital),[38] what are the relative merits of the forms of capital in gaining employment in public and private management, how does the distribution of cultural and symbolic capital give rise to the reproduction of a hierarchy of tastes and socioeconomic positions. Ultimately, however, the language of quantification is employed with an exact analogy with the conversion of one form of economic value to another, as in the "'exchange rate' (or 'conversion rate') among the different forms of capital" and "the determination of the relative value and magnitude of the different forms of power" (Bourdieu 1996b, p. 265).[39]

These characteristics of Bourdieu's use of capital represent a clear extension of the scope of the concept in response to the (conceptual) fluidity of capital previously outlined. Significantly, for example, where Marx views the display of wealth as a necessary condition for the functioning capitalist, an expenditure of revenue distinct from capital, Bourdieu (1986a, p. 287) considers it as a form of symbolic capital itself, apparently drawing upon Marx for analytical support (capital?):

> The members of the professions ... find in smart sports and games, in receptions, cocktails and other society gatherings not only intrinsic satisfaction and edification but also the select society in which they can make and keep up their "connections" and accumulate the capital of

---

37 See also Calhoun (1993, p. 65) and Postone et al (1993, p. 5): "Economic capital can be more easily and efficiently converted into symbolic (that is, social and cultural) capital than vice-versa, although symbolic capital can ultimately be transformed into economic capital".

38 Ryan (1991, p. 50) puts the issue well: "The problem for capital is that *commoditisation* of cultural objects erodes those qualities and properties which constitute them as cultural objects, as use values in the first place". See also Slater's (1997, p. 71) reference to Gresham's law of cultural taste, a parallel with money suggested by F.R. Leavis, in which the good is driven out of circulation by the bad. This paradox can, however, be exaggerated as is revealed by Haug's notion of the aesthetic illusion being turned to commercial gain. See Fine and Leopold (1993, Chapter 2) for a discussion.

39 See Wu (1998) for the notion that corporate spending on the arts is a way of accumulating cultural capital.

honourability they need in order to carry on their profession. This is only one of the cases in which luxury, "a conventional degree of prodigality", becomes, as Marx observed, "a business necessity" and "enters into capital's expenses of representation" as "an exhibition of wealth and consequently as a source of credit".

In effect, there is a double fluidity in Bourdieu's notion of capital which is quite independent of the fluidity of capital itself as an economic category. On the one hand, as just illustrated, the notion of *economic* capital lacks depth, precision and rigour. On the other hand, this inadequate concept of economic capital is extrapolated to the other forms of capital even if these are endowed with a distinctive content of their own.[40]

In this light, it is worth examining how Bourdieu's notion of capital differs from that offered by Becker, as it has been suggested here that each has been analytically seduced by the fluidity of capital. Bourdieu and Wacquant (1992, p. 118) consider the issue directly and argue that, "the only thing I share with economic orthodoxy ... are a number of words". Although recognising that economics is a diverse field, he considers that it displays "all kinds of reductionisms, beginning with economism, which recognizes nothing but material interest and the deliberate search for the maximization of monetary profit" (Bourdieu and Wacquant 1992, p. 118). This, and other commentary on Becker, as in Bourdieu (1996b, p. 275/6 and 1986b, p. 255), show that Bourdieu has not kept abreast with the developments in Becker's own thinking let alone with those neoclassical economists who are more adept at constructing a theory of social structures and strategies on the basis of methodological individualism.

More specifically, Bourdieu adopts the stance that reference to the social is sufficient to separate him from the reductionism and economism of human capital theory. This is a consequence of his notion that the reproduction and inheritance of social, cultural and symbolic capital is obscured by the processes that take place, for example, within the family.[41] Indeed, it is an irony in Bourdieu's work that his fluid and ambiguous, if not illegitimate, extension of the concept of capital to the non-economic arena leads him to consider

---

40 Thus, as Lamont and Lareau (1988, p. 156) lament: "In Bourdieu's global theoretical framework, cultural capital is alternatively an informal academic standard, a class attribute, a basis for social selection, and a resource for power which is salient as an indicator/basis of class position". See also Calhoun (1993, p. 65).

41 Most notably in Bourdieu (1986b, pp. 244/5) for cultural capital. See also Bourdieu (1994, p. 127), and Bourdieu (1986a, p. 177) for the hidden capital that generates distinct tastes for food.

that the presence of such capital has been obscured – the invention of the non-existent is inevitably compatible with a theory of its invisibility! But, as has been seen above, the factors to which Bourdieu points have proved highly visible to Becker in his theories of personal and social capital.

The same is even more so of the new economic sociology in which considerable emphasis is placed upon the social as networks.[42] As Wacquant observes, with copious references (Bourdieu and Wacquant 1992, p. 118):

> There exist obvious and large zones of overlap and convergence between Bourdieu's older and newer work ... and the concerns of the "New Economic Sociology".

Quite apart from how acceptable this might be to Becker, the following definition of social capital fits extremely comfortably within the framework offered by Granovetter (1985), discussed below, and his followers (Bourdieu 1986b, p. 248/9):

> Social capital is the aggregate of the actual or potential resources which are linked to possession of a durable network ... The volume of the social capital possessed by a given agent thus depends on the size of the network of connections he can effectively mobilize and on the volume of the capital ... possessed by a given agent, or even by the whole set of agents to whom he is connected.

This is not to suggest that Bourdieu's work is reducible to such network theory. His methodology sets him apart in two closely related ways. First, he is conscious of the need to define the meaning of the social in its historically-specific context. It is not sufficient to establish the presence of a network but also its content in practice. Such is the basis on which those such as Zelizer (1988) and DiMaggio (1990) have criticised the new economics sociology for its failure to interrogate the cultural content of the objects of study rather than taking this as self-evident by virtue of the interactions that are consolidated and even congealed. It is an accusation that cannot be levelled against Bourdieu.[43]

---

42   For overviews of the new economic sociology, see collections edited by Swedberg.
43   Note, however, that DiMaggio (1991) provides evidence for the interpretation offered here of a transition away from the extremes of postmodernism in which concepts of capital play a leading role. In the context of cultural production but of more general applicability, p. 153: "The received terminology of lay and academic cultural criticism – phrases such as mass society, highbrow/lowbrow, postmodernism – will not get us very far in addressing such issues. Terms that have entered the sociological vocabulary during the

Second, Bourdieu adopts a particular stance towards empirical work. Whilst he uses statistical techniques to establish connections between the various forms of capital, the various correlations involved are considered meaningless in the absence of an understanding of the meanings of the correlates themselves (Bourdieu 1986a, p. 18). His methodology involves the use of categories that are investigative in intent and only become systematic with use. Tracing the intellectual genealogy of such concepts is considered to be pointless as each proves to be a "temporary construct which takes shape for and by empirical work" (Bourdieu and Wacquant 1992, p. 161).[44] This contrasts with the use of (mathematical) models with well-defined components whose meaning and interactions are deemed to be able to be fully, and timelessly, explored or tested empirically.

Bourdieu's methodology, then, attempts to strike a balance between economism, by which is meant the treatment of non-economic forms of capital as if they were equivalent to the economic, and retaining a hold on the specificity of non-economic forms of capital without ignoring the "brutal fact of universal reducibility to economics" (Bourdieu 1986b, p. 252/3). In this way, the fluidity of capital, its convertibility, poses a central methodological conundrum (Bourdieu 1986b, p. 252/3):[45]

> The real logic of the functioning of capital, the conversions from one type to another, and the law of conservation which governs them cannot be understood unless two opposing but equally partial views are superseded: on the one hand, economism, which, on the grounds that every type of capital is reducible in the last analysis to economic capital,

---

past two decades – cultural capital, cultural industry systems, and others developed by Pierre Bourdieu ... will provide more leverage. What such recent progress promises is an analytic sociology of culture, distinct from criticism and textual interpretation, sensitive to the structural and pragmatic aspects of the symbolic economy, rigorously empirical in method and temperament, and thus capable of a comprehension of contemporary cultural change".

44 It is noted that this leads to a chicken and egg problem as far as the definition of the field of a particular type of capital is concerned and its distribution, Bourdieu and Wacquant (1992, p. 108). It should also be observed that Bourdieu's categories of capital have proved far from temporary in his and other hands and that it is essential that their genealogy be uncovered irrespective of how temporary they are for him.

45 Note the Althusserian overtones and also that Bourdieu frequently does degenerate into economic reductionism, in part because this is immanent in the notion of convertibility between the various types of capital, so that one is equivalent to another (whether in changing form, as in the profit of non-economic capital, or in the balance of conflict where one form is set against another).

ignores what makes the specific efficacy of the other types of capital, and on the other hand, semiologism ... which reduces social exchanges to phenomena of communication.

As McLennan (1998) has sharply clarified, Bourdieu's motivation in positing different types of capital – and the *fields* they create and the *habitus* that are brought to them – is to avoid crude determinism in social theory, both in what is caused and how. To have attempted to do so by appeal to different forms of capital is, however, symbolic of failure in two respects. On the one hand, there is the creation of a chaotic concept of capital itself and, on the other hand, a metaphorical slippage into reductionism to the as if economic (as the functioning of various types of "capital").

4 From Bourdieu to Coleman – With Intermediate Stops

For Bourdieu, then, despite seduction by the fluidity of capital,[46] the social remains a necessary starting point and is not reducible to methodological individualism.[47] Taken seriously, his work would be incapable of supporting the colonisation of the social sciences by economics. But what Bourdieu says and how he is interpreted and used is another matter. The fluid use of capital is turned to other purposes so that cultural capital, in particular, is simply used as the basis for investigating the empirical relationship between social stratification and cultural activity, no doubt encouraged by Bourdieu's own case studies along these lines. As Lamont and Lareau (1988, p. 161) observe in surveying the US literature:

> In general, American researchers have abstracted the concept of cultural capital from the micro-political framework in which it was originally

---

46 In many ways, much of the content of Bourdieu's approach is captured in the following (Bourdieu 1996b, p. 318): "Symbolic capital consisting of recognition, confidence, and, in a word, legitimacy has its own laws of accumulation that are distinct from those of economic capital ... (Such) durable capital tends to be ... misrecognised, recognised legitimate capital ... through conversion into better concealed forms of capital, such as works of art or education".

47 This methodological commitment is made more secure by Bourdieu's pre-occupation with cultural studies. The symbolic is perceived as the most complex form of capital and "his whole work may be read as a hunt for its varied forms and effects" (Bourdieu and Wacquant 1992, p. 119).

embedded. From a tool for studying the process of class reproduction, the concept became a tool for examining the process of status attainment.

In short, cultural capital becomes a property of individuals even if it is shared in common by socioeconomic groups, and Bourdieu is bowdlerised.

Since the survey of Lamont and Lareau, there has been an explosion of such studies in which statistical study tends to be supplemented by more or less cursory commentary on social theory. Cultural or social capital attached by proxy to individuals is correlated with the incidence of other variables. Hirabayashi (1993), for example, treats migrant networks as a form of social capital. Similarly, Sanders and Nee (1996) perceive social capital of immigrants to the USA in terms of their human capital, family networks, and access to finance whether from their country of origin or newly found credit associations.[48] Swartz (1996) examines the cultural capital attached to religion. But there is a mass of studies. In principle, and at times in practice, it is possible for more sophisticated statistical techniques to be adopted which hold out the impression of being more rooted in social determinants. For example, the presence of a network can be taken as a variable and associated with other individual or network variables.[49] Nonetheless, the inter-network relations are themselves built up and mutually reproduced on the basis of methodological individualism however much this may be concealed or unrecognised.[50]

A major difference in such empirical work, however, is that it no longer needs to draw upon Bourdieu for its inspiration. It can also refer to the theories of social capital that are associated with James Coleman or the new economic sociology which correspond, respectively, to the weaker (Becker) and stronger versions (asymmetric information) through which economics is colonising the social sciences. Significantly, for example, Kelly (1994) studies the incidence of Afro-American pregnancy in West Baltimore by reference to the distribution of social and cultural capital, a notion, it is argued, that has been reclaimed

---

48   They seek to explain relative success in self-employment. To address capital proper, they would need to examine access to exploitative labour markets, presumably equally dependent on ethnic networks and family membership!

49   See Anheier and Gerhards (1995), for example, who use blockmodelling to examine the social and cultural capital of German writers to determine their membership or not of the elite.

50   In principle, of course, a network of relationships could be studied between network relations and so on with fleas on fleas. Ultimately, this rests on a cascade of structured binary interactions between individuals.

from classical sociology by Bourdieu in the 1970s and Coleman in the 1980s.[51] Labour market analysis offers an excellent avenue for bringing together the different notions of capital in view of sociological and economic traditions, with credentialism and social closure complementing human capital, respectively, as observed by Brown (1995).[52]

Coleman is Professor of Sociology at the University of Chicago and, as such, the counterpart to Becker as economist with whom he has been jointly running a seminar for many years to promote the application of the economic approach to the other social sciences. Coleman's (1987) article appears to mark the first appearance of his use of the term "social capital". Given that it has subsequently given rise to his own book, Coleman (1990) running to a thousand pages, it is disarmingly simple. Social capital simply represents the extent to which an appropriate solution has been found to the problem of public goods (from which all can consume without cost but none has an incentive to provide unless charging an inefficiently high cost) and externalities (where the actions of individuals have direct repercussions for others). The capacity to deal with these issues reflects a balance between satisfying individual interests and exercising control over them (to prevent free-riding). Once such arrangements are internalised by individuals, they represent norms of behaviour. Coleman (1987, p. 153) appears to consider that putting these elementary insights together constitutes a dramatic discovery both for economics and sociology:[53]

---

51 Note that the two authors come together in the nineties in Bourdieu and Coleman (eds) (1991). In his epilogue, Bourdieu (1991, p. 373) considers the enterprise to have been a success in otherwise potentially breaching a dialogue of the mutually deaf. Despite his claims to the contrary, as argued here, the only potential for a constructive outcome is essentially in the form of an eclectic notion of "capital" in which the economic approach surreptitiously becomes more influential.

52 See also Sanders and Nee (1996) who refer to the work of Coleman (1988 and 1990), Granovetter (1985) and Bourdieu (1993) in addressing social capital.

53 It is commonplace for respective ignorance of one another's disciplines to be cited as an obstacle for integration of economics and sociology. This needs to be established in terms of the dynamics of both disciplines and the incentives to overcome such ignorance. A more secure consequence of the latter appears to be the dramatic discovery of the elementary as far as the other discipline is concerned. For another example of Coleman's profound ignorance of neoclassical economics, see the bizarre statement of his fundamental difference with it on the grounds that it should use a Cobb-Douglas utility function rather than one of general functional form (Swedberg (ed.) 1990, p. 57). He also inappropriately berates it for being incapable of making interpersonal comparisons. Note that Coleman's (1991) history is equally inventive with, by his account, no apparent constructed social organisations prior to the thirteenth century, p. 4, and a shift, "in the past century from subsistence economies of households", p. 11. On a different tack, in a review of his book, Frank (1992, p. 148) rebukes Coleman mildly for lack of originality and/or scholarship in failing to refer to Schelling's (1978) work, with Coleman's volume,

> But just as neoclassical economics was slow in recognizing the fundamental differences introduced by externalities and public goods, those who use "exchange theory" in sociology have been slow in recognizing that many social actions and transactions generate externalities or have the character of public goods or bads. This has meant that exchange theory in sociology has been incorrectly individualistic, failing to recognize that externalities create an interest in exercising control ... It is in this sense that social norms constitute social capital.

From such humble beginnings, Coleman's work has appealed to rational choice to explain the whole of social science (Swedberg (ed.) 1990, p. 53).[54] The social system can be built up out of an agglomeration of relations between individuals in which control and interest are fundamental categories, readily deployed in problems involving fallacy of composition, principal-agents, etc. At times, if only for convenience, it is permissible to take collective agencies as given but not in fundamental theory (Swedberg (ed.) 1990, p. 51/2):

> One can, I think, take corporate actors as given ... for certain kinds of theoretical purposes. At the same time, for other purposes, one has to take them as problematic. In other words, I say that methodological individualism can work at more than one level. True methodological individualism takes natural persons ... as the only starting point ... (But) the micro-to-macro framework is a *relative* framework. At whatever level one finds actors acting purposively, one can take that as a micro level and examine the functioning of the system of those actors. But, as I say, for the fundamental explanation, one also wants to take those actors as problematic.

Coleman's contingent concession to the corporate actor provides the point of departure for the less individualistic approaches both to economics and sociology and to the relationship between them. Before addressing this directly, consider how Coleman as a sociologist is distinguished from Becker as an

---

[54] "if not a clone of Schelling's, then at least its fraternal twin". In his book, Coleman (1990) ultimately credits Loury (1977 and 1987) with introducing the concept of social capital. The possible exception is psychology since it is concerned with "the action of a natural person" (Swedberg (ed.) 1990, p. 53). Even so, Coleman seems to think that it is possible that, "the same structure exists *internal* to the individual, and the values of particular resources or events for the system are his interests, since he is the system". Elsewhere, Coleman (1991) sees constructed social organisation by way of physical analogy, as in nuclear fission and genetic engineering.

economist despite the unswerving commitment of each to methodological individualism. Apart from the trivial and erroneous differences detailed in an earlier footnote, the differences are merely ones of starting point from within their respective disciplines. As Frank (1992) observes, Coleman is not committed to reliance upon a representative individual (which is not really required by Becker either but for the obsession for explaining everything on the basis of one given set of underlying preferences). More important, whilst Becker starts from the equilibrium exchange models of neoclassical economics and extends them to situations without monetary exchange,[55] the reverse is the case for Coleman. He is concerned with the variety of social exchanges that take place in the absence of money and which are treated as a variety of barters with social capital serving, by way of analogy, as a form of credit on which individuals can draw so long as the mechanisms exist for them to pay back.

Of course, such differences in starting points should not be emphasised at the expense of overlooking what the two share in common, a commitment to rational choice.[56] The acknowledged difference by other writers from within both economics and sociology in that the optimising agent is not taken as the starting point. Baron and Hannan (1994, p. 1117) set up the problem as follows:

> First, motivations, preferences and behaviors are molded (and thus must be understood) in social context. Second, individualism, rationality as an approved standard of behavior and the infrastructure supporting markets (eg property rights) are themselves *social and historical products*, not timeless abstractions.

For sociologists such as Granovetter (1985), emphasis is placed on the social and historical, as networks of interpersonal relations become congealed or embedded and, consequently, more important than the antediluvian individualism that might be construed as having created them at some point in the distant past. Thus, more or less as an analytical manifesto (Granovetter 1990, p. 95/6) asserts:

> (1) action is always socially situated and cannot be explained by reference to individual motives alone, and (2) social institutions do not

---

55 Although, as observed above, his exchange economy has no money.
56 As Becker observes (Swedberg (ed.) 1990, p. 50): "I think the differences between the various schools (of economics and sociology) are much smaller than the similarities. Basically, what the rational choice people do is to start with some unit of behavior or actor that they assume is behaving rationally".

arise automatically in some inevitable form but rather are "socially constructed".

So, the social can be taken as historically given as the basis for examining the individual, as in the notion that (Granovetter 1992, p. 10):

> The general principle may be that the actor whose network reaches into the largest number of relevant institutional realms will have an enormous advantage.

Consequently, Becker is perceived to adopt too simple an approach and "very narrow" for neglecting the "particular history in a relationship" which is "embedded in networks" (Swedberg (ed.) 1990, p. 100).

Exactly the same critical stance to rational choice can be observed from within economics in which George Akerlof is seen as one of the leading protagonists. He sees himself as always doing "the opposite of what Becker does" (Swedberg (ed.) 1990, p. 73). As Elster observes, Swedberg (ed.) (1990, p. 238):[57]

> Becker and Akerlof … represent two different trends. There is the imperialist trend of economics, which I would say just ignores sociological theory in its attacks on sociological problems. And then there is the trend that Akerlof represents, which takes sociological theory seriously and uses it to study economic problems.

In this vein, there is considerable hostility to, even contempt for, Becker although it tends to be tempered by admiration for his technical virtuosity.[58] For Akerlof, on Becker-type analysis, there is reference to the comment made of Friedman by Samuelson, that he learnt how to spell "banana" but did not know where to stop (Swedberg (ed.) 1990, p. 73);[59] Elster refers to "the mindless application of rational choice theory to everything" (Swedberg (ed.) 1990, p. 238); Sen observes that, "Becker's tools have been chosen on the ground of

---

57 See also Swedberg (ed.) (1990, p. 194) where Schelling suggests in contrast to Becker that: "George Akerlof is more creative. He has a great curiosity … (he) is almost the opposite of economic imperialism. He looks into sociology for concepts that he can import into economics".

58 In Bourdieu's terms, Becker clearly has accumulated considerable cultural and symbolic capital in inverse proportion to his critical faculties and powers of independent thought.

59 Taramasalata is even better. My own preferred parable is the child whose first toy is a hammer and who presumes that everything in the world is a nail.

their alleged success in economics, but they are too narrow and do not have much predictive and explanatory power even in economics" (Swedberg (ed.) 1990, p. 264); Schelling admits, "I myself don't find Becker's work so helpful ... he is completely satisfied with the traditional economic model of rational behavior ... what annoys me about Becker, and maybe your term, 'imperialism', somewhat catches it, is that he doesn't think there is anything to learn from outside economics" (Swedberg (ed.) 1990, p. 193/4); and for Solow, "my nagging feeling is that what he gets ... oscillates between the obvious and the false" (Swedberg (ed.) 1990, p. 276).

5   The Revolution Portrayed

In short, there are three corresponding and inter-related oppositions in the literature: is economics being taken to sociology or vice-versa; is analysis based on the individual or the social; and what is the analytical status of the historically or socially given factors if taken independent of rational choice.[60] These considerations have correctly been understood in the past as posing substantive barriers between the disciplines. The burden of the argument here is that the opposite is now the case as a result of the reaction against the extremes of postmodernism, the colonising designs of economics whether in the forms offered by Becker or Akerlof, Coleman or Granovetter, and the conflation of concepts induced by the previously discussed fluidity of capital.[61]

In their review article, itself significant for appearing in the *Journal of Economic Literature*, Baron and Hannan (1994, p. 1123) observe that Becker has progressed from use of human capital to capital for any type of activity, emphasising that such invention is far from new for sociologists, referring explicitly to Bourdieu's notions of linguistic and cultural capital which are perceived to merge Marxian ideas on class reproduction with economic notions of human capital – Bourdieu is Beckered![62]

They also explicitly suggest limited progress for economics imperialism as far as sociology is concerned (and vice-versa) in view of the evidence of limited

---

60   Note that Bourdieu (1991) essentially views such oppositions as obstacles to analytical progress.
61   Note that Lindenberg (1990) suggests that sociological models of behaviour had become exhausted by the 1960s and paved the way for a renewal of interest in economic models albeit in unclean forms.
62   See Calhoun (1993, p. 84) who observes: "Despite his disclaimers Bourdieu does indeed share a great deal with Gary Becker and other rational choice theorists".

mutual citations from the Social Science Citation Index. Perhaps they are correct and, in primarily presenting the logical case for colonisation by economics, the argument here is inevitably selective and incapable of assessing the extent of advance and momentum relative to the persistence of continuing traditions and the creation of new ones independent of a colonising economics.

There are, however, five counter-arguments to such objections. First, as is evidenced by the use of the term human capital, it can enter into the vocabulary of social science as a whole without necessarily its origins and implications being acknowledged or accepted. Second, economic colonisation is in its early stages – Coleman dates from the late 1980s and Granovetter from the mid-eighties. The basis for the assault is also relatively recent within economics. Interestingly, Becker gave his first paper treating children as a consumer durable in 1960 to laughter from economists as well as sociologists and demographers (Swedberg (ed.) 1990, p. 33). Akerlof's first, now classic, paper, dating from 1966, on the market for "lemons", dealing with the market structure arising out of informational asymmetries, was rejected by the *American Economic Review* and the *Journal of Political Economy*![63] Third, the fluidity of the conceptualisation of capital is permissive of a common language which, together with analytical eclecticism, has created a Trojan horse out of economics as far as the other social sciences are concerned. Fourth, the colonisation is advancing with new developments across a broad front and is not confined to sociology even if this has been the focus in the previous discussion.

The fifth and most important argument in support of the idea of a forward march of economics into other social sciences is to observe just how much has happened since the appearance of the review of Baron and Hannan, even within the field of social capital alone. Survey articles, such as those of Harriss and de Renzio (1997) and Woolcock (1998) have already appeared. The latter identifies seven areas of application.[64] The point at the moment is less to examine the notion of social capital critically, as have many contributions, as to highlight the conduit that it provides for the colonisation of other social sciences by economics. Significantly and prominently, political science has been added to the lexicon of social capital, most notably through the work

---

63 More generally, see Akerlof (1984). Becker claims to have applied the economic approach to politics in a paper rejected by the *Journal of Political Economy* in the early 1950s. Although such a paper was published in 1958, "nobody paid it much attention … I was applying economics to politics as early as anyone. But the rejection hurt" (Swedberg (ed.) 1990, p. 33).

64 And, in what must be one of the longest ever footnotes, provides a bibliography.

FROM BOURDIEU TO BECKER   101

of Putnam.[65] In this respect, Putnam is the network counterpart to Becker-type rational choice politics, or the new political economy, as originating with Olson (1965) and taken up by Bates (1981 and 1988).[66] Peter Evans (1996a and b) and his collaborators also correspond within politics to the more sociologically inclined such as Granovetter, with the notion of the developmental state being reinterpreted through social capital, on which see later.

Not surprisingly, the advance of economics is also to be found within geography where it has always sat relatively comfortably whether in mainstream versions or as the political economy of space. In this respect, what sets geography apart from economics is that it has been profoundly influenced by postmodernism. As Zukin (1996) has observed, this has given rise to two schools of thought on the built environment. The traditional focuses on the political economy of land use whereas the more recent addresses the symbolic economy, visual representation and inclusion/exclusion in the production of space.[67] In bringing the two schools together, it is hardly surprising that the influence of the fluidity of capital should be felt, with notions of cultural and social capital being deployed freely and flexibly, further encouraged by the resonances between capital as wealth and as city.[68] For Kearns (1993, p. 50), cultural capital is tied

---

65   See Putnam (1993a and b and 1995), for example. The work of Putnam is also correctly seen as the counterpart to that of Coleman in terms of the relative emphasis of the role of the state in crowding in or crowding out social capital in the form of networks, so that this debate is itself raised to a higher political level in terms of social capital. Putnam explicitly derives his use of the latter from Coleman (1990), p. 167, although, in his final chapter, where he addresses social capital *after* completing his case study, he draws freely upon any author or notion from the literature. Ultimately, this leads to the conclusion, p. 177: "Stocks of social capital, such as trust, norms, and networks, tend to be self-reinforcing and cumulative. Virtuous circles result in social equilibria with high levels of cooperation, trust, reciprocity civic engagement, and collective well-being ... Defection, distrust, shirking, exploitation, isolation, disorder, and stagnation intensify one another in a suffocating miasma of vicious circles. This argument suggests that there may be at least *two* broad equilibria toward which all societies that face problems of collective action (that is *all* societies) tend to evolve and which, once attained, tend to be self-reinforcing".
66   Note that Olson was trained and is a professor in economics (Swedberg (ed.) 1990, p. 177): "I like to get down, whenever possible, to the primitive entity of economic and social life: *the individual*".
67   If not through notions of post-Fordism. Thrift and Glennie (1993) correctly criticise the use of the universal categories "modern" Fordist production and "postmodern" flexible production as logical and chronological categories for their undermining of the ability to assess continuity and change in consumption. This can be perceived as confirming the weakness of post-Fordism as a postmodern category, placing it as geography firmly within the camp of the political economy of land use.
68   Kearns and Philo (1993, p. ix) point to, "*cultural capital* where 'capital' refers both to money and to 'capital' or sizeable cities".

up in historic sites and images, Crilley (1993, p. 234) views buildings as functioning as "symbolic capital", Philo and Kearns (1993, p. 16) consider property-ownership and fancy possessions as the surface badges of cultural capital, and Goodwin (1993, p. 146) argues, in an inversion of the truth, that "urban capital is in the end valorised like any other form of capital".[69]

Otherwise, where academics tread, pretentious popularisers are quick to follow. In his article entitled "Social Capital and the Global Economy", Fukuyama (1995, p. 103) typically paints a future in terms which have long since become fashionable:

> The most important distinctions between nations are no longer institutional but cultural ... culture will be the key axis of international differentiation – though not necessarily an axis of conflict. The traditional argument between left and right over the appropriate role of the state, reflected in the debate between the neomercantilists and neoclassical economists, misses the key issue concerning civil society. The left is wrong to think that the state can embody or promote meaningful social solidarity. Libertarian conservatives, for their part, are wrong to think that strong social structures will spontaneously regenerate once the state is subtracted from the equation. The character of civil society and its intermediate associations, rooted as it is in nonrational factors like culture, religion, tradition and other premodern sources, will be key to the success of modern societies in a global economy.

As social theory falls under the spell of economics, the opposite illusion emerges spontaneously as if use of terms such as social capital were the denial of the new economics (imperialism) rather than its perfection. But it is hardly surprising that the end of history should seamlessly give way to the triumph of economics. And, just as economics confidently confronts the non-economic from a position of ignorance, so non-economists return the compliment. For Fukuyama (1996, p. 13):

---

69 The strength of radicalism within economic geography, pioneered by David Harvey and Doreen Massey, may have diminished the appeal of the longstanding what might be termed the old economic geography. But the new economic geography, inspired by Paul Krugman, was awaiting in the wings and about to take off with a vengeance. See Fine (2010b) but also note that Krugman's novelty lies in market imperfections based on returns to scale and scope as opposed to informational imperfections most closely associated with Stiglitz.

Over the past generation, economic thought has been dominated by neoclassical or free market economists, associated with names like Milton Friedman, Gary Becker, and George Stigler. The rise of the neoclassical perspective constitutes a vast improvement from earlier decades in this century, when Marxists and Keynesians held sway. We can think of neoclassical economics as being, say, eighty percent correct; it has uncovered important truths about the nature of money and markets because its fundamental model of rational, self-interested human behavior is correct about eighty percent of the time. But there is a missing twenty percent of human behavior about which neoclassical economics can give only a poor account. As Adam Smith well understood, economic life is deeply embedded in social life, and it cannot be understood apart from the customs, morals, and habits of the society in which it occurs. In short, it cannot be divorced from culture.

On a more serious, and even more recent, note, the notion of social capital has been picked up by the World Bank, and it is worth concluding by discussing the reasons for this.[70] For almost two decades, the debate over development has been dominated by the Washington Consensus, with the IMF and the World Bank adopting a neo-liberal position on the analytical agenda set in terms of market versus the state. Broadly, if simplifying, the alternative position in the debate, favouring state intervention in policy and in explaining successful economic development, has been attached to the notion of the developmental state. This approach has itself fallen into two separate schools, the economic school identifying why and how the state must intervene, and the political school studying the conditions under which the state can intervene appropriately.[71]

Currently, there is a shift in the position of the World Bank, which is rapidly gaining momentum, most remarkably signified by the aggressive interventions being made by Stiglitz, Deputy President and Chief Economist to the World Bank.[72] Stiglitz has long been a representative of the new developments in the microeconomics of market failure. He has proposed a post Washington Consensus on this basis. At the same time, the World Bank has set up a Satellite

---

70 Fine (1999b) provides a more detailed account.
71 See Fine and Stoneman (1996) and Fine and Rustomjee (1997). For latest contribution with references to those earlier, see Fine and Pollen (2018).
72 See especially, Stiglitz (1998) and for critique Fine et al (eds) (2001) and Bayliss et al (eds) (2011).

Group on social capital within its Task Force on Social Development (Harriss and de Renzio 1997, p. 930).

What is the connection between these developments?[73] First, as critical assessments of social capital have observed, it can be anything and, consequently, provides a framework for the re-running of old debates – whether at the macro-level in terms of the meanings and role of civil society or at any number of micro-levels.[74]

Second, even so, the decanting of old wine into new bottles reflects ideological and analytical shifts. On the one hand, there is a more progressive content relative to the old Consensus. It is accepted that state intervention is justified in case of microeconomic, market failures for which corrective action can be shown to be beneficial. On the other hand, in contrast to notions of modernisation, Keynesianism and welfarism, whatever their respective merits, the analytical framework is one of focusing upon micro- rather than macro-relations which, consequently, remain unexamined. It is, for example, astonishing how little notions of social capital have even addressed the issue of globalisation despite the extent to which it has emerged to prominence in economic and social theory. Much the same is true of the role of power, especially as social capital holds out the promise of something for nothing and the placing of conflicts of interest into the background.

Third, more specifically at the level of policy, the old Consensus has been caught in an ideological dilemma. In arguing against state intervention (even if as an ideological cover for what has been the promotion of discretionary intervention in the form of austerity and liberalisation), it becomes impossible to argue positively about what the state should do. Consequently, as has become apparent in latest issues of the World Bank's World Development Report, a new state-friendly stance allows for even greater influence over the economic and non-economic policies to be adopted by developing countries.

Fourth, the emergence of social capital has had the effect of allowing the World Bank to sidestep completely the weight of criticism that has been built up against it during the era of the Washington Consensus. Irrespective of its conceptual merits, the developmental state in one form or another has been a major rallying call for those who have opposed the simplistic nostrums of the old Consensus. The corresponding literature was totally ignored by the World Bank. Now, by embracing the notion of social capital, it can continue to proceed as if that literature never existed.

---

73   Some of the points that follow are very neatly caught in Hildyard (1998).
74   See Harriss and de Renzio (1997) and Woolcock (1998).

Fifth, even worse, the notion of social capital has the capacity to incorporate and re-interpret the developmental state literature in its own image, reducing its radical and macro content. Further, it will induce many within the critical tradition to work within such a framework, with the post Washington Consensus dominating the agenda on development as did the old Consensus. In short, social capital, the move to a post Washington Consensus, and the colonising of other social sciences by economics are all closely related. It is imperative, as social theory (re)incorporates the economic in retreating from the excesses of postmodernism, that it does so on the basis of an appropriate political economy rather than succumbing to the far from seductive charms of the dismal science. Section 2, pointing to fluidity, structures, relations, and tendencies, highlighted the analytical elements through which this can be done on the basis of the realities of capital itself, rather than appealing to the invented and chaotic notion of social capital.

6 Concluding Remarks

The previous section concludes on an appropriate note of continuing relevance, especially with regard to the study of development. Whilst social capital offered an early and leading edge into the latest phase of economics imperialism – let's call everything (social or other type of) capital and include it in a production function or a statistical equation to be estimated. Such adventurous steps still remained predominantly prospective as well as their extension to social variables whether attached to capital or not. This is not least because some economists, understandably of an older generation, remained conservative over stretching the use of the term capital in its scope of both definition and application.[75] Given that capital is thing-like, its use should be confined to what can genuinely and legitimately be considered an element in production functions, a stock that can be added to or drawn down by identifiable flows. And its use should be confined to what can be considered production as in growth theory.

---

75 See especially Arrow (1999) and Solow (1999) in a World Bank initiative that set aside their reservations in its continuing work. Note that social capital was used as a means to explain the Solow residual in a form of (new) growth theory with which Solow, to say the least, has been far from enamoured, in part again because of reservations over the legitimate scope of application of neoclassical economics. See Fine and Dimakou (2016) for a discussion.

References

Akerlof, G. (1984) *An Economic Theorist's Book of Tales*, Cambridge: Cambridge University Press.

Anheier, H. and J. Gerhards (1995) "Forms of Capital and Social Structure in Cultural Fields – Examining Bourdieu Social Topography", *American Journal of Sociology*, vol 100, no 4, pp. 859–903.

Arrow, K. (1999) "Observations on Social Capital", in Dasgupta and Serageldin (eds) (1999), pp. 3–5.

Arthur, C. (1998) "The Fluidity of Capital and the Logic of the Concept", in Arthur and Reuten (eds) (1998), pp. 95–128.

Arthur, C. and G. Reuten (eds) (1998) *The Circulation of Capital: Essays on Volume Two of 'Capital'*, London: MacMillan.

Baron, J. and M. Hannan (1994) "The Impact of Economics on Contemporary Sociology", *Journal of Economic Literature*, vol XXXII, no 3, Sept, pp. 1111–46, reproduced in Swedberg (ed.) (1996), pp. 530-66..

Bates, R. (1981) *Markets and States in Tropical Africa: the Political Basis of Agricultural Policies*, Berkeley: University of California Press.

Bates, R. (1988) *Towards a Political Economy of Development: a Rational Choice Perspective*, Berkeley: University of California Press.

Bayliss, K. and B. Fine (2021) *A Guide to the Systems of Provision Approach: Who Gets What, How and Why*, Basingstoke: Palgrave MacMillan.

Bayliss, K., B. Fine and M. Robertson (eds) (2018 *Material Cultures of Financialisation*, London: Routledge, reproduced from special issue of *New Political Economy*, vol 22, no 4, 2017.

Bayliss, K., B. Fine and E. Van Waeyenberge (eds) (2011) *The Political Economy of Development: the World Bank, Neoliberalism and Development Research*, London: Pluto.

Bebbington, A. (2004) "Social Capital and Development Studies 1: Critique, Debate, Progress?", *Progress in Development Studies*, vol 4, no 4, pp. 343–49.

Bebbington, A., S. Guggenheim, E. Olson and M. Woolcock (2004) "Grounding Discourse in Practice: Exploring Social Capital Debates at the World Bank", *Journal of Development Studies*, vol 40, no 5, pp. 33–64.

Bebbington, A., Woolcock, M., Guggenheim, S. and E. Olson (eds) (2006) *The Search for Empowerment: Social Capital as Idea and Practice at the World Bank*, Bloomfield: Kumarian Press.

Becker, G. (1996) *Accounting for Tastes*, Cambridge: Harvard University Press.

Berman, M. (1982) *All That Is Solid Melts into Air: the Experience of Modernity*, New York: Simon and Schuster.

Bourdieu, P. (1981) "Men and Machines", in Knorr-Cetina and Cicourel (eds) (1981), pp. 304–317.

Bourdieu, P. (1986a) *Distinction: a Social Critique of the Judgement of Taste*, London: Routledge, first published in French in 1979.

Bourdieu, P. (1986b) "The Forms of Capital", in Richardson (ed.) (1986), first published in German in 1983, pp. 241–58.

Bourdieu, P. (1987) "What Makes a Social Class? On the Theoretical and Practical Existence of Groups", *Berkeley Journal of Sociology*, vol XXXII, pp. 1–17.

Bourdieu, P. (1991) "Epilogue: on the Possibility of a Field of World Sociology", in Bourdieu and Coleman (eds) (1991), pp. 373–87.

Bourdieu, P. (1993) "Concluding Remarks: for a Sociogenetic Understanding of Intellectual Works", in Calhoun et al (eds) (1993), pp. 263–275.

Bourdieu, P. (1994) *Towards a Reflexive Sociology*, Cambridge; Polity Press, first published in French from 1987 onwards.

Bourdieu, P. (1996a) *The Rules of Art: Genesis and Structure of the Literary Field*, Cambridge: Polity Press, first published in French in 1992.

Bourdieu, P. (1996b) *The State Nobility: Elite Schools in the Field of Power*, Cambridge: Polity Press, first published in French in 1989.

Bourdieu, P. and J. Coleman (eds) (1991) *Social Change for a Changing Society*, Boulder: Westview Press.

Bourdieu, P. and H. Haacke (1995) *Free Exchange*, Cambridge: Polity Press, first published in French in 1994.

Bourdieu, P. and L. Wacquant (1992) *An Invitation to Reflexive Sociology*, Cambridge: Polity Press.

Brenner, R. and M. Glick (1991) "The Regulation School and the West's Economic Impasse", *New Left Review*, no 188, July/Aug, pp. 45–119.

Brown, P. (1995) "Cultural Capital and Social Exclusion – Some Observations on Recent Trends in Education, Employment and the Labour Market", *Work, Employment and Society*, vol 9, no 1, pp. 29–51.

Calhoun, C. (1993) "Habitus, Field and Capital: the Question of Historical Specificity", in Calhoun et al (eds) (1993), pp. 61–88.

Calhoun, C., E. LiPuma and M. Postone (eds) (1993) *Bourdieu: Critical Perspectives*, Cambridge: Polity Press.

Campbell, M. (1998) "Money in the Circulation of Capital", in Arthur and Reuten (eds) (1998), pp. 129–58.

Carrier, J. and D. Miller (eds) (1998) *Virtualism: the New Political Economy*, London: Berg.

Christoforou, A. (2022) "Social Capital and Civil Society in Public Policy, Social Change, and Welfare", *Journal of Economic Issues*, vol 56, no 2, pp. 326–34.

Coleman, J. (1987) "Norms as Social Capital", in Radnitzky and Bernholz (eds) (1987), pp. 133–55.

Coleman, J. (1988) "Social Capital in the Creation of Human Capital", *American Journal of Sociology*, vol 94, Supplement, pp. 95–120, reproduced in Swedberg (ed.) (1996), pp. 319-44.

Coleman, J. (1990) *Foundations of Social Theory*, Cambridge: Harvard University Press.

Coleman, J. (1991) "Prologue: Constructed Social Organization", in Bourdieu and Coleman (eds) (1991), pp. 1–14.

Crilley, D. (1993) "Architecture as Advertising: Constructing the Image of Redevelopment", in Kearns and Philo (eds) (1993), pp. 127–163.

Damodaran, S., S. Gupta, S. Mitra and D. Sinha (eds) (2023) *Development, Transformations and the Human Condition: Volume in Honour of Professor Jayati Ghosh*, New Delhi: Routledge, forthcoming.

Dasgupta, P. and S. Serageldin (eds) (1999) *Social Capital: a Multifaceted Perspective*, Washington, DC: World Bank.

DiMaggio, P. (1990) "Cultural Aspects of Economic Action and Organization", in Friedland and Robertson (eds) (1990), pp. 113–136.

DiMaggio, P. (1991) "Social Structure, Institutions, and Cultural Goods: the Case of the United States", in Bourdieu and Coleman (eds) (1991), 133–166.

Evans, P. (1996a) "Introduction: Development Strategies across the Public-Private Divide", *World Development*, vol 24, no 6, pp. 1033–37.

Evans, P. (1996b) "Government Action, Social Capital and Development: Reviewing the Evidence on Synergy", *World Development*, vol 24, no 6, pp. 1119–32.

Fine, B. (1975) "The Circulation of Capital, Ideology and Crisis", *Bulletin of the Conference of Socialist Economists*, no 12, October, pp. 82–96.

Fine, B. (1980) *Economic Theory and Ideology*, London: Edward Arnold.

Fine, B. (1992) *Women's Employment and the Capitalist Family*, London: Routledge.

Fine, B. (1995a) "Flexible Production and Flexible Theory: the Case of South Africa", *Geoforum*, vol 26, no 2, pp. 107–19.

Fine, B. (1995b) "From Political Economy to Consumption", in Miller (ed.) (1995), pp. 127–163.

Fine, B. (1997a) "The New Revolution in Economics", *Capital and Class*, no 61, Spring, pp. 143–48. See also Chapter 4.

Fine, B. (1997b) "Playing the Consumption Game", *Consumption, Markets, Culture*, vol 1, no 1, pp. 7–29.

Fine, B. (1997c) "Value Theory: a Personal Account", *Utopia*, no 28, pp. 9–27, in Greek.

Fine, B. (1998a) *Labour Market Theory: a Constructive Reassessment*, London: Routledge.

Fine, B. (1998b) "The Triumph of Economics: or 'Rationality' Can Be Dangerous to Your Reasoning", in Carrier and Miller (eds) (1998), pp. 49–73.

Fine, B. (1998c) "A Question of Economics: Is It Colonising the Social Sciences?", vol 28, no 3, 1999, pp. 403–25. See also Chapter 7.

Fine, B. (1999a) "From Becker to Bourdieu: Economics Confronts the Social Sciences", *International Papers in Political Economy*, vol 5, no 3, pp. 1–43.

Fine, B. (1999b) "The Developmental State is Dead - Long Live Social Capital", *Development and Change*, vol 30, no 1, 1999, pp. 1–19, reproduced in Moore (ed.) (2007) with afterword, pp. 121–44.

Fine, B. (2001) *Social Capital versus Social Theory: Political Economy and Social Science at the Turn of the Millennium*, London: Routledge.

Fine, B. (2008) "Social Capital in Wonderland: the World Bank behind the Looking Glass", *Progress in Development Studies*, vol 8 no 3, pp. 261–69.

Fine, B. (2010a) *Theories of Social Capital: Researchers Behaving Badly*, London: Pluto Press.

Fine, B. (2010b) "Flattening Economic Geography: Locating the World Development Report for 2009", *Journal of Economic Analysis*, vol 1, no 1, pp. 15–33, http://users.ntua.gr/jea/JEA%20Vol.%20I,%20No%20I,%202010/jea_volume1_issue1_pp15_33.pdf.

Fine, B. (2012) "Revisiting Rosa Luxemburg's Political Economy", *Critique*, vol 40, no 3, pp. 423–30.

Fine, B. (2020) "Framing Social Reproduction in the Age of Financialisation" in Santos and Teles (eds) (2020), pp. 257–72.

Fine, B. (2023) "Social Capital: the Indian Connection", in Damodaran et al (eds) (2023), forthcoming.

Fine, B. and O. Dimakou (2016) *Macroeconomics: a Critical Companion*, London: Pluto.

Fine, B., M. Heasman and J. Wright (1996) *Consumption in the Age of Affluence: the World of Food*, London: Routledge.

Fine, B., C. Lapavitsas and J. Pincus (eds) (2001) *Development Policy in the Twenty-First Century: Beyond the Post-Washington Consensus*, London: Routledge.

Fine, B. and E. Leopold (1993) *The World of Consumption*, London: Routledge, revised edition, 2002.

Fine, B. and G. Pollen (2018) "The Developmental State Paradigm in the Age of Financialisation', in Hyland and Munck (eds) (2018), pp. 211–27.

Fine, B. and Z. Rustomjee (1997) *South Africa's Political Economy: from Minerals-Energy Complex to Industrialisation*, Johannesburg: Wits University Press.

Fine, B. and A. Saad Filho (2010/2016) *Marx's 'Capital'*, London: Pluto, sixth edition, 2016; fifth edition in French, Paris: Raisons d'Agir, 2013.

Fine, B. and C. Stoneman (1996) "Introduction: State and Development", *Journal of Southern African Studies*, vol 22, no 1, March, pp. 5–26.

Fleury, J.-B. and A. Marciano (2017) "The Making of a Constitutionalist: James Buchanan on Education", Available at SSRN: https://ssrn.com/abstract=2994683 or http://dx.doi.org/10.2139/ssrn.2994683.

Frank, R. (1992) "Melding Sociology and Economics: James Coleman's *Foundations of Social Theory*", *Journal of Economic Literature*, vol XXX, no 1, March, pp. 147–70, reproduced in Swedberg (ed.) (1996), pp. 345-68.

Friedland, R. and A. Robertson (eds) (1990) *Beyond the Marketplace: Rethinking Economy and Society*, New York: Walter de Gruyter.

Fukuyama, F. (1995) "Social Capital and the Global Economy", *Foreign Affairs*, vol 74, no 5, pp. 89–103.

Fukuyama, F. (1996) *Trust: the Social Virtues and the Creation of Prosperity*, London: Penguin.

Goodwin, M. (1993) "The City as Commodity: the Contested Spaces of Urban Development", in Kearns and Philo (eds) (1993), pp. 145–62.

Granovetter, M. (1985) "Economic Action and Social Structure: the Problem of Embeddedness", *American Journal of Sociology*, vol 91, no 3, Nov, pp. 481–510, reproduced in Swedberg (ed.) (1996), pp. 239-68.

Granovetter, M. (1990) "The Old and the New Economic Sociology: a History and an Agenda", in Friedland and Robertson (eds) (1990), pp. 89–112.

Granovetter, M. (1992) "Economic Institutions as Social Constructions: a Framework for Analysis", *Acta Sociologica*, vol 35, no 1, pp. 3–11, reproduced in Swedberg (ed.) (1996), pp. 269-77.

Haldar, A. and J. Stiglitz (2016) "Group Lending, Joint Liability, and Social Capital: Insights from the Indian Microfinance Crisis", *Politics and Society*, vol 44, no 4, pp. 459–497.

Harriss, J. and P. de Renzio (1997) "'Missing Link' or Analytically Missing?: the Concept of Social Capital, an Introductory Bibliographic Essay", *Journal of International Development*, vol 9, no 7, pp. 919–37.

Harvey, D. (1989) *The Condition of Postmodernity: an Enquiry into the Origins of Cultural Change*, Oxford: Blackwell.

Hildyard, N. (1998) *The World Bank and the State: a Recipe for Change?*, London: Bretton Woods Project.

Hirabayashi, L. (1993) *Cultural Capital: Mountain Zapotec Migrant Associations in Mexico City*, Tucson: University of Arizona.

Hyland, M. and R. Munck (eds) (2018) *Handbook on Development and Social Change*, Cheltenham: Edward Elgar.

Jameson, F. (1998) *The Cultural Turn: Selected Writings on the Postmodern, 1983–1998*, London: Verso.

Kearns, G. (1993) "The City as Spectacle: Paris and the Bicentenary of the French Revolution", in Kearns and Philo (eds) (1993), pp. 49–102.

Kearns, G. and C. Philo (1993) "Preface", in Kearns and Philo (eds) (1993), pp. ix–x.

Kearns, G. and C. Philo (eds) (1993) *Selling Places: the City as Cultural Capital*, Oxford: Pergamon Press.

Kelly, M. (1994) "Towanda's Triumph – Social and Cultural Capital in the Transition to Adulthood in the Urban Ghetto", *International Journal of Urban and Regional Research*, vol 18, no 1, pp. 88–111.

King, A. (ed.) (1996) *Re-Presenting the City: Ethnicity, Capital and Culture in the 21st Century Metropolis*, London: MacMillan.

Knorr-Cetina, K. and A. Cicourel (eds) (1981) *Advances in Social Theory and Methodology: Toward an Integration of Micro- and Macro-Sociologies*, London: Routledge Kegan Paul.

Kolankiewicz, G. (1996) "Social Capital and Social Change", *British Journal of Sociology*, vol 47, no 3, special issue for Lockwood, pp. 427–441.

Lamont, M. and A. Lareau (1988) "Cultural Capital: Allusions, Gaps and Glissandos in Recent Theoretical Developments", *Sociological Theory*, vol 6, no 2, Fall, pp. 153–68.

Lindenberg, S. (1990) "Homo Socio-Oeconomicus: the Emergence of a General Model of Man in the Social Sciences", *Journal of Institutional and Theoretical Economics*, vol 146, no 4, pp. 727–48.

Loury, G. (1977) "A Dynamic Theory of Racial Income Differences", in Wallace and Le Mund (eds) (1977), pp. 153–86.

Loury, G. (1987) "Why Should We Care about Group Inequality", *Social Philosophy and Policy*, vol 5, no 1, pp. 249–71.

Mavroudeas, S. (1990) "Regulation Approach: a Critical Assessment", PhD Thesis, University of London.

McLennan, G. (1998) *"Fin de Sociologie?* The Dilemmas of Multidimensional Social Theory", *New Left Review*, no 230, July/Aug, pp. 58–90.

Miller, D. (ed.) (1995) *Acknowledging Consumption*, London: Routledge.

Mirowski, P. and D. Plehwe (2015) *The Road from Mont Pèlerin: The Making of the Neoliberal Thought Collective*, with a new preface, Cambridge: Harvard University Press.

Moore, D. (ed.) (2007) *The World Bank: Development, Poverty, Hegemony*, Scotsville: University of KwaZulu-Natal Press.

Olson, M. (1965) *The Logic of Collective Action*, Cambridge: Harvard University Press.

Philo, C. and G. Kearns (1993) "Culture, History, Capital: a Critical Introduction to the Selling of Places", in Kearns and Philo (eds) (1993), pp. 1–32.

Porter, R. (1993) "Baudrillard: History, Hysteria and Consumption", in Rojek and Turner (eds) (1993), pp. 1–22.

Postone, M., E. LiPuma and C. Calhoun (1993) "Introduction: Bourdieu and Social Theory", in Calhoun et al (eds) (1993), pp. 1–13.

Putnam, R. (1993a) *Making Democracy Work: Civic Traditions in Modern Italy*, Princeton: Princeton University Press.

Putnam, R. (1993b) "The Prosperous Community: Social Capital and Public Life", *The American Prospect*, no 13, pp. 35–42.

Putnam, R. (1995) "Bowling Alone: America's Declining Social Capital", *Journal of Democracy*, vol 6, no 1, pp. 65–78.
Putnam, R. (2000) *Bowling Alone: the Collapse and Revival of American Community*, New York: Simon & Schuster.
Radnitzky, G. and P. Bernholz (eds) (1987) *Economic Imperialism: the Economic Method Applied Outside the Field of Economics*, New York: Paragon House Publishers.
Richardson, J. (ed.) (1986) *Handbook of Theory and Research for the Sociology of Education*, New York: Greenwood Press.
Robbins, D. (1991) *The Work of Pierre Bourdieu*, Buckingham: Open University Press.
Rojek, C. and B. Turner (1993) "Introduction: Regret Baudrillard", in Rojek and Turner (eds) (1993), pp. ix–xviii.
Rojek, C. and B. Turner (eds) (1993) *Forget Baudrillard*, London: Routledge.
Ryan, B. (1991) *Making Capital from Culture: the Corporate Form of Capitalist Cultural Production*, New York: Walter de Gruyter.
Sanders, J. and V. Nee (1996) "Immigrant Self-Employment – the Family as Social Capital and the Value of Human Capital", *American Sociological Review*, vol 61, no 2, pp. 231–49.
Santos, A. and N. Teles (eds) (2020) *Financialisation in the European Periphery: Work and Social Reproduction in Portugal*, London: Routledge.
Schelling, T. (1978) *Micromotives and Macrobehavior*, New York: W. W. Norton.
Slater, D. (1997) *Consumer Culture and Modernity*, Cambridge: Polity Press.
Smith, T. (1998) "The Capital/Consumer Relation in Lean Production: the Continued Relevance of Volume Two of 'Capital'", in Arthur and Reuten (eds) (1998), pp. 67–94.
Solow, R. (1999) "Notes on Social Capital and Economic Performance", in Dasgupta and Serageldin (eds) (1999), pp. 6–12.
Stanley, C. (1996) *Urban Excess and the Law: Capital, Culture and Desire*, London: Cavendish Publishing Company.
Stiglitz, J. (1998) "More Instruments and Broader Goals: Moving Toward the Post-Washington Consensus", the 1998 WIDER Annual Lecture, January 7th, Helsinki.
Stiglitz, J. (1999) "Formal and Informal Institutions", in Dasgupta and Serageldin (eds) (1999), pp. 59–70.
Swartz, D. (1996) "Bridging the Study of Culture and Religion: Pierre Bourdieu and the Political Economy of Symbolic Power", *Sociology of Religion*, vol 57, no 1, pp. 71–85.
Swedberg, R. (ed.) (1990) *Economics and Sociology, Redefining their Boundaries: Conversations with Economists and Sociologists*, Princeton: Princeton University Press.
Swedberg, R. (ed.) (1996) *Economic Sociology*, Cheltenham: Edward Elgar.
Thrift, N. and P. Glennie (1993) "Historical Geographies of Urban and Modern Consumption", in Kearns and Philo (eds) (1993), pp. 33–48.

Tommasi, M. and K. Iurelli (eds) (1995) *The New Economics of Human Behaviour*, Cambridge: Cambridge University Press.

Wacquant, L. (1996) "Foreword" to Bourdieu (1996b), pp. ix–xxii.

Wallace, P. and A. Le Mund (eds) (1977) *Women, Minorities, and Employment Discrimination*, Lexington: Lexington Books.

Woolcock, M. (1998) "Social Capital and Economic Development: Toward a Theoretical Synthesis and Policy Framework", *Theory and Society*, vol 27, no 2, pp. 151–208.

World Bank (1993) *The East Asian Miracle: Economic Growth and Public Policy: a World Bank Policy Research Report*, Oxford: Oxford University Press.

Wu, C. (1998) "Embracing the Enterprise Culture: Art Institutions since the 1980s", *New Left Review*, no 230, July/Aug, pp. 28–57.

Zelizer, V. (1988) "Beyond the Polemics on the Market: Establishing a Theoretical and Empirical Agenda", *Sociological Forum*, vol 3, no 4, pp. 614–34, reproduced in Swedberg (ed.) (1996), pp. 298-318.

Zukin, S. (1996) "Space and Symbols in an Age of Decline", in King (ed.) (1996), pp. 43–59.

CHAPTER 6

Economics Imperialism as Kuhnian Revolution?

Postscript as Personal Preamble

Soon after I first began to study economics as a postgraduate in 1969, I recall a flurry of interest in the application of Kuhn's theory of scientific revolution to economics, with some attention to Ward (1972) in particular. Understandably, given the title of this volume, *What's Wrong with Economics?*, there was an appeal to heterodox economists determined to bring down mainstream economics as it was, and replace it with a new "paradigm". By contrast, as observed below, the mainstream itself sought to rely upon Kuhn to legitimise its status as "normal" science. Even so the moment was also open to be interpreted as marking the end of the Keynesian revolution and the beginnings of the monetarist counter-revolution.

In other words, revolution was in the air or, at least, in our thoughts. But almost three decades had to pass before I put forward the hypothesis of an as yet mainly unobserved revolution in the making in and around economics, that involving economics imperialism and specifically in its new form associated with market imperfections. With the leisure to study this in depth and breadth thanks to a two-year ESRC Professorial Fellowship, leaving me able to focus on research alone, it was a natural step in general to question what constitutes a revolution in thought/scholarship and, in particular, if and how economics imperialism represents such a revolution able to stand comparison with the marginalist, Keynesian and monetarist (counter)revolutions. It was equally understandable that I should revisit Kuhn in some level of detail and interrogate to what extent his approach could apply to economics imperialism and, vice-versa, what light could be shed on Kuhn in view of economics imperialism?[1]

---

1 Taking an approach and seeing what insight it provides for a topic/case study but, then, turning the tables, and critically assessing the approach in light of the empirics and/or salient variable (whether present or not, and how treated) is a favoured advice given to research students. The results are much more likely to be favourably received if teasing out what positive contributions might be made as opposed to being confined to crucial dismissal on grounds of analytical flaws. I should have learned this lesson earlier myself. Make friends before you make enemies but, to be fair to my younger self, most mainstream economists are unswerving and dismissive enemies, and some heterodox economists can be even worse.

For mainstream economics, the Kuhnian revolution was at most a passing moment. And, if to a lesser degree, the same applies to heterodoxy. To a large extent, then, this chapter might be dismissed as a nostalgic indulgence. Nonetheless, apart from marking the passage of the Kuhnian fad,[2] there is also at least an implicit, if necessarily partial, account of the trajectory of economics imperialism or, more accurately to the extent that the two diverge, the increasing scope of my explicit acknowledgement of it by topic and by discipline. More examples are listed than previously with one of them, finance addressed, possibly in anticipation of, if not in name, the rise to prominence of financialisation across the economy and the social sciences.[3] The terminology of imperfect-market economics as ushering in a new phase (or stage) of economics imperialism is consolidated, tending to displace the old based on as if perfectly working markets. And this all carries the implications, re-emphasised or emphasised for the first time: how weak is mainstream methodology; how weak is its understanding and knowledge of the history of economic thought; how economics imperialism involves bringing back in (BBI) what was necessarily excluded to allow for mainstream focus on production and utility functions, individualistic optimisation, (in)efficiency and equilibrium; and last, but by no means least, the mainstream is dubbed as parasitic, arrogant, ignorant and contemptuous in its relations with other disciplines, and more heavily exposed as such as it seeks to colonise them, see Fourcade et al (2015) for the supposed (self-belief in) superiority.

1 Introduction[4]

It is now forty years since Thomas Kuhn laid out his theory of scientific revolution. Kuhn was initially concerned to explain how science changed, drawing a distinction between normal, smoothly evolving science within a given paradigm and revolutionary science that blazes a shorter, if not short, sharp shift between paradigms. As a result, Kuhn's language, especially the notion of a paradigm for example, has become commonplace even as substantive

---

2 But see Dow (2023).
3 See especially Mader et al (eds) (2020) and, for my own latest contribution, Fine (2022).
4 Main text based on Fine (2001c). This paper was written whilst in receipt of a Research Fellowship from the UK Economic and Social Research Council (ESRC) under award number R000271046 to study The New Revolution in Economics and Its Impact upon Social Sciences. An earlier version was presented at the METU Annual Economics Conference, Ankara, September, 2000.Thanks to those who gave comments. See also Fine (2002 and 2004a).

understanding of his contribution, and (constructive) criticisms of it, have declined. Further, in the scholarly literature, more than enough time has passed for his approach to have been fully traversed, if not forgotten, territory in understanding the sources and nature of intellectual change. For those economists who participated, even if merely as an audience, in the Kuhnian revolution, it ought in retrospect to stand out as a remarkably rare period of self-examination of a discipline that is notoriously unaware of, and uninterested in, its own history and methodological underpinnings.[5] Whilst primarily concerned with the history of science, Kuhnian notions were readily transposed to the social sciences without economics standing on the sidelines as an exception, even if primarily aloof, as has been so for other intellectual fashions such as postmodernism in the more recent period.[6]

This is not, then, to suggest that the Kuhnian project was readily assimilated without modification within the dismal science. But it did receive a surprisingly broad welcome across the discipline, from both orthodoxy and heterodoxy. The mainstream, for example, could claim that it practised such a successful and appropriate brand of normal science that it need fear no subsequent revolution, the Keynesian having complemented the marginalist revolution (with the monetarist counter-revolution only on the horizon). Thus, for Gordon (1965, p. 123/6):[7]

> [Adam] Smith's postulate of the maximizing individual in a relatively free market and the successful application of this postulate to a wide variety of specific questions is our basic paradigm. It created a "coherent scientific

---

5　de Vroey (1975) observes, for example, correct from my own memory, how influential Kuhn had become in discussions of history of economic thought. In preparing this paper, however, I have been struck by how little Kuhn's influence has been reflected in practice in journal publications in economics.

6　For Kuhn applied across the social sciences, see Gutting (ed.) (1980). Khalil (1987) reviews the application of Kuhn to economics but see also Gordon (1965), Coats (1969), Bronfenbrenner (1971), Kunin and Weaver (1971), Karsten (1973), Ward (1972), Stanfield (1974), de Vroey (1975), Blaug (1975), Chase (1983), Dow (1985), Argyrous (1992 and 1994) in debate with Dow (1994).

7　No doubt evidence for the last sentence is (not) provided by those that come before it, and their extraordinary misrepresentation of the classics. See also Davis (1997, p. 289): "Since the *History of Political Economy* appeared nearly three decades ago, it seems as if most historians of economic thought have concluded that they no longer speak to other economists, and might accordingly focus entirely on thought that is no longer actively pursued by contemporary economists and on which history has closed the door". Further, just as economics as normal science misrepresents the history of economics thought, so it misrepresents economic realities. With continuing relevance for contemporary economics, see Perelman (2000) for a striking critique of Adam Smith's failure to confront the economic, political and ideological realities attached to "a relatively free market". Finally, note that Coats (1969) reckons that Gordon is the first to apply Kuhn to economics.

tradition" (most notably including Marx) and its persistence can be seen by skimming the most current periodicals ... I conclude that economic theory is much like a normal science and that, like a normal science, it finds no necessity for including its history as a part of professional training.

Whilst the mainstream used the Kuhnian concepts of normal science to puff out its chest with pride and confidence, radical political economy found much within the Kuhnian framework with which to assault the mainstream as both abnormal and non-scientific by its own, let alone other, standards. It saw the prospect of itself prospering by way of alternative, Ward (1972) for example.

Such dreams have now been lost rather than fulfilled with the decline of radical political economy and other heterodoxies. Indeed, as argued elsewhere, not only has the mainstream strengthened its stranglehold on the discipline but there is also currently a revolution going on in or, more exactly, around economics. In brief, it is colonising the social sciences as never before giving rise to what its own practitioners have dubbed economic or economics imperialism.[8] On the basis of the new information-theoretic economics, the new micro-foundations purports to examine both the imperfections of the market as well as the non-market responses to them, in the form of institutions, customs, collective action, etc. The latter feature is what enables economics to encroach upon previously unchartered or, at least, hostile territory traditionally occupied and dominated by the other social sciences. Such developments are reflected in the proliferation of "new" fields of economics – the new institutional economics, the new household economics, the economic sociology, the new political economy, the new growth theory, the new labour economics, the new economic geography, the new financial economics, the new development economics, and so on.

The use of the term revolution to describe the current phase of economics imperialism arises out of its reversing, at least in one respect, the marginalist revolution of the 1870s.[9] Irrespective of other differences, economics

---

8 See Fine (1997a, 1998a and b, 1999a, 2000a-f, and 2001a and b) – and Fine (1999b) in debate with Bowden and Offer (1994, 1996 and 1999) and Fine (1999c) with Thompson (1997 and 1999), and Fine and Lapavitsas (2000) with Zelizer (2000) – for the general argument as well as for specific case studies. For evidence from the mainstream itself, see Becker (1996) and Lazear (2000), both of whom refer to economic imperialism and Olson and Kähkönen (2000) who prefer the telling metaphor of economics as metropolis and other social science as the suburbs. See also Frey (1999) who attracts praise from Nobel Laureates Becker, Stigler and Buchanan. I prefer the term economics imperialism, as well as colonisation of the other social sciences, as opposed to economic imperialism. The latter is favoured by the mainstream despite total neglect of its incidence in reality, on which see Perelman (2000).
9 Note, though, that Khalil (1987, p. 119) observes that Stigler, Schumpeter, Blaug and others have all denied that there was a marginalist *revolution* (leading to neoclassical economics), as

was consolidated as a separate academic discipline from the other social sciences, and the economy as market as a separate object of study. Now, the new information-theoretic economics purports once again to examine both economic and non-economic phenomena in tandem, with both understood as responses to informational imperfections. In one respect at least, the marginalist revolution has been reversed, in reuniting the market with the non-market. But the purpose of this article is not, as the reader might be beginning to anticipate, to consider economics imperialism as a more or less exemplary study of a Kuhnian revolution within economics or across the social sciences more generally. There will not be an answer to the question – does the current phase of economics imperialism represent a Kuhnian revolution? It does not seek to establish whether economics imperialism represents a new paradigm, representing a revolutionary shift from the old.

Indeed, as will be seen in Section 2, the debate around Kuhn was drawn to the conclusion that his approach was fundamentally flawed, and that his key concepts did not stand up well either to close analytical or empirical scrutiny. In short, it is not appropriate in general to examine and understand intellectual change in broad Kuhnian terms. However, this does not mean that the Kuhnian approach, and the debate it inspired, should be discarded – much like the mainstream's disregard for the history of economic thought. Rather, the intention here is to revisit the debate over Kuhn for the light that it sheds on the way in which intellectual changes occur. For, both the critical and warm reception that Kuhn received is itself explained by the important insights that he offered or prompted even though his overall framework has, ultimately, been rejected. Methodology has moved on since Kuhn, not least through the influence of postmodernism and notions of social construction, de-construction and re-construction. It is, then, inappropriate to charaterise economics imperialism as a Kuhnian revolution but it is fruitful to consider it against the debate that his notion has inspired. This is done through the following four sections. Section 2 provides a brief overview both of the Kuhnian stance on scientific progress and some of the features of the current phase of economics imperialism. Section 3 bounces off the Kuhnian notions of paradigm and normal science in order to investigate what is distinctive about

---

do heterodox economists, if from different perspectives, such as Hodgson (2011) and Lawson (2013) – with Milonakis and Fine (2012) and Fine (2015), respectively, for response and forthcoming volume on heterodox economics for further discussion. But also see de Vroey (1975) for a telling and wide-ranging contrast on a before and after basis in favour of the unavoidable, if not instantaneous, reality of a marginalist revolution. For a latest restatement of his views, see Lawson (2021).

economics imperialism. Section 4 turns to revolutionary science and how there are shifts between schools of thought. Section 5 asks why schools change and provides some illustrative examples of the differential impact of economics imperialism. The concluding remarks look to the future.

2 Preliminaries

It is worth beginning with a brief account of the two elements, Kuhnian scientific revolution and economics imperialism, that are being set off against one another. For the former, a useful summary is provided by Suppe (1977) on which I draw freely.[10] Central to Kuhn is the notion of paradigm, with science proceeding through discontinuous breaks between them rather than through a continuous evolution, as is suggested by Toulmin (1972) in critique of Kuhn. A paradigm is multi-faceted, ranging from exemplars (or standard applications) to disciplinary matrix (or world view), "but according to Kuhn the scientist obtains his disciplinary matrix from the study of exemplars, and they in large part determine that matrix", p. 139. For Kuhn, the matrix is not acquired "through the study of explicitly formulated methodological rules ... and a theory always is advanced in conjunction with various exemplars which are presented as archetypal applications of the theory to phenomena", p. 140. Further, generalisations are not explicitly and formally specified but proceed through implicitly acquired skill in interpretation. So, there is a need for apprentices both to learn exemplars and obtain the skills to extend them. "It follows that two scientific communities whose symbolic generalizations are the same or employ some of the same theoretical terms, but possess significantly different exemplars, will attach different meanings to the theoretical terms and thereby interpret their generalizations differently", p. 141. Suppe cites Kuhn to the effect that, exemplars "are achievements sufficiently unprecedented to attract an enduring group of adherents away from competing modes of scientific activity [which are] ... sufficiently open-ended to leave all sorts of problems for the redefined group of practitioners to resolve", p. 143. This all occurs in response to mounting theoretical or empirical anomalies produced, often unintentionally, within previous paradigms. The weight of anomalies leads to cumulative switch to other exemplars and, ultimately, to logical incompatibility between disciplinary matrices, differences in prediction, differences in vocabulary, and

---

10   Page references are to him but see also Barbour (1980) for an excellent précis of Kuhn and the debate that he induced.

to "an argument over competing world views and competing ways of doing science". With a division into competing camps, without common assumptions, persuasion rather than logic becomes decisive in commitment to one or other paradigm. The new matrix has "changed meanings attached to theoretical terms" possibly with the old as approximation, p. 147.

So much for Kuhn for the time-being; now for economics imperialism. It is far from new since there have been longstanding attempts to treat all social phenomena as if they were reducible to the economic, with Gary Becker especially in the forefront. This has depended on what I have called the non-revolutionary route – of treating non-market phenomena *as if* they were governed by a market and, thereby, imposing economic rationality upon them in the form of atomised and optimising individuals. In terms of colonising other social sciences, this has the distinct disadvantage of denying the social other than as aggregation over individuals or as externally given and unexplained. Nor are market imperfections new to "traditional" neoclassical economics (with implication of a rationale for state or other intervention) since they have long been recognised, especially but not exclusively within partial equilibrium, alongside transaction costs, say, as an influence on the organisation of firms and other institutions. What is more fundamentally innovative within the new microeconomics of informational asymmetry (the new approach as I will call it as opposed to the old) is its ability to examine social structure and customs, albeit on the continuing basis of the peculiar form taken by methodological individualism. Utility maximisation is the ultimate rationale for both economic (and market) and non-economic (and non-market) behaviour, with equilibrium reproduction or evolution of the social on the basis of aggregate individual behaviour. Relative to the old, the new approach adds market imperfections in the form of informational asymmetries but, on this basis alone, it also extends the scope of the analysis more or less indefinitely across the social sciences.

It does so, without going into details, through the use of informational imperfections to explain why markets might be inefficient, might not clear (supply and demand remain out of equilibrium), or might not emerge at all.[11] As a result, whilst still drawing upon a methodology of optimising individuals, it is able to suggest why economic *structures* might arise – as, for example, in the division between the employed and unemployed when the labour market does not clear. Whilst a significant result *within* mainstream economics,

---

11   For details, probably unnecessary for those trained in economics, see any of references cited in footnote 8.

even more important are the implications for other social sciences. For non-economic or non-market behaviour is now understood as the rational, i.e. individual optimising behaviour, response to market imperfections. It is appropriate in face of informational, and hence market, imperfections to form social structures, as reflected in collectives, institutions and the state, and to engage in what would otherwise appear to be non-rational behaviour, as in customs, trust and norms.

Such simple analytical advances considerably expand the capacity of economics to colonise the other social sciences, not least because of the formal and abstract nature of the models employed within economics – they apply in principle to any imperfect (non-)market situation. Accordingly, the principles involved have no historical nor social roots other than in the language deployed. For, in content, they rely entirely upon categories such as utility, production, inputs and informational uncertainties, quite apart from the timeless and rootless optimising of individuals, themselves located in history and society only by virtue of the preceding optimising of their ancestors. Thus, the new, like the old, approach is characterised in its starting point by excising social and historical content in anything other than name. Consequently, such content can be (re)introduced formally as path dependence in some form but informally on the basis of the continuing traditions and concerns of the colonised disciplines and topics. The social is the non-market response to market imperfections. Further, such incursions tend to be informal, adopting the language rather than the models of economics, as in reference to human capital in any number of applications and rent-seeking and collective action when discussing institutions. Of course, it is also possible for formal economic models to be directly applied theoretically and empirically to other disciplines or non-economic topics without such informalities.

In the latter case, economics tends merely to draw upon other disciplines for definition of an issue and on which to exercise its models. As such, the colonisation of the other social sciences by economics is particularly open to being parasitic, arrogant, ignorant and contemptuous. These are harsh words, rarely if ever raised in the context of normal science, although possibly wielded as revolutionary science seeks to replace an old by a new paradigm. Why are they justifiably attached to economics imperialism? The parasitism of colonisation arises out of the lack of social and historical content that characterises the underlying theory. Its origins within economics mean that it has been applied first to market imperfections in isolation in order to explain why markets may be inefficient, fail to clear, or be absent altogether. It is then extended to non-market forms and to any other problem in the social sciences – with the exception of anything involving the social construction of meaning for which it is powerless. But, by its nature, the theory does not construct problems; it only offers solutions to problems that already exist, together with the corresponding concepts with which they have been posed. Within economics, the problems are why is it that markets might not work perfectly and why is the market not the only form of social organisation. These are well-established problems within economics, especially outside the mainstream, with a correspondingly wide range of answers, varying from different versions of Keynesianism to different schools of political economy that share in common a rejection of methodological individualism. Otherwise, in the other social sciences, any number of theoretical issues and concepts can be appropriated and reinterpreted within the new information-theoretic approach. Of course, all analytical advances are liable to confront, draw upon, and even revolutionise traditional scholarship. As a result of its reductionism, however, the new approach can only do this in the form of reinterpretation on the basis of its own understanding of informational imperfections.

In much colonisation by economics of the other social sciences, such parasitism is also associated with arrogance in two respects. For, having exploited the other social sciences for their problems and concepts, the results of previous scholarship are reproduced as if innovative by virtue of having been based upon informational imperfections. At times, this borders on the farcical with naïve economists claiming to have shown, for example, that institutions matter and that labour markets differ from other markets as if this were not already well-known from a variety of other perspectives. In addition, though, as the second form of arrogance, it is precisely the failure of previous analyses to have proceeded from informational imperfections which leads them to be perceived, from the perspective of economics imperialism, as both deficient and lacking theoretical rigour. For these, in the hands of economic theorists, always means mathematical modelling irrespective of conceptual coherence and validity. And where theory ends, statistical methods in the form of econometrics are taken as the only benchmark by which to assess theory, as if falsifiability as a criterion of science had never been questioned.

With respect to ignorance, the colonisation of social sciences by economics has been marked by total disregard for the scholarship of the appropriated disciplines and that attached to the object of analysis other than for the parasitical purposes outlined previously. It is simply a matter of investigating sources of, and applications for, models of informational imperfections. At best, earlier contributions are filtered for this purpose. Finally, in colonising the other social sciences, economics reveals its contempt for them by the sum of the previously outlined features, with the sum greater than the individual parts. For anything that does not conform to its approach is dismissed as lacking "rigour" and "science", terms that are well-known within economics as a superficial code for policing anything that does not ultimately rest on a mathematical model and/or statistical testing.[12]

Ironically, as discussed below, economics as a discipline has engaged in its own version of Kuhnian normal science whilst becoming decreasingly detached from a sense of its own methodology and discussion of methodology, whether of economics or more generally. Its own claims to be scientific depend upon an antediluvian view of science, certainly one that is both pre-Kuhnian, and widely discredited on all sides.[13] As Kuhn (1970a, p. 235) argued some thirty years ago:

> Philosophers of science will need to follow other contemporary philosophers in examining, to a previously unprecedented depth, the manner in which language fits the world, asking how terms attach to nature, how those attachments are learned, and how they are transmitted from one generation to another by the members of a language community.

Economists do not appear to have heeded his advice. They remain as unconscious as ever of the ideological content of the concepts and methods they use. These are taken to be self-evident, unproblematic and universally applicable. As Amariglio and Ruccio (1999, p. 23) put it:

> Academic economists tend to privilege the form of reasoning associated with economic science – the 'economic way of thinking' ... the formal methods that serve to guarantee scientific rigor.

Nonetheless, despite its claims to be scientific, in contrast to other social sciences, especially in light of its (mathematical) rigour and empirical testing, as is obvious even from casual oversight, the mainstream always sacrifices both rigour and empirical evidence when it is a choice between them and its own theoretical and conceptual predilections – assuming, for example, that general equilibrium exists and is unique, efficient and stable despite the assumptions shown to be necessary for this, that a single-good production function can

---

12   Lazear (2000) is salutary reading in this respect, putting into print in an issue of a leading journal devoted to the current state of economics, what is commonly to be heard from economists as a matter of course. For a critique of Lazear, see Fine (2000d).
13   Boylan and O'Gorman (1995, pp. 27 fwd) refer to a post-positivism phase as prevailing in economic methodology over the last quarter of a century, characterised by a desperate but unsuccessful attempt to rescue falsifiability.

represent the economy as a whole, that individuals have (given) utility maximisation as their (only) goal, there is only risk not uncertainty (the unknowable), there are no externalities nor increasing returns to scale or scope, there are given, perfectly competitive prices, technology is fixed, etc, etc.[14]

3   Paradigm Lost or (Re)Gained?

As observed, if there is the use of one concept that particularly marked the arrival of Kuhn's influence, it is that of paradigm. It has entered the scholarly lexicon and is used freely as an analytical rationale, often without reference to and, possibly, knowledge of its dependence on Kuhn. You have your paradigm and I have mine. It's just a matter of taste.[15] Thus, as on the canvas of Marxism which, at about the same time, began to attach itself to the Althusserian notion of "problematic", it became commonplace for all and sundry across the academic world to locate themselves as working within one or other paradigm, or as engaging in their own versions of normal science. As Masterman (1970, p. 60) puts it:

> That there is normal science – and that it is exactly as Kuhn says it is – is the outstanding, the crushingly obvious fact which confronts and hits any philosophers of science who set out, in a practical or technological manner, to do any actual scientific research. It is because Kuhn – at last – has noticed this central fact about all real science … that it is normally a

---

14   Other examples include conditions necessary for comparative advantage to be meaningful (as the basis for trade theory) and the theory of the second best. Perversely, these breaches with the assumptions often needed to establish the core elements of the mainstream, let alone to deploy it, have subsequently been used to apply those core elements to the conditions under which they are not defined, itself the basis for extending economics imperialism. See, for example, Fine (2009) for the study of identity on the basis of utility functions. But any sensible treatment of identity rejects the notion of its foundation from a given individual utility function as starting point.

15   Note that Kuhn (1970a) himself, in the absence of objective and universal criteria of theory choice, rejects a simple and liberal version of relativism, as in his dismissal of Paul Feyerabend who "provides the exception that proves the rule … [for] he at once concludes to the intrinsic irrationality of theory-choice", p. 234. This is because theory choice, for Kuhn, is not a matter of individual choice but follows from "the nature of the scientific group, discovering what it values, what it tolerates, and what it disdains", p. 238. On the other hand, he rejects the accusation that might is right in what passes for normal science but, equally, reiterates that neither inner logic nor external criteria alone can decide what passes for science (although all play a part). See also later discussion.

habit-governed, puzzle-solving activity, not a fundamentally upheaving or falsifying activity ... that actual scientists are now, increasingly reading Kuhn instead of Popper ... in new scientific fields particularly, 'paradigm' and not 'hypothesis' is now the 'O.K. word'.

There are a number of further points here as far as current developments within economics are concerned. First consider methodology. The current phase of economics imperialism has primarily reverted to the image of the discipline as engaging in falsifying activity and posing and testing hypotheses. According to Lazear (2000, p. 102/3), for example, whose article and its title celebrate economics imperialism:[16]

> The power of economics lies in its rigor. Economics is scientific; it follows the scientific method of stating a formal refutable theory, testing the theory, and revising the theory based on the evidence. Economics succeeds where other social sciences fail because economists are willing to abstract. The old joke about a stranded, starving economist assuming a can opener to open a can of food pokes fun at our willingness to assume away what we believe to be unimportant or difficult details. Economists are used to posing the counterfactual question to do an analysis. What would one expect in the absence of the hypothesized effect? What would be observed? Do the data allow us to choose between various hypotheses? Economists are not alone among social scientists in following this method, but this form of enquiry has become standard for economic research.

In this light, the impact of Kuhn on economic methodology within the discipline has even been perverse. Initially, to the extent that there was a response to Kuhn, it was a shift towards recognising the difficulties in principle and in practice of holding to positivism or the less stringent Popperian standards of falsifiability. Paradoxically, Kuhn thereby had the effect of justifying an unchanged practice of proceeding as if on the falsifiability track whatever its deficiencies, on the grounds that this constituted normal science. Economics as a discipline has rarely shown any interest in methodology, as observed by Blaug (1975) in commenting on the Kuhnian revolution,[17] and the prick of conscience prompted by Kuhn did little to upset its normal practices in this

---

16   Note that his assertions about what economists do have long been known to be a false image of themselves. See Blaug (1980), McCloskey (1986) and Lawson (1997), for example.
17   See also Argyrous (1992).

respect nor in its attachment in principle to falsifiability. Indeed, the post-Kuhn movement in economic methodology has had the effect of removing it even further from the practice and knowledge of economists.[18] In short, what, from the perspective of critical realism, Lawson (1997) dubs the deductivist method characteristic of mainstream economics has, if anything, strengthened since Kuhn.[19] Consequently, a shift in methodology does not mark the current phase of economics imperialism. It is more of the same on, if anything, an even shallower basis, with less likelihood of critical self-reflection.

Second, on a more mundane level, to what extent has economics imperialism been associated with a shift in "habit-governed, puzzle-solving activity"? On the face of it, very little has changed. Whatever its methodological deficiencies, mainstream economics has remained firmly committed to an unchanging method – one attached to methodological individualism of a special type, utility maximisation, to equilibrium as an organising concept, and to considerations of efficiency, the three distinctive scientific elements emphasised by Lazear (2000). In addition, the technical apparatus and the barrage of associated techniques has at most become a little more sophisticated and extensive – with the fundamentals in terms of production and utility functions being instantly recognisable.

Third, neither of the previous points sheds any light directly on what a paradigm (in economics) is and whether the current phase of economics imperialism represents or is best understood as a paradigm shift. In this respect, it is worth recording that Masterman's contribution is most often cited for highlighting the ambiguity of Kuhn's own use of the term paradigm. She is credited with having discovered at least twenty-one different ways in which Kuhn has used the term. She does, however, assign these to three broad types, the sociological, the metaphysical and the construct. The last two of these correspond, respectively, to the common previously observed distinction to be found in the literature, one suggested by Kuhn himself – between paradigm as world view or "disciplinary matrix" and paradigm as exemplar. Here, the distinctive character of economics imperialism does emerge. Masterman (1970, p. 70) understands a "construct paradigm" as an "artefact":

> For only with an artefact can you solve puzzles.

---

18 As Lawson (1997, p. 12) quotes Frank Hahn in advising young economists, "to 'avoid discussion of "mathematics in economics" like the plague', and to 'give no thought at all to methodology'".

19 This leads to the conclusion that methodology is the Achilles' heel of mainstream economists. For an alternative view, see Fine (2004b).

With puzzle-solving as normal science, it is not difficult to identify the artefact associated with the new phase of economics imperialism. It is the notion of asymmetric information and the consequences this has for market and non-market outcomes. Indeed, the founding artefact is an exemplary exemplar – the market for "lemons", or second-hand cars, as laid out by Akerlof (1970).[20] It solves a number of puzzles – why the market might not work perfectly despite optimising individuals and no exogenous impediments to market clearing. As observed, there are three possible outcomes – markets clear but are Pareto-inefficient (there are buyers and sellers who would like to exchange at some other price but do not), they do not clear (those on the short side of the market do not have incentive to change price in their favour), or there is no market at all (undermined by presence of moral hazard or adverse selection for example).

Following Akerlof, information-theoretic economics has proceeded by accumulating different types of informational asymmetries and applying them across an equally diverse range of markets. Although with the physical sciences in mind, Masterman (1970, p. 70) astonishingly and unwittingly anticipates recent developments within economics, as economists have searched out applications for asymmetric information:[21]

> A normal-scientific puzzle always has a solution which is guaranteed by the paradigm, but which it takes ingenuity and resourcefulness to find.

Further, as Chase (1983, p. 816) observes, a paradigm fills out a new analytical terrain:

> The acceptance of a new exemplary paradigm by a community of scientists will often require a redefinition of the corresponding science ... some old problems may be relegated to another science or declared

---

20 More generally, see Akerlof (1984 and 1990), and Fine (2001a, Chapter 3) for comparison of Akerlof and Becker as economic imperialists, revolutionary and non-revolutionary, respectively, although Becker has become more revolutionary, and in the vanguard, with his adoption of social capital (Becker 1996). See also Fine (2019) most recently.

21 See also Chase (1983, p. 817): "Normal science is a highly productive mechanism since, *within the context of the accepted exemplary paradigm*, it is keenly focused and goal-oriented". Stiglitz (1994) provides a striking illustration. He poses and solves the problem of the economics of socialism from the perspective of information-theoretic economics, referencing over one hundred of his own problem-solving articles along the way. As discussed later, his attention has subsequently moved to solving the problems of development by the same process.

entirely 'unscientific', while others that were previously nonexistent or trivial may ... become the very archetypes of scientific achievement.

In case of economics imperialism, a wider definition of economic science is involved since it is not simply a matter of explaining market imperfections but also of incorporating the non-market responses to them, thereby establishing a presence within the other social sciences. Masterman suggests that a paradigm is established by taking an exemplar, A, and finding other applications for it, B, by analogy whereby B becomes A-like. This is precisely what has been characteristic of economics imperialism – for economic and social analyses have been reduced, respectively, to market imperfections and the non-market responses to them. From "lemons", or the market for second hand cars, the entire terrain of economic and social theory is opened up!

Interestingly, Masterman (1970) considers that the exemplar attached to a paradigm is more important than its world view, or metaphysical element, and this seems to be borne out by the "disciplinary matrix" attached to information-theoretic economics. How does the new information-theoretic economics differ from what went before? It takes as its point of departure the model of perfectly competitive equilibrium. In its place is posited an imperfectly competitive world, with imperfect markets and imperfect information, leading both to inefficiencies and to non-market responses to them (whether these correct market imperfections or not, or even make them worse). In other words, the vision of the new approach is its micro-foundations writ large. In case of development economics, for example, Stiglitz and Hoff (1999) argue that:[22]

> In leaving out history, institutions, and distributional considerations, neoclassical economics was leaving out the heart of development economics. Modern economic theory argues that the fundamentals {resources, technology, and preferences} are not the only ... determinants of economic outcomes ... even without government failures, market failures are pervasive, especially in less developed countries.

---

22   This was previously anticipated by Stiglitz (1989) and formalised with his launching, as Chief Economist at the World Bank, of the post Washington Consensus (Stiglitz 1998a). Note the title of his subsequent major contribution in this vein, "Towards a New Paradigm for Development: Strategies, Policies and Processes" (Stiglitz 1998b) and how both economic history and development economics, and development studies more generally, come under the Stiglitz orbit. See Fine (2001b) for critique but also forthcoming volume on development.

Further, with casual reference to the Black Plague, as an illustrative accident of history (like AIDS today?), and multiple equilibria, an explanation is provided for the fundamental problem of why "developed and less developed countries are on different production functions":

> We emphasize that accidents of history matter ... partly because of pervasive complementarities among agents ... and partly because even a set of dysfunctional institutions and behaviors in the past can constitute a Nash equilibrium from which an economy need not be inevitably dislodged.

This appears an ideal illustration of Kuhn's (1970b) own understanding of how paradigms are generated by, and transformed into, an evolving disciplinary matrix. There are symbolic generalisations, of which production functions and Nash equilibria are archetypal. The metaphysical content of 'modern economic theory' is one of 'failures' – market, government or otherwise – as opposed to the ideal, perfectly competitive, world of 'neoclassical economics'. Values within a paradigm are of two types – those concerning predictions and puzzle formulation, and those attached to overall consistency, simplicity and plausibility. For the new approach, there is a common reliance with the old both upon econometrics and upon a method of optimising individuals. But the puzzles are about how the market understandably works imperfectly rather than how it diverges from perfection because of externally imposed constraints.

The third broad category of meaning of paradigm identified by Masterman (1970) is the sociological as opposed to the metaphysical (world view) or the construct (exemplar). This refers to the community of scientists and their common practices which, in retrospect, Kuhn (1970b) confesses he would have taken as his analytical and expositional starting point whilst recognising that paradigm and scientific community set up a vicious definitional circle in terms of who does what. Paradoxically, although the new approach appropriately presents itself as less dogmatic than the model of perfect competition that it has sought to replace, it has prospered in an intellectual climate in which economics as a discipline has become even more intolerant of alternatives. Radical political economy has been considerably depleted and, even where it has not, the modelling and statistical techniques of the orthodoxy are increasingly imperative as a condition of entry to the profession, to the exclusion of almost all else. Blaug (1998a, p. 12) reports from John Hey, previously managing editor of the *Economic Journal*, that there is a 'journal game', based on use of irrelevant material, the stylised facts observed by an author, and designed to demonstrate cleverness rather than address crucial economic problems. Blaug (1998b, p. 45) himself opines:

I am very pessimistic about whether we can actually pull out of this. I think we have created a locomotive. This is the sociology of the economics profession. We have created a monster that is very difficult to stop.

Blaug (1998a, p. 11) also reports from a survey of a lack of interest in the real world on the part of elite graduate economics students as opposed to honing their skills in the latest econometrics and mathematical economics.[23] Particularly striking is the degree of Americanisation of economics, as a source of training and of peer research.[24] Thus, theory is not a matter of individual choice but follows from "the nature of the scientific group, discovering what it values, what it tolerates, and what it disdains" (Kuhn 1970a, p. 238). Tacit knowledge plays a major role, with membership of the profession, "learned by doing science rather than by acquiring rules for doing it" (Kuhn 1970b, p. 191). Despite the emphasis upon econometrics in contemporary economics, there must be considerable doubt about whether it is conducive to a dialogue between theory and the real world in anything other than a formal sense. This point is illustrated, for example, by Barro-type regressions for the new growth theory and the corresponding methodology involving the inclusion of as many variables as possible to test (conditional) convergence and to assess the impact of these on economic performance.[25]

There can be little doubt, as Garnett (1999) observes, that mainstream economics continually and dogmatically reasserts its scientific status and superiority relative to other forms of economic discourse, thereby creating boundaries for definition of the profession, entry conditions, and associated benefits in employment, prestige, financial support and intellectual independence. But, why as a discipline should it seek to extend its supposedly superior form of science to other disciplines, over and above its enhanced capacity to do so in light of the new information-theoretic economics? It is possible to posit a certain maturing in the current dynamic of the discipline and its

---

23 See also Khalil (1987, p. 126) who, in drawing upon Leijonhufvud, observes: "Isolating practitioners in an ivory tower allows the aesthetic criterion to play a role in theoretical endeavours ... (with) beauty and elegance rather than empirical corroboration as the basis of theory selection".

24 On all of this, see Coats (ed.) (1996), Hodgson and Rothman (1999), Bernstein (1999) and Lee and Harley (1998), for example. For more recent evidence of the dominance of US by its monoeconomics, see Aigner (2021).

25 More or less the same is true for testing the impact of trade liberalisation, financial liberalisation, etc. For a critique of the new growth theory on these and more general scores, see Fine (2000a). For an account of the continuing corresponding flaws in econometrics, see Wible and Sedgley (1999).

disciples. First, observe that the conditions of entry to the intellectual vanguard of the profession are extremely technically demanding. As the degree of mathematical and statistical sophistication has been ratcheted up, so existing professionals who do not conform have found themselves marginalised to a greater or lesser extent. On the other hand, the newly-trained academic economists have been highly tuned in the techniques and are growing in numbers. On casual observation, and discussion with colleagues, there is now no shortage of "American-trained" economists, searching out careers.

Second, in a world in which publish or perish and a doctorate is not enough, the new recruits need outlets for their abilities, satisfied to some extent by the emergence of new journals. But a crucial intellectual factor is involved here. This is that the analytical and technical *principles* underlying the new information-theoretic approach are demanding but, once commanded, are limited in scope and economic application. It is simply one market imperfection after another. Whether by virtue of intellectual boredom of those who are already well-established – one more market, one more twist on a technique – or the search for new avenues by those who have yet to establish themselves, the other social sciences provide a virgin terrain on which to play out those skills that would otherwise exhibit rapidly declining marginal productivity! In effect, neo-liberalism is the death of economics because, if the market works perfectly, there is no need to study it. By contrast, the market imperfection, information-theoretic approach keeps the discipline alive but only at the expense of intensifying technical virtuosity, relying upon ever more esoteric models and, most important in reserves of potential, by extension to non-market applications.

Third, academia in general increasingly depends upon external research funding. Compared to their colleagues in business, accounting, marketing and finance, academic economists are generally unsuited to serving the needs of the private sector. Where they are able to oblige, the rewards they can command by being within the private sector itself heavily outweigh those of remaining within academia. On the other hand, economists have also been less than willing and attractive participants in more publicly-minded research, not least because of being unworldly. As Balakrishnan and Grown (1999, p. 135) reveal in their study of foundation support for economic research:

> When the Ford Foundation funded multidisciplinary graduate programs in social science and health, for example, it found it impossible to convince economists to join the effort. Similarly, when the MacArthur Foundation sponsored a competition for multidisciplinary research on

the human dimensions of global environmental change, economists were generally absent from the teams of investigators.

However, in deploring this absence of economics, Balakrishnan and Grown are heartened by "recent developments in economics and philanthropy [that] provide new openings to reexamine and renegotiate this relationship". They refer specifically to, "lively interest in the economics of information and incentive problems due to asymmetric information in settings as varied as the provision of public services, labour markets, credit markets, insurance markets, and Third World agriculture", p. 124/5. Thus, intellectual, professional and personal imperatives have been conducive to the outward thrust of economics imperialism, consolidating a paradigm of market imperfections extended to non-market outcomes. It allows for (competition for) jobs, publications and research funding!

4   Paradigm Shift?

In short, it does appear to be possible to argue that there is a new paradigm within economics, one that emphasises market (as informational) imperfections at micro– and macro-levels, one that is deeply embedded within mainstream neoclassical methodology, and one that addresses the non-economic as well as the economic. Yet, given that the ways of characterising a paradigm are so multifarious, it is hardly surprising that it is possible to fit it in various ways to the new approach. Within the debate over Kuhn, however, whether and how shifts take place *between* paradigms has been more problematic. Indeed, Toulmin (1972, p. 107) suggests that:

> The theory of scientific revolution is, thus, quite independent of the theory of paradigms. This, rather than the term 'paradigms', is the distinctive feature of Kuhn's analysis.

For scientific revolution, a standard account of Kuhn would point to the fruitfulness of a paradigm in throwing up and solving problems as a matter of normal science. But the paradigm also has its dark side in creating empirical and theoretical anomalies that it is incapable of accommodating. Once these become too heavy in number or weight, they create the potential for a new paradigm to emerge that is capable of resolving the anomalies of the old. In other words, normal science proceeds within a given paradigm through incremental change until a revolutionary change gives rise to a shift between paradigms.

This framework for understanding shifts between paradigms has been subject to considerable criticism for science, let alone for social science. First, it has been observed that the difference between paradigms is not so sharp in content. As Toulmin (1972, p. 105/6) has put it:[26]

> We must face the fact that paradigm-switches are never as complete as the fully-fledged definition implies; that rival paradigms never really amount to entire alternative world-views; and that intellectual discontinuities on the theoretical level of science conceal underlying continuities at a deeper, methodological level.

Such is certainly true of the emergence of the new approach to economics, with its predominantly breaking with the old only by introducing informational imperfections and broadening the scope of application to the non-economic. Second, it is argued that the break between paradigms is much less dramatic, bringing the distinction between normal and revolutionary science into question, with all change proceeding through incremental shift and self-criticism. As Bronfenbrenner (1971, p. 150) observes for economics:

> Important advances tend to be major *accretions* without any corresponding rejections of existing paradigms.

Again, such reservations are appropriate in describing the emergence of the new approach. This is especially so in view of the limited extent to which it challenges the methodology of the old approach. Kuhn's account of the sharp break between paradigms both in outlook and passage between them is dependent upon two important features. On the one hand, empirical observation of the same phenomena would be interpreted differently. On the other hand, the criteria for judging theory would also be incompatible across paradigms. Kuhn (1970a, p. 234) observes critically of Popper that:[27]

---

26 He continues, "This done, we must ask ourselves whether the use of the term 'revolution' for such conceptual changes is not itself a rhetorical exaggeration". The same has been suggested to me in terms of perceiving economics imperialism as a revolution! See also Stigler (1969, p. 225): "If vast changes in the subject and techniques of a science can be accommodated within a paradigm, and hence do not constitute a revolution, Kuhn's assertion that a crisis is necessary to the emergence of a new paradigm is virtually a tautology".

27 See, though, Dow (1985, p. 24): "Kuhn's position was rendered ambiguous, however, when he set out five criteria by which theories may be appraised, referring to the following characteristics: accuracy, consistency, breadth of scope, simplicity and fruitfulness ...

He and his followers share with more traditional philosophers of science the assumption that the problem of theory-choice can be resolved by techniques which are semantically neutral ... canons of rationality thus derive exclusively from those of logic and linguistic syntax. ... [and] the existence of a vocabulary adequate to neutral observation reports.

In short, both observation and theory-choice are paradigm-dependent. Whilst Kuhn has been criticised for neglecting the extent to which both observation and criteria can be commonly accepted across different paradigms, the new approach seems identical to the old in these respects.

Kuhn's response to the criticisms reported in this section – that the distinctions between paradigms and between normal and revolutionary science are not sufficiently sharp – has been to suggest that revolutionary science is more not less common than generally supposed. This ultimately leads Toulmin (1972, p. 117) to conclude that, as all theoretical change becomes potentially revolutionary, "on his latest reinterpretation, Kuhn's account of 'scientific revolution' rests on a logical truism and – as such – is *no longer a theory of conceptual change at all*". Possibly, in anticipation of such a charge, given his assessment of an increasing frequency of revolutionary as opposed to normal science, Kuhn (1970a, p. 252) suggests, "the gist of the problem is that to answer the question 'normal or revolutionary?' one must first ask, 'for whom?'".[28]

This is particularly germane to economics imperialism. Much of the thrust of the previous discussion points to the limited extent to which it represents a Kuhnian revolution *within* economics, even if the notion could be accepted as appropriate.[29] Indeed, far from the new information-theoretic economics serving as a break, as it sees itself, with the new classical economics with its reliance upon perfectly working markets, the rational expectations hypothesis can be seen as an important stepping stone between the two approaches. As Davis (1997, p. 299) remarks of the New Classicals:

Although he provided no rational justification for these criteria, the fact that they were put forward as something transcending individual paradigms appears to weaken the incommensurability of paradigms and at the same time opens the door to the *development* of a rationale for universal criteria".

28   Thus, he suggests that the Copernican was for everyone but the discovery of oxygen was for chemists and not for mathematical astronomers.
29   Kunin and Weaver (1971) advise of dual difficulties – the adequacy of Kuhn for science together with its mechanical application to economics.

Their sudden repopulation of the world with a new type of economic agent simultaneously made extinct an older type of being: the naïve victim of money illusion, whose expectations adapted but gradually to changing circumstances.

This is particularly germane to the new approach given that market imperfections are far from new to mainstream economics. In opposition to the New Classicals, though, they have to be endogenised, and how appropriate to do so on the basis of perfect calculation in face of informational imperfections. So the significance of the new approach does not lie primarily in its impact upon economics. It is more important for its influence upon other social sciences, reinforcing the presence of a rational choice methodology and/or reducing the social to the consequences of informationally-based market imperfections.

5 Paradigm Lost, Regained or Reconstructed?

The previous two sections have focused upon what distinguishes one paradigm from another and how shifts take place between them. This section is more concerned with why those shifts take place and with providing illustrations of economics imperialism in action. For the former, whilst some attention has been placed on needing to overcome the individual and professional inertia created by an existing paradigm, and its associated community of scientists whose outlook is incompatible with a newly emerging paradigm,[30] this cannot be exclusively decisive. For, otherwise, there would never be any intellectual change, nor could its direction be determined.[31] Two further explanatory elements have been decisive in the literature, the role of external and internal factors, otherwise understood as relativist or absolutist approaches, respectively, to intellectual change.[32] The absolutist position

---

30 But note that Toulmin (1972) questions whether revolutionary science is based on a conceptual rupture between incompatible paradigms rather than a cumulative and gradual process of debate. Referring to the Newton/Einstein transition, he argues that the physicists who lived through the period from 1890 to 1930 were unaware of a breakdown in communication, even over such an extended time. The same applies for a longer period for the Copernican changeover.
31 Hence the incompleteness of Fischer's (1993) account, following Zupan (1991), in explaining the persistence of general equilibrium because of its serving as heuristic device, theoretical norm and system of logic. These are presumed to interact with personal commitment, itself explained by role of start-up costs, free-rider problems in view of paradigm as public good, and network externalities.
32 For the latter, in the context of economics, see Chalk (1967).

understands intellectual change as arising out of the inner logic of the discipline itself.[33] In the case of the new information-theoretic approach, it is not difficult to identify the inner source that prompted it as a response. With the rise of the new classical economics, and its assumptions of rational expectations and perfect market clearing, economic fluctuations were explained entirely in terms of random and unanticipated shocks. There would also be no impact from government intervention, as its intentions would be neutralised by economic agents deploying available information and models of the economy optimally. It is hardly surprising that the new micro-foundations should take the two crucial assumptions of the new classical economics as its point of departure. On the one hand, information is asymmetric between agents (a point already recognised in a perverse way by the new classical economics insofar as government as an economic agent could affect outcomes with a surprise, or unanticipated, policy package). On the other hand, this can be used to explain, rather than to assume as in earlier microeconomics, why markets might not clear perfectly.[34]

The rest, as the saying goes, is partially history of economic thought. But the rise of the new approach, even in absolutist terms, is marked by two anomalies or special features. First, it explicitly set itself the goal of restoring the earlier paradigm that preceded the new classical economics, namely Keynesianism. To do so, however, it had to reconstruct it on micro-foundations, complementing earlier fixed price models (the reappraisal or disequilibrium (re)interpretation of Keynes) with an explanation for why prices might be inflexible. Second, it opened up the non-economic as the non-market response to market imperfections, paving the way for a new phase of economics imperialism. In addition, as already mentioned, developments within the discipline have been associated with the driving out of alternative approaches, or incorporating them on its own terms, especially those attached to radical political economy.

To explain all of this requires some movement towards the relativist approach – how intellectual developments are influenced by socio-economic conditions in the external environment. The rise of the new classical economics is heavily associated with the broader emergence of neo-liberalism and the idea that government is both bad and too extensive. The market should be

---

33 Some have argued that Kuhn needs to be interpreted as a dialectic, with normal science as thesis, anomalies as antithesis, and new paradigm as synthesis. See Karsten (1973) and Chase (1983), and Kunin and Weaver (1971) and Khalil (1987) for the dialectic in the broader context of external circumstances, the socio-psychological evolution of intellectual communities, and so on.

34 For a fuller account in the context of labour markets, see Fine (1998a, Chapter 2).

allowed to prevail wherever possible, seeking to mould the world in the virtual image of perfect competition,[35] and, not surprisingly, the non-market should be understood as far as possible as if it were a market as in the economic analysis promoted by Gary Becker. With the collapse of the socialist economies, the new approach has been perfectly placed to offer a more palatable and progressive alternative – charting a course between socialist planning and neo-liberalism, and constructing a virtual world of market imperfections and the non-market responses to them.[36]

But, for economics imperialism to have any success outside the discipline of economics, other disciplines had to be receptive to its incursions. Previously, other than for rational choice approaches, which had gained ground unevenly across the social sciences in the wake of neo-liberalism, there have been two major stumbling blocks for a colonising economics. One has been overcome to some extent. This has been the need previously for economics to take the social, the structural, the institutional, the customary as given or even irrational. Now, albeit on the continuing basis of methodological individualism, this is no longer so – the social can be explained as the rational, longer-term response to market and informational imperfections. The second impediment is insurmountable and loomed large as neo-liberalism prevailed. Postmodernism has placed considerable emphasis on the social (and individual) construction of the meaning of things, the consumption of the sign of things, for example, rather than the things themselves. As a result, in the extreme, the associated subjectivity has predominated over, and excluded, close examination of the material processes involved in social (de- and re-) construction. On the other hand, economics has traditionally taken all objects at face value and as unproblematic within its own vernacular of utility, inputs, production, etc. Postmodernist social science and economics are simply incompatible, although postmodernism had the perverse effect of abandoning economic analysis to the economists.[37] Now, however, across the social sciences, there has been something of a retreat from postmodernism and a wish to refocus upon material, including economic, factors. With mainstream economics currently able to claim that history, institutions, and customs matter, it has made advances across other social sciences

---

35 See Carrier and Miller (eds) (1998).
36 However, later work would argue that information-imperfect economics and the corresponding new phase of economics imperialism corresponds to the second phase of (Third Wayism) neoliberalism and, only in this sense, in opposition to first phase of everything as if perfect market economics and first shock therapy phase of neoliberalism. See Fine (2019).
37 Post-Fordism represents a minor exception.

despite its continuing but veiled methodological deficiencies from the perspective of alternative disciplines.

It is crucial to recognise, however, how recent and faltering are these shifting parameters in the external (intellectual) environment with which economics imperialism interacts. Equally, as with the past influence of postmodernism, whether by topic or discipline, the impact has been both uneven and diverse, as will be the retreat from its excesses. Yet, as has been seen with the bringing of the social back into economics, the ex ante "paradigm" is not liable to be restored. Departure from it will even be greater than before. Thus, to adopt the Kuhnian terminology, the prospects for paradigm shifts across the social sciences as they accommodate or confront the retreats from postmodernism and neo-liberalism as well as the colonising designs of economics, are uncertain. As will be argued, they are still to be contested.

At a general level, this is to raise a question that has been notable for its absence from Kuhnian discussion, especially across the social sciences. Here, it has been more or less taken for granted that interdisciplinary boundaries are sacrosanct. It is simply a matter of one approach taking over the given subject matter from another, even if giving frameworks, methods, concepts, theories and evidence a tweak or two. Economics imperialism, of course, is about something else, seeking to disregard interdisciplinary boundaries. But, in doing so, does it move the boundaries by incorporating the previous subject matter of other disciplines or does it merely violate these boundaries, bringing economics to bear within continuing interdisciplinary demarcations?

There is no general answer as will be illustrated by two examples taken from success under the "old" economics imperialism. One of the most prominent has been human capital theory. Initially, it met with considerable opposition. As Becker (1993, p. xix) observes in proud retrospect, "a dozen years ago, this terminology would have been inconceivable". The obstacle to acceptability of the approach centred on aversion to the notion of education as comparable to an accumulated physical asset with productive potential.[38] This objection has not so much been dissipated as overlooked. For, despite continuing to flourish within economics on the same basis, human capital is used in entirely different and heterogeneous ways across the other social sciences, thereby

---

38   A similar reception is recorded by Fleury (2010, p. 1) for "*The Economics of Discrimination* (1957) [which] was Gary Becker's first published work using microeconomic tools to investigate supposedly non-economic phenomena". Fleury also perceptively observes, as for most other applications of the first phase of economics imperialism, that this was not the first time economic analysis was used, citing Myrdal, but the first to confine it to a purely economic analysis.

reflecting their concerns and traditions. As a result, human capital has not primarily brought the subject matter of other disciplines under its wings. Rather, it has spread its influence across disciplinary boundaries. Thus, in sociology, human capital has been used as an element in social stratification. As such, its application in identifying the origin, nature and reproduction of social classes is inconsistent with its origins in the methodological individualism of mainstream economics, and the notion of education, etc as an input or output in some or other production function.[39]

A totally different outcome is represented by the case of finance. This is now more or less taken as granted to be a sub-discipline of economics, especially as far as high-level theory and empirical work are concerned. As Harrison (1997, pp. 174/5) remarks:

> For a long time, the study of financial markets was not done by economists ... that economists did not do research on financial markets ... is not completely to say that no research was done on them. Nonacademic "how-to" books of investing, written by practitioners, were plentiful. Academic insights were sparser.

This is illustrated by the fate of Harry Markowitz, who received a Nobel prize in economics in 1990 for his work on finance, but who completed his first work in the form of his University of Chicago (successful) doctoral dissertation in 1955. As reported by Harrison (1997, p. 176), citing Bernstein (1992), Milton Friedman's comment on Markowitz's work was as follows:

> Harry, I don't see anything wrong with the math here, but I have a problem. This isn't a dissertation in economics, and we can't give you a Ph.D. in economics for a dissertation that's not economics. It's not math, it's not economics, it's not even business administration.

Harrison provides an account of how, from these shaky beginnings, finance became incorporated within economics through reliance upon arbitrage and perfectly working markets, parodying the process itself as one of intellectual arbitrage. Thus, p. 180:[40]

---

39 See Fine and Rose (2001) for fuller discussion. Note also the unjustified and possibly inexplicable neglect of human capital as a (direct) source of utility as opposed to a factor in production and productivity.

40 See also p. 180/1: "The Modigliani-Miller theorem, for instance, relies on an arbitrage argument to prove its point ... Modigliani and Miller rely on 'perfect capital markets'".

> From the standpoint of an academic economist, financial markets had been converted from the most tangled underbrush to the pristine ideal of textbooks. Here were perfect markets – a market where the power of arbitrage was supreme, where thousands of individuals with millions of dollars in incentives were pursuing information and pouncing on arbitrage opportunities. The traded good was almost as generic as a widget; there was plethora of publicly available information, there was easy entry and exit; and trading was relatively costless and free from other frictions. The theoretical implication of such perfectly functioning markets was that they were efficient. The invisible hand would enforce not only the 'right' price but also the 'right' allocation of resources. The casino could be trusted. What more inviting place for economists to venture?

Further, from a position of lying outside economics, finance as a sub-discipline of economics has not only been transformed but has leapfrogged into the vanguard, p. 182/3:[41]

> Regardless of whether economics was profoundly changed, finance certainly was ... In fact, finance has become the 'proving ground' for new price theory and econometric technique. This puts the field at the forefront of the technical envelope, as measured by the use of mathematics and computers. Because of the availability of large quantities of data, because of the desirable properties of stock prices, and because of the monetary rewards to a 'successful' innovation, it is still the most ideal 'real world' market. But this has created some kind of a feedback effect, where innovations in finance have found their way back to the 'rest' of economics. In particular, this is true for statistical and computer techniques.

Now it would be worthwhile investigating in greater depth how and why finance has become comprehensively incorporated into economics, but

---

41   Strangely, although Harrison remarks that the new financial economics has been put to practical use, not least in the Black-Scholes formula, he does not raise the issue of whether the disproportionate growth and change of financial markets themselves has had an effect on attaching finance to economics as academic disciplines. It is also worth noting that, although he does not mention Kuhn, the new finance as a research programme is raised, p. 183: "The ongoing defense of the EMH [efficient market hypothesis] corresponds closely to Lakatos's description of the protection of the background presumptions that make up the unquestioned 'hard core' of what he calls a 'scientific research program'".

applications of human capital have not.[42] This is not the intention here. Rather it is to highlight two factors that these illustrations share in common despite their different outcomes. First, by choice, they are both examples of the old economics imperialism, having established themselves in the Becker-type, more generally Chicago-like, mould of an as if world of perfect markets. Yet, each has also moved on effortlessly from that old to the new world of market, especially informational, imperfections. In the case of human capital, it now prospers despite, even because of, acknowledgement of such imperfections in the provision (in schools) and use (in labour markets) of human capital. Paradoxically, one of the leading proponents of the economics of education, Mark Blaug (1987), was converted from a "True Believer" in view of market imperfections, especially labour market screening. Nonetheless, human capital has steamed ahead with market imperfections being used, as argued by Fine and Rose (2001), as a way of bringing back in on a selective basis some of what has been left out – the specificity of education and of labour markets.

For the economics of finance, the impact of the new information-theoretic economics has been even more dramatic. Whilst the incorporation of finance into economics might have originated with, and been founded upon, the implications of perfectly working markets, the forefront of the sub-discipline is now entirely concerned with the implications of imperfectly working financial markets. These extend to the non-market, thereby providing a theory of financial systems, archetypically Anglo-American or market-based and German-Japanese or bank-based, according to the extent of non-market relations between borrowers and lenders in dealing with market (informational and contractual) imperfections.[43]

A second general feature shared by human capital and the economics of finance is that they have marched forward only by displacing existing analyses – initially by cutting insights out altogether and, then, by reincorporating

---

42   Contrast with neuroeconomics which proceeds as if it can go wherever it likes. For an early assessment, see Fine (2011), with appendix entitled, "Attaching economics to the brain or from free to choose ... to 'motor responses to brain chemistry'", quotation taken from Hands (2010, p. 644): "Milton and Rose Friedman titled their popular book Free to Choose (1980) not 'motor responses to brain chemistry' or 'conditioned response in the marketplace'". For a useful recent account of the trajectory of neuroeconomics, and behavioural economics more generally, in the context of interdisciplinarity, see Truc (2022), although economics imperialism does not figure, but see also Koshovets (2019) and Primrose (2022).

43   For a critique of the new financial economics, see Fine (1997b) and Ayber and Lapavitsas (2001). For a fully referenced contribution from sociology, viewing the financial system from a network perspective, see Uzzi (1999).

them on a selective basis within the framework of market imperfections. As already emphasised, both are established through as if perfect market as starting point. For education, as argued by Fine and Rose (2001) amongst others, this leads to the closing of two black boxes. One is the provision of education itself – it is merely reduced to a stream of costs and benefits. The other is the workings of the labour market – it becomes like any other in serving both as a factor input and a direct source of (dis)utility (Fine 1998a). What is notably absent is any idea of education and the labour market as *systems* as emphasised for example in traditional educational and industrial relations literature. Nonetheless, systemic features are re-introduced as (the results of) market imperfections.

Much the same is true of finance, not least in the progress from as if perfect to as if imperfect markets to which systemic differences have been explicitly reduced. As a consequence, longstanding literature on the nature of financial systems, and their contribution to growth and development, have been studiously ignored. It is as if the debate over Perry Anderson's hypothesis of the peculiarity of the English simply did not exist.[44] Such literature – in dealing with the economic, political and ideological power of a financial fraction of capital – is not readily amenable to interpretation as market imperfections! In this respect, it is worth highlighting Crafts' (1999) comment on Gerschenkron who emphasised how state intervention, especially to mobilise finance for investment, is crucial to "latecomer" economic development:[45]

> Gerschenkron on development from conditions of economic backwardness still deserves to be read and might usefully be revisited from the perspective of modern microeconomics.

It is apt to close discussion of finance with Crafts for he is a leading British (new) economic historian. Economic and social history has also experienced a longstanding dialogue with economics imperialism. The new economic history is now entering its fifth decade. Again, its initial phase was marked by an approach on the basis of an as if perfect market. As a result, a wedge was driven

---

44   The idea that the power of finance has held back British domestic industry, originating in part with Anderson (1964). See also Fine and Harris (1985, Chapters 1 and 4) and Ingham (1984).

45   Further, for Crafts (1999), whilst Gerschenkron "can be construed in terms of modern microeconomics ... [this] does not mean that his underlying view of the role of the state in the development process is acceptable", because of his neglect of sources of total factor productivity and the dangers of government as opposed to market failure.

between social and economic history, one emphasising culture, institutions and so on, and the other the relentless forward march of supply and demand and more propitious property rights. Significantly, in the United States where economics and economic history have traditionally been located within the same department, this accentuated the division between the two approaches in personnel, professional associations and journals (Lamoreaux 1998). As Livingston (1994, p. xv) suggests, this created "fields that stopped talking to each other around twenty years ago, when the 'new economic history' and the 'new social history' partitioned the discipline and encouraged the settlement of their respective territories". A rampaging cliometrics was, thereby, caught on the horns of a dilemma. For economics as a discipline was becoming more history-less. Not only, as previously discussed, did it have a decreasing interest in its own history as a discipline, but it also had no need to study history at all.[46] Economics could hardly take over history by eliminating it other than as a source of data and loosely formed hypotheses!

The new information-theoretic economics has played a major part in seeking to renegotiate the impasse between the two schools of history, as evidenced by a series of edited volumes emanating from Brookings (see Temin (ed.) 1991; Lamoreaux and Raff (eds) 1995; and Lamoreaux et al (eds) 1999). [47] They accept that the old cliometrics was wrong to have excluded history in the form institutions, customs, culture and the like. But these can be brought back in as the non-market response to market imperfections, with history taking the form of path dependence of various sorts. Indeed, on this basis, the ambitions of the "newer" economic history are no less than those of the old cliometrics. For Lamoreaux et al (1999, p. 10):[48]

> Although ... previous volumes dealt with learning processes, the present volume moves this theme to center stage by asking explicitly how firms, industries, and even nations can learn to overcome uncertainty ... The essays in this volume thus mark a transition from focussing on problems

---

46 Indicative is the set of papers given at the AEA meetings in December 1984, organised to deal with the issue, "Economic History: A Necessary though not Sufficient Condition for an Economist". Kindleberger (1986, p. 83) describes it as "one of the most enthusiastically received sessions on the program" but expresses concern that the technicalities attached to economics will squeeze out "a true contact with the facts", p. 90.

47 See Fine (2000b), and also Fine and Milonakis (2000), for a critique of what they term the newer economic history. See also forthcoming volume on economic history.

48 See also Lamoreaux et al (1999, p. 14/5): "More than any other factor, the ability to collect and use information effectively determines whether firms, industry, groups, and even nations will succeed or fail".

that are common to a whole class of firms or industries to explaining why firms, groups, and nations can differ in important and persistent ways.

Recent developments in cliometrics, then, reinforce the point that the current phase of economics imperialism is about negotiating the re-introduction of the social and historical into economics irrespective of whether this leads to shifts of, or across, disciplinary boundaries. The same applies, if in a different way, to economic geography. For, during the phase of postmodernism, it was marked by a distinctive rhythm and content, especially when compared to economic and social history. In particular, the influence of postmodernism led to an intensive focus upon the social construction and meaning of space itself. By the same token, further incursions of mainstream economics – with a longer standing presence than for history – were stoutly resisted with an ill-concealed and general contempt. As a result, political economy established a powerful presence within the discipline, giving rise to a cultural turn but not at the expense of the economic.[49]

What implications does this have for the arrival of the new information-theoretic economics upon the scene? First, there has been the emergence of an associated new economic geography, especially associated with Paul Krugman. It has been sufficiently successful to warrant a contribution to the *Journal of Economic Surveys* (Schmutzler 1999). His is, unwittingly, a telling testimony to the themes of this chapter. In this light, it is worth reproducing his conclusions at length, p. 373:

> First, history matters in the development of agglomerations. Cumulative processes generated by positive externalities can lead to the development of core-periphery structures even when no region has natural advantages. Second, transportation costs, the strength of scale economies and the importance of footloose industries are important factors determining whether such industrial concentration is likely to develop. Third, continuous changes in such parameters can lead to a discontinuous change in economic structure. Fourth, there are possible implications for trade: if positive externalities play a role, increasing economic integration affects both the distribution of manufacturing and the geographical distribution within the manufacturing sector. Fifth, there are interactions between the trade policy and the regional structure of an economy: increasing

---

49 This is marked in the work and influence of David Harvey (1982, 1985 and 1989), for example. See also Lee and Wills (eds) (1997).

integration may lead to decreasing concentration within the economy. Sixth, models with transportation costs are helpful ways to understand the causes and consequences of multinationals.

Further, he confesses, p. 357, "no single one of these aspects is new to spatial economics".

Significantly, none of this has anything to do with geography other than in the limited adoption of some of the vernacular, even of a radical disposition as in reference to core-periphery and the spatial. As a result, the new economic geography can only contribute in a negative sense to the discipline as sharply elaborated by Martin (1999) in his devastating critique.[50] For he points to what is the stripped-down restoration of what has been legitimately rejected and the omission of what is essential, p. 77. In terms of the incorporation of history, for example, p. 76:[51]

> The 'history' referred to is not real history: there is no sense of the real and context-specific periods of time over which actual spatial agglomerations have evolved (and, in many cases, dissolved) ... Thus, while the claim that "history matters" is certainly correct, the treatment of history in the new economic geography is more metaphorical than real and, despite the importance assigned to path dependence, this notion remains a conceptual and explanatory black box.

In addition, Martin highlights Krugman's view that geography had lost five traditions that the latter intends to restore – location theory, gravity and potential models, cumulative causation, land use and land rent models, and local external economies. Here is an economist delving into the history of thought and getting it wrong. For, as Martin argues, these traditions were not lost but rejected, p. 81:

> They were deliberately abandoned on philosophical and epistemological grounds, as part of the large-scale movement away from logical positivism that occurred in geography at that time. The location-theoretic, regional science models were cast aside not because the mathematics of maximization-and-equilibrium had (temporally) reached their limits,

---

50 A further telling critique, of general applicability once mainstream and much other economics confronts the international, is the impoverished notion of what constitutes the national and the nation state.

51 See also Gaspar (2016).

nor because geographers were unable intellectually to elaborate those mathematical tools, but precisely because of the realisation that formal mathematical models impose severe limits on our understanding. Geographers became more interested in real economic landscapes, with all their complex histories, local contexts and particularities, and less entranced by abstract models of hypothetical space economies.

Thus, Martin concludes, the new economic geography is "neither that new, nor is it geography. Instead, it is a reworking (or re-invention) – using recent developments in formal (mathematical) mainstream economics – of traditional location theory and regional science", p. 65.

As such, Martin is concerned that the new economic geography is both flourishing and capable of being turned to policy issues.[52] Significantly, though, in terms of interdisciplinary boundaries and intra-disciplinary content, the impact of economics imperialism in this case is potentially indirect, not involving economics directly but the relations between economic geography and regional science. Thus, this and the other examples presented in this section, illustrate the diversity in extent, content and outcome as far as economics imperialism is concerned. The Kuhnian approach to paradigm shift, including the idea of an attached community of practitioners, has been unduly pre-occupied with the displacement of one by another set of scholars and their beliefs. Whatever its other merits and deficiencies, this leaves it ill-equipped to address the shifting boundaries and content across disciplines.

The separation of the social sciences into disciplines is, after all, extraordinarily recent in the sweep of intellectual history. Whilst the divisions between them were created, or strengthened, more or less at the same time, alongside the marginalist revolution within economics, their subsequent paths have been different and variously influenced. In case of sociology, for example, Velthuis (1999) has shown how sociology was distinguished from economics in the eyes of Talcott Parsons, the leading functionalist of the discipline, by its method rather than by its subject matter – dealing in the social as opposed to the individual. Further, Connell (1997) has shown how the initial impetus to sociology was given by confrontation with those other worlds revealed by imperialist expansion, raising the issue of what characterised the modernity of

---

52 Compare, though, with the later assessment of Schmutzler (1999, p. 374), "Finally, of course, the new economic geography literature has one great shortcoming: so far, it has hardly generated any policy recommendation", p. 374. This is not surprising since it shares this characteristic with the new, endogenous growth theory of which it is more or less a partial replica.

the colonising powers by way of contrast. Only after such concerns had been safely set aside, not least with the horrors of civilisation associated with interwar fascism, could the enduring classics of sociology – Marx, Weber, Durkheim, etc – be sanitised and canonised as dealing exclusively with the social relations, structures and even conflicts of modernity. Meanwhile anthropology was consolidated as a separate discipline to deal, primarily ethnographically with the intellectually initiating world that had been abandoned by sociology.

According to the model that economics imperialism has of itself, such considerations are simply irrelevant. It really does not matter how the other disciplines got where they are; it is only necessary to recognise that economics can and should sweep across them in view of its superior science and rigour. Such a model of its influence on social science is, however, totally inappropriate irrespective of its own false claims as scientific. For, as heavily emphasised by Callon in his work on science and technology, the "overflowing" of concepts from one application, frame of reference or expertise to another involves a transformation of those concepts.[53] They have a different meaning and application when used by others, whether as experts or not in their own fields of endeavour. Further, those meanings are contested however they may or may not be incorporated. In other words, the impact of economics imperialism and of the economic within the other social sciences remains open, subject no doubt to external influences, but also to the internal dynamic of intellectual debate itself.

6 Concluding Remarks

As mentioned at the outset, the goal here has not been to apply Kuhn to economics imperialism nor to resurrect Kuhnian notions of scientific change. If anything, this chapter has reinforced the criticisms of Kuhn that have previously been made in terms of the co-existence of paradigms, the lack of sharp differentiation between them and normal and revolutionary science, and the lack of capacity for both observation (or empirical work) and criteria for assessing analysis to be common across paradigms. Nonetheless, the significance of Kuhn, now as before, is in its emphasis upon perceiving science as the social construct of a community, not governed primarily, let alone exclusively, by its own or an absolute standard of truth. Indeed, the main message of

---

53   Thus, translation is defined as "the methods by which an actor enrols others" and "a common form of translation in science is that of problematisation", itself defined as "an equivalence between two problems that requires those who wish to solve one to accept a proposed solution for the other", Callon et al (1986, p. xvii).

this chapter is that very small changes have taken place *within* economics with the new approach. As far as exemplars are concerned, those of perfect competition have been set against those of imperfect information. For disciplinary matrix, deviation from perfect competition, as world view, due to economic and social impediments to the market, has been challenged by a vision of market outcomes based on imperfect information and non-market responses to them. Pretty much everything else is and is recognisably the same, other than the even more severe exclusion of alternatives and the ever more demanding technical standards of the profession.

Yet, on such a limited basis, economics imperialism is prospering as never before. Lest this be considered an exaggeration despite all the new fields shooting up in and around the discipline, it is worth acknowledging how human capital, a talisman of the old approach, has spread its influence across the social sciences despite initial reservations. The same is already happening with social capital, with its leading proponent, Robert Putnam, reputedly the most cited author across the social sciences in the 1990s (Fine 2001a, Chapter 6). This is not to suggest that social capital is purely or primarily an artefact of economists. It is, however, open to capture by them, as the catch-all for the non-economic. Otherwise, social capital is used by non-economists to avoid, at most to shadow box with, economics in suggesting that civil society, institutions, customs and values, or whatever are important and have been neglected by economics. But this is no longer the case, and almost all social capital analysis is subject to capture and re-interpretation by a colonising economics, even as social capital itself is used to appropriate and transform social theory in its own image.

In short, economics might be thought of as like the Roman Empire, continuing to expand even as it is subject to intellectual decay from within. In this light, we are not only confronted by the barbarianism of economics imperialism but also, in a more constructive vein, by the task of restoring political economy as a central component of the social sciences. It was initially excised by the marginalist revolution and, subsequently, by the extremes of postmodernism. It now has the potential to prosper once more. It is an opportunity that must be grasped, with an appropriate understanding to the fore both of capitalism in general and of its contemporary character.

References

Aigner, E. (2021) "Global Dynamics and Country-Level Development in Academic Economics: An Explorative Cognitive-Bibliometric Study", Department of

Socio-Economics, Institute for Multi-Level Governance & Development, Vienna University of Economics and Business, Social-Ecological Discussion Paper in Economics, no 7, https://www-sre.wu.ac.at/sre-disc/sre-disc-2021_07.pdf.

Akerlof, G. (1970) "The Market for 'Lemons': Quality Uncertainty and the Market Mechanism", *Quarterly Journal of Economics*, vol 84, no 3, pp. 488–500.

Akerlof, G. (1984) *An Economic Theorist's Book of Tales*, Cambridge: Cambridge University Press.

Akerlof, G. (1990) "George A. Akerlof", in Swedberg (ed.) (1990), pp. 61–77.

Amariglio, J. and D. Ruccio (1999) "The Transgressive Knowledge of 'Ersatz' Economics", in Garnett (ed.) (1999), pp. 19–36.

Anderson, P. (1964) "The Origins of the Present Crisis", *New Left Review*, no 23, pp. 11–52.

Arestis, P. and M. Sawyer (eds) (2004) *The Rise of the Market*, Camberley: Edward Elgar.

Argyrous, G. (1992) "Kuhn's Paradigms and Neoclassical Economics", *Economics and Philosophy*, vol 8, no 2, pp. 231–48.

Argyrous, G. (1994) "Kuhn's Paradigms and Neoclassical Economics: Reply to Dow", *Economics and Philosophy*, vol 10, no 1, pp. 123–26.

Ayber, S. and C. Lapavitsas (2001) "Financial System Design and the Post-Washington Consensus", in Fine et al (eds) (2001), pp. 28–51.

Balakrishnan, R. and C. Grown (1999) "Foundations and Economic Knowledge", in Garnett (ed.) (1999), pp. 124–38.

Barbour, I. (1980) "Paradigms in Science and Religion", in Gutting (ed.) (1980), pp. 223–45.

Becker, G. (1957) *The Economics of Discrimination*, Chicago: Chicago University Press.

Becker, G. (1993) *Human Capital: a Theoretical and Empirical Analysis, with Special Reference to Education*, London: University of Chicago Press, third edition.

Becker, G. (1996) *Accounting for Tastes*, Cambridge: Harvard University Press.

Bernstein, M. (1999) "Economic Knowledge, Professional Authority, and the State: the Case of American Economics During and After World War II", in Garnett (ed.) (1999), pp. 124–38.

Bernstein, P. (1992) *Capital Ideas: the Improbable Origins of Modern Wall Street*, New York: Free Press.

Blaug, M. (1975) "Kuhn versus Lakatos, or Paradigms versus Research Programmes in the History of Economics", *History of Political Economy*, vol 7, no 4, pp. 399–433.

Blaug, M. (1980) *The Methodology of Economics: or How Economists Explain*, Cambridge: Cambridge University Press.

Blaug, M. (1987) *The Economics of Education and the Education of an Economist*, New York: New York University Press.

Blaug, M. (1998a) "Disturbing Currents in Modern Economics", *Challenge*, vol 41, no 3, pp. 11–34.

Blaug, M. (1998b) "The Problems with Formalism: Interview with Mark Blaug", *Challenge*, vol 41, no 3, pp. 35–45.

Bowden, S. and A. Offer (1994) "Household Appliances and the Use of Time: the United States and Britain since the 1920s", *Economic History Review*, vol XLVII, no 4, pp. 725–48.

Bowden, S. and A. Offer (1996) "The Technological Revolution That Never Was: Gender, Class, and the Diffusion of Household Appliances in Interwar England", in de Grazia and Furlough (eds) (1996), pp. 244–74.

Bowden, S. and A. Offer (1999) "Household Appliances and 'Systems of Provision' – a Reply", *Economic History Review*, vol LII, no 3, pp. 563–67.

Boylan, T. and P. O'Gorman (1995) *Beyond Rhetoric and Realism in Economics: Towards a Reformulation of Economic Methodology*, London: Routledge.

Bronfenbrenner, M. (1971) "The 'Structure of Revolutions' in Economic Thought", *History of Political Economy*, vol 3, no 1, pp. 136–51.

Callon, M., J. Law and A. Rip (1986) "Glossary", in Callon et al (1986), pp. xiii–xvii.

Callon, M., J. Law and A. Rip (eds) (1986) *Mapping the Dynamics of Science and Technology: Sociology of Science in the Real World*, London: MacMillan.

Carrier, J. and D. Miller (eds) (1998) *Virtualism: the New Political Economy*, London: Berg.

Chalk, A. (1967) "Relativist and Absolutist Approaches to the History of Economic Theory", *Southwestern Social Science Quarterly*, vol 48, pp. 5–12.

Chase, R. (1983) "The Kuhnian Paradigm Thesis as a Dialectical Process and Its Application to Economics", *Rivista Internazionale di Scienze Economiche e Commerciali*, vol XXX, no 9, pp. 809–28.

Coats, A. (1969) "Is There a 'Structure of Scientific Revolutions' in Economics?", *Kyklos*, vol 22, no 2, pp. 289–96.

Coats, A. (ed.) (1996) *The Post-1945 Internationalization of Economics*, *History of Political Economy*, vol 28, Supplement, Durham, NC: Duke University Press.

Connell, R. (1997) "Why Is Classical Theory Classical?", *American Journal of Sociology*, vol 102, no 6, pp. 1511–57.

Crafts, N. (1999) "Development History", Symposium on Future of Development Economics in Perspective, Dubrovnik, 13–14th May.

Davis, J. (1997) "New Economics and Its History: a Pickeringian View", in Davis (ed.) (1997), pp. 289–308.

Davis, J. (ed.) (1997) *New Economics and Its History*, *History of Political Economy*, vol 29, Supplement 1, Durham, NC: Duke University Press.

De Grazia, V. and E. Furlough (eds) (1996) *The Sex of Things: Gender and Consumption in Historical Perspective*, London: University of California Press.

De Vroey, M. (1975) "The Transition from Classical to Neoclassical Economics: a Scientific Revolution", *Journal of Economic Issues*, vol IX, no 3, pp. 415–39.

Dow, S. (2023) "Political Economy as a Methodological Approach", *Review of Political Economy*, vol 35, no 1, pp. 98–110.

Dow, S. (1985) *Macroeconomic Thought: a Methodological Approach*, Oxford: Basil Blackwell.

Dow, S. (1994) "Kuhn's Paradigms and Neoclassical Economics", *Economics and Philosophy*, vol 10, no 1, pp. 119–22.

Fasenfest, D. (ed.) (2022) *Marx Matters*, Leiden: Brill.

Fine, B. (1997a) "The New Revolution in Economics", *Capital and Class*, no 61, Spring, pp. 143–48. See also Chapter 4.

Fine, B. (1997b) "Industrial Policy and South Africa: a Strategic View", NIEP Occasional Paper Series, no 5, Johannesburg: National Institute for Economic Policy.

Fine, B. (1998a) *Labour Market Theory: a Constructive Reassessment*, London: Routledge.

Fine, B. (1998b) "The Triumph of Economics: Or 'Rationality' Can Be Dangerous to Your Reasoning", in Carrier and Miller (eds) (1998), pp. 49–74.

Fine, B. (1999a) "From Becker to Bourdieu: Economics Confronts the Social Sciences", *International Papers in Political Economy*, vol 5, no 3, pp. 1–43. See also Chapter 5.

Fine, B. (1999b) "A Question of Economics: Is It Colonising the Social Sciences?", *Economy and Society*, vol 28, no 3, pp. 403–25. See also Chapter 7.

Fine, B. (1999c) "'Household Appliances and the Use of Time: the United States and Britain since the 1920s'– a Comment", *Economic History Review*, vol LII, no 3, pp. 552–62.

Fine, B. (2000a) "Endogenous Growth Theory: a Critical Assessment", *Cambridge Journal of Economics*, vol 24, no 2, pp. 245–65, a shortened and amended version of identically titled, SOAS Working Paper, No 80, February 1998.

Fine, B. (2000b) "New and Improved: Economics' Contribution to Business History", longer version of original SOAS Working Paper in Economics, no 93.

Fine, B. (2000c) "Bringing the Social Back into Economics: Progress or Reductionism?", Department of Economics Research Paper, no 731, University of Melbourne, enlarged and amended version, *History of Economics Review*, vol 32, no 1, pp. 10–35, 2000.

Fine, B. (2000d) "'Economic Imperialism': a View from the Periphery", *Review of Radical Political Economics*, vol 34, no 2, pp. 187–201.

Fine, B. (2000e) "Globalisation in Light of the Political Economy of Finance and the Political Economy of the Welfare State", paper presented to METU Annual Economics Conference, Ankara, September.

Fine, B. (2000f) "Consumption for Historians: an Economist's Gaze", SOAS Working Paper in Economics, no 90.

Fine, B. (2001a) *Social Capital versus Social Theory: Political Economy and Social Science at the Turn of the Millennium*, London: Routledge.

Fine, B. (2001b) "Neither Washington or Post-Washington Consensus: an Introduction", in Fine et al (eds) (2001), pp 1–27.

Fine, B. (2001c) "Economics Imperialism as Kuhnian Revolution?", *International Papers in Political Economy*, vol 8, no 2, pp. 1–58.

Fine, B. (2002) "Economics Imperialism and the New Development Economics as Kuhnian Paradigm Shift", *World Development*, vol 30, no 12, pp. 2057–70.

Fine, B. (2004a) "Economics Imperialism as Kuhnian Revolution", in Arestis and Sawyer (eds) (2004), pp. 107–44.

Fine, B. (2004b) "Addressing the Critical and the Real in Critical Realism", in Lewis (ed.) (2004), pp. 202–26.

Fine, B. (2009) "The Economics of Identity and the Identity of Economics?", *Cambridge Journal of Economics*, vol 33, no 2, pp. 175–91.

Fine, B. (2011) "Prospecting for Political Economy", in *International Journal of Management Concepts and Philosophy*, vol 5, no 3, pp. 204–17.

Fine, B. (2015) "Neoclassical Economics: an Elephant Is Not a Chimera but Is a Chimera Real?", in Morgan (ed.) (2015).

Fine, B. (2019) "Economics and Interdisciplinarity: One Step Forward, N Steps Back?" *Revista Crítica de Ciências Sociais*, no 119, pp. 131–48.

Fine, B. (2022) "From Marxist Political Economy to Financialisation or Is It the Other Way about?", in Fasenfest (ed.), pp. 43–66.

Fine, B. and L. Harris (1985) *The Peculiarities of the British Economy*, London: Lawrence and Wishart.

Fine, B. and C. Lapavitsas (2000) "Markets and Money in Social Theory: What Role for Economics?", *Economic and Society*, vol 29, no 3, pp. 357–82.

Fine, B., C. Lapavitsas and J. Pincus (eds) (2001) *Development Policy in the Twenty-First Century: beyond the Post-Washington Consensus*, London: Routledge.

Fine, B. and D. Milonakis (2000) "From New to Newest: the Economic History of Douglass North", mimeo, published in revised parts as "From Principle of Pricing to Pricing of Principle: Rationality and Irrationality in the Economic History of Douglass North", with D. Milonakis, *Comparative Studies in Society and History*, vol 45, no 3, pp. 120–44, 2003, and "Douglass North's Remaking of Economic History: a Critical Appraisal", *Review of Radical Political Economics*, with D. Milonakis, vol 39, no 1, pp. 27–57, 2007.

Fine, B. and P. Rose (2001) "Education and the Post-Washington Consensus", in Fine et al (eds) (2001), pp. 155–81.

Fischer, C. (1993) "On the 'Stickiness' of the Economic Equilibrium Paradigm: Causes of Its Durability", *American Journal of Economics and Sociology*, vol 52, no 1, pp. 51–62.

Fleury, J.-B. (2010) "Drawing New Lines: Economists and Other Social Scientists on Society in the 1960s", *History of Political Economy*, vol 42, Supplement 1, pp. 315–42.

Fourcade, M., E. Ollion and Y. Algan (2015) "The Superiority of Economists", *Journal of Economic Perspectives*, vol 29, no 1, pp. 89–114.

Frey, B. (1999) *Economics as a Science of Human Behaviour: Towards a New Social Science Paradigm*, extended second edition of that of 1992, Boston: Kluwer Academic Publishers.

Friedman, M and R. (1980) *Free to Choose: a Personal Statement*, New York: Harcourt Brace Jovanovich.

Garnett, R. (1999) "Economics of Knowledge: Old and New", in Garnett (ed.) (1999), pp. 1–16.

Garnett, R. (ed.) (1999) *What Do Economists Know?: New Economics of Knowledge*, London: Routledge.

Gaspar, J. (2016) "New Economic Geography: History and Debate", FEP-UP, Working Paper, no 580, School of Economics and Management, University of Porto.

Gordon, D. (1965) "The Role of the History of Economic Thought in the Understanding of Modern Economic Theory", *American Economic Review*, vol 55, no 2, pp. 119–27.

Gutting, G. (ed.) (1980) *Paradigms and Revolutions: Applications and Appraisals of Thomas Kuhn's Philosophy of Science*, Notre Dame: Notre Dame University Press.

Hands, D. (2010) "Economics, Psychology and the History of Consumer Choice Theory", *Cambridge Journal of Economics*, vol 34, no 4, pp. 633–648.

Harrison, P. (1997) "A History of an Intellectual Arbitrage: the Evolution of Financial Economics", in Davis (ed.) (1997), pp. 172–187.

Harvey, D. (1982) *The Limits to Capital*, Oxford: Blackwell.

Harvey, D. (1985) *The Urbanisation of Capital*, Oxford: Blackwell.

Harvey, D. (1989) *The Condition of Postmodernity: an Enquiry into the Origins of Culture*, Oxford: Basil Blackwell.

Hodgson, G. (2011) "Sickonomics: Diagnoses and Remedies", *Review of Social Economy*, vol 69, no 3, pp. 357–76.

Hodgson, G. and H. Rothman (1999) "The Editors and Authors of Economics Journals: a Case of Institutional Oligopoly?", *Economic Journal*, vol 109, no 453, pp. 165–86.

Ingham, G. (1984) *Capitalism Divided*, London: MacMillan.

Karsten, S. (1973) "Dialectics and the Evolution of Economic Thought?", *History of Political Economy*, vol 5, no 2, pp. 399–419.

Khalil, E. (1987) "Kuhn, Lakatos, and the History of Economic Thought", *International Journal of Social Economics*, vol 14, no 3, pp. 118–31.

Kindleberger, C. (1986) "A Further Comment", in Parker (ed.) (1986), pp. 83–92.

Koshovets, O. (2019) "Neuroeconomics: New Heart for Economics or New Face of Economic Imperialism", *Journal of Institutional Studies*, vol 11, no 1, pp. 6–19.

Kuhn, T. (1970a) "Reflections on My Critics", in Lakatos and Musgrave (eds) (1970), pp. 231–278.

Kuhn, T. (1970b) *The Structure of Scientific Revolutions*, Chicago: Chicago University Press, second edition with postscript, original of 1962.

Kunin, L. and F. Weaver (1971) "On the Structure of Scientific Revolutions in Economics", *History of Political Economy*, vol 3, no 2, pp. 391–97.

Lakatos, I. and A. Musgrave (eds) (1970) *Criticism and the Growth of Knowledge*, Cambridge: Cambridge University Press.

Lamoreaux, N. (1998) "Economic History and the Cliometric Revolution", in Molho and Wood (eds) (1998), pp 59–84.

Lamoreaux, N., D. Raff and P. Temin (1999) "Introduction", in Lamoreaux et al (eds) (1999), pp. 1–19.

Lamoreaux, N. and D. Raff (eds) (1995) *Coordination and Information: Historical Perspectives on the Organization of Enterprise*, Chicago: Chicago University Press.

Lamoreaux, N., D. Raff and P. Temin (eds) (1999) *Learning by Doing: in Markets, Firms, and Countries*, Chicago: Chicago University Press.

Lawson, T. (1997) *Economics and Reality*, London: Routledge.

Lawson, T. (2013) "What Is This 'School' Called Neoclassical Economics?", *Cambridge Journal of Economics*, vol 37, no 5, pp. 947–983.

Lawson, T. (2021) "Whatever Happened to Neoclassical Economics?", *Revue de Philosophie Economique*, vol 22, no 1, pp. 39–84, cited from https://www.researchgate.net/publication/356832620_Whatever_happened_to_neoclassical_economics/link/61b07b361a5f480388c187e4/download.

Lazear, E. (2000) "Economic Imperialism", *Quarterly Journal of Economics*, vol 115, no 1, pp. 99–146.

Lee, F. and S. Harley (1998) "Peer Review, the Research Assessment Exercise and the Demise of Non-Mainstream Economics", *Capital and Class*, no 66, pp. 23–51.

Lee, R. and J. Wills (eds) (1997) *Geographies of Economies*, London: Arnold.

Lewis, P. (ed.) (2004) *Transforming Economics: Perspectives on the Critical Realist Project*, London: Routledge.

Livingston, J. (1994) *Pragmatism and the Political Economy of Cultural Revolution, 1850–1940*, Chapel Hill: University of North Carolina Press.

Mader, P., D. Mertens and N. Van der Zwan (eds) (2020) *International Handbook of Financialization*, London: Routledge.

Martin, R. (1999) "The New 'Geographical Turn' in Economics: Some Critical Reflections", *Cambridge Journal of Economics*, vol 23, no 1, pp. 65–91.

Masterman, M. (1970) "The Nature of a Paradigm", in Lakatos and Musgrave (eds) (1970), pp. 59–90.

McCloskey, D. (1986) *The Rhetoric of Economics*, Brighton: Wheatsheaf.

Milonakis, D. and B. Fine (2012) "Interrogating Sickonomics, from Diagnosis to Cure: a Response to Hodgson", *Review of Social Economy*, vol 70, no 4, pp. 477–91.

Molho, A. and G. Wood (eds) (1998) *Imagined Histories: American Historians Interpret the Past*, Princeton: Princeton University Press.

Morgan, J. (ed.) (2015) *What Is This 'School' Called Neoclassical Economics?: Debating the Origins, Meaning and Significance*, London: Routledge.

Olson, M. and S. Kähkönen (2000) "Introduction: The Broader View", in Olson and Kähkönen (eds) (2000), pp. 1–36.

Olson, M. and S. Kähkönen (eds) (2000) *A Not-So-Dismal Science: a Broader View of Economies and Societies*, Oxford: Oxford University Press.

Parker, W. (ed.) (1986) *Economic History and the Modern Economist*, Oxford: Basil Blackwell.

Perelman, M. (2000) *The Invention of Capitalism: Classical Political Economy and the Secret History of Primitive Accumulation*, Durham: Duke University Press.

Primrose, D. (2022) "Behavioural Economics and Neuroeconomics", in Stilwell et al (eds) (2022), pp. 390–410.

Schmutzler, A. (1999) "The New Economic Geography", *Journal of Economic Surveys*, vol 13, no 4, pp. 355–79.

Stanfield, R. (1974) "Kuhnian Scientific Revolutions and the Keynesian Revolution", *Journal of Economic Issues*, vol VIII, no 1, pp. 97–109.

Stigler, G. (1969) "Does Economics Have a Useful Past?", *History of Political Economy*, vol 1, no 2, pp. 217–30.

Stiglitz, J. (1989) "Markets, Market Failures and Development", *American Economic Review*, vol 79, no 2, pp. 197–202.

Stiglitz, J. (1994) *Whither Socialism?*, Cambridge: MIT Press.

Stiglitz, J. (1998a) "More Instruments and Broader Goals: Moving Toward the Post-Washington Consensus", the 1998 WIDER Annual Lecture, January 7th, Helsinki.

Stiglitz, J. (1998b) "Towards a New Paradigm for Development: Strategies, Policies and Processes", *Prebisch Lecture*, UNCTAD, Geneva.

Stiglitz, J. and K. Hoff (1999) "Modern Economic Theory and Development", Symposium on Future of Development Economics in Perspective, Dubrovnik, 13-14th May.

Stilwell, F., D. Primrose and T. Thornton (eds) (2022) *Handbook of Alternative Theories of Political Economy*, Cheltenham: Edward Elgar.

Suppe, P. (1977) *The Structure of Scientific Theories*, Urbana: University of Chicago Press, second edition.

Swedberg, R. (ed.) (1990) *Economics and Sociology, Redefining Their Boundaries: Conversations with Economists and Sociologists*, Princeton: Princeton University Press.

Temin, P. (ed.) (1991) *Inside the Business Enterprise: Historical Perspectives on the Use of Information*, Chicago: Chicago University Press.

Thompson, G. (1997) "Where Goes Economics and the Economies?", *Economy and Society*, vol 26, no 4, pp. 599–610.

Thompson, G. (1999) "How Far Should We Be Afraid of Conventional Economics? A Response to Ben Fine", *Economy and Society*, vol 28, no 3, pp. 426–33.

Toulmin, S. (1972) *Human Understanding: the Collective Use and Evolution of Concepts*, Princeton: Princeton University Press.

Truc, A. (2022) "Interdisciplinary Influences in Behavioral Economics: a Bibliometric Analysis of Cross-Disciplinary Citations", *Journal of Economic Methodology*, vol 29, no 3, pp. 217–51.

Uzzi, B. (1999) "Embeddedness in the Making of Financial Capital: How Social Relations and Networks Benefit Firms Seeking Financing", *American Sociological Review*, vol 64, no 4, pp. 481–505.

Velthuis, O. (1999) "The Changing Relationship between Economic Sociology and Institutional Economics: from Talcott Parsons to Mark Granovetter", *American Journal of Economics and Sociology*, vol 58, no 4, pp. 629–49.

Ward, B. (1972) *What's Wrong with Economics?*, New York: Basic Books.

Wible, J. and N. Sedgley (1999) "The Role of Econometrics in the Neoclassical Research Program", in Garnett (ed.) (1999), pp. 169–90.

Zelizer, V. (2000) "Fine-Tuning the Zelizer View", *Economy and Society*, vol 29, no 3, pp. 383–89.

Zupan, M. (1991) "Paradigms and Cultures: Some Economic Reasons for Their Stickiness", *American Journal of Economics and Sociology*, vol 50, no 1, pp. 99–103.

CHAPTER 7

A Question of Economics: Is It Colonising the Social Sciences?

Postscript as Personal Preamble

To mark the 25th anniversary of the founding of *Economy and Society*, the political economist and one of the journal's leading editors, Grahame Thompson, gave a talk upon the nature of, and prospects for, economics, published as Thompson (1997). Inevitably, it attracted my attention and solicited the response that is offered here. I offered a critique not only of Thompson's characterisation of the mainstream as such but also for his relative neglect of my posited revolution in or around the mainstream, by then gathering momentum if not yet in full swing.

Commendably, Thompson (1999) responded to my critique.[1] In doing so, he did not add much that was not already to be found in his earlier contribution, discussed below. However, it is worth rehearsing some of his arguments. First, he sees neoclassical economics as in crisis, in part because of its failure to specify the Keynesian multiplier, in part because of the unexplained crisis of 1997/98, in part because of loss of confidence in real business cycle theory, and in part because of the opening up of such aspects to critique from other disciplines.[2] With the benefit of even more hindsight than available at the time, this is, however, to overlook that every crisis of self-confidence in the mainstream since the Keynesian revolution has witnessed an increase in its stranglehold over the discipline, not least following the Global Financial Crisis of 1997/98 (for which it could not see it coming and ex ante denied it could happen). This

---

1 Note the title of this piece, with dismissive reference to being "afraid" of conventional economics.
2 Following the Global Financial Crisis of 2007/8, the economics panel of the UK's Economic and Social Research Council was pressed by non-economists to set up a heterodox macroeconomics research programme. They did so, despite an extraordinarily well-organised bid from genuinely heterodox economists, by handing it over to those involved in agency-based modelling. Tellingly, the heterodox bid was criticised for failing to engage sufficiently with mainstream economists, although it did maximally and successfully despite the refusal of many mainstreamers to be involved. If ever there was a Catch 22 ... we need heterodox research because orthodox will not do it, but we need orthodox to do it in order to allow or legitimise it!.

is not to say nothing changes, far from it, as evidenced by the shifts between different phases of economics imperialism.

Second, Thomson positively welcomes the positive contribution that can be made by the mainstream, for example in organisational economics, in the use of biological models by way of analogy with the economy, and the work of Elinor Ostrom and social capital as useful contributions in and of themselves and as a means of interdisciplinary dialogue. Once again, with the benefit of hindsight, this has led us to the new, newer and newest institutional economics, see forthcoming volume on economic history, as leading examples of economics imperialism. As for biological models, we now have the rapidly expanding field of neuroeconomics for which, to understand the workings of the economy, we no longer refer to the isolated individual but, instead, look inside his or her brain.[3] On the other hand, Nobel Laureate, Robert Shiller (2019) explains the economy by economic rumours akin to a pandemic, as in his *Narrative Economics: How Stories Go Viral and Drive Major Economic Events*. And Hausmann and Rodrik (2003) persist in understanding technical change as self-discovery, akin to monkeys swinging from tree to tree in the forest in search of nuts and fruit, with policy confined to making it easier for them to do so.[4]

Third, favour as a potential participant in a reconstructed, interdisciplinary economics is bestowed upon the mainstream so long as it departs from engaging purely with rational agents, with the acknowledged need for socially constructed individuals. But, upon word searches through his article, such social construction leads to no mention of class (except within "neoclassical"), power, hierarchy, nor structure (except for genetics).

Fourth, there is an undertone of unwarranted criticism. By claiming himself to be pragmatic and pluralist (why not use the words unduly compromising and eclectic), there is a presumption by Thompson otherwise of others being dogmatic and seeking to displace one dogma with another, whether it

---

3   Koshovets (2019, p. 6) sees: "[neuroeconomics] as a specific version of economic imperialism claiming that the brain can be modeled using the principles of standard economic theory … Turning 'choice' and its 'economic relatives' into the key concepts for interpreting the neural structures and their activity would open the way for neuroeconomics to become an imperial science on human life or even nature itself". Or, on a wider terrarin, as in his book's title (Barro 2003) "Nothing Is Sacred: Economics Ideas for the New Millennium".

4   See Fine (2009a and b) for critique in a South African context. Elinor Ostrom offered major contributions both to institutional economics and social capital. But, strangely, her work across these two areas rarely if ever intersected although they are essentially the same except that the good side of social capital is emphasised over the bad, whereas (at least with neoliberals) the bad over the good for institutions (see Fine 2010b).

be Sraffian, post-Keynesian or Marxist. There is also his claim of undue dismissal of neoclassical economics, especially for the potentially positive contribution that it can make – yet, my own work has drawn extensively and critically on the mainstream to reconstruct political economy through exposing its deficiencies.

What is, however, remarkable in Thompson's contribution is his anticipation not only of the pluralist turn in economics but also of a much more general and wide-ranging (and illegitimate) critique of heterodoxy that was to emerge a decade or more later – especially around its failures both to engage more fully with what is perceived to be a disintegrating and increasingly open mainstream and to develop a meaningful and positive research programme of its own rather than simply snapping at the heals of the mainstream.[5]

In the context of economics imperialism, these issues are taken up more fully in the next volume on economics imperialism. Interestingly, though, after some delay, Peter Nielsen and Jamie Morgan (2005) offered a commentary upon the debate between Thompson and myself, characterising it as a dialogue of the deaf.[6] This is because Thompson is, rightly, perceived to be adopting a broad pluralist/pragmatist philosophical position whereas my understanding of the field of mainstream economics is seen as combining methodological analysis of theoretical innovation and a broad critical sociology. Otherwise, on more or less every aspect of my account, Nielsen and Morgan appear to agree with my assessments of what is happening within economics and its relationship with the other social sciences, and the validity of my propositions seem to be borne out even more so over the next couple of decades. Their one major reservation is to avoid undue determinism[7] – how can I have both an open methodology and presume that the future is fixed or set on economics imperialism – although, to be fair, my own emphasis is upon variegated outcomes of economics imperialism across the social sciences according to subject matter, discipline and evolving inner traditions and outer influences, with the implication that economics imperialism is a tendency and not, in some sense, nuclear destruction of the social sciences with rebuild by economics.

Otherwise, my main difference with Nielsen and Morgan is more, then, with the undertones, especially ones in which a supposed balance is set against a supposed extreme. The claim that the debate with Thompson is one of the deaf carries with it the implication that I am neither pragmatic nor pluralist. But

---

5   See Chester and Jo (eds) (2023) and forthcoming volume on heterodox economics.
6   Note that, in the electronic version of the title of the paper, I appear as "fine" not "Fine".
7   This misunderstanding is reproduced in Nik-Khah and Van Horn (2012), see discussion in second volume on economics imperialism.

nothing could be further from the truth as is evidenced by a fifty year career in and against mainstream economics rather than departing for easier and more rewarding contexts. But both pragmaticism and pluralism have to be grounded in realities. And the thrust of my analyses is that those realities involve an overwhelming dominance of the discipline of economics by an intolerant mainstream whose main, if limited, form of tolerance is repressive through, at most, incorporation, distortion and dilution of insights whether from heterodoxy or interdisciplinarity. Neither pluralism nor pragmatism can be considered let alone pursued in a world of such extremes of intellectual dominance and intolerance. Pursuit of pragmatism and pluralism must take this context into account. Further, from the perspective of most other (social) sciences, mainstream economics is at the unacceptable and unthinkable extremes of methodology, methods, theory, conceptualisation and realism. How is it possible to be pluralist and pragmatic other than through critical reconstruction in such circumstances, as opposed to a bit of this and that through analytical and strategic balance or compromise.

And, as far as determinism of the outcomes of economics imperialism is concerned, if things were otherwise, and mainstream economics genuinely engaged in pluralism, with corresponding pragmatism in its relations with heterodoxy and other disciplines, it would immediately be rendered unrecognisable in more or less every aspect of its intellectual and institutional existences. In a word or two, the conditions of existence of mainstream economics do not allow it to be pluralist nor accept pragmatism other than through subordination of heterodoxy and other disciplines.[8]

1   Introduction[9]

The purpose of this contribution is to suggest that there is currently a revolution under way in or, more exactly, around economics. In brief, I argue that economics is now engaged in a process of colonising the other social sciences.

---

8 This is said tongue in cheek as, with Barry Hindess, Paul Hirst, a collaborator with Grahame Thompson, was (in)famous for focusing upon conditions of existence (of social formations, of which, no doubt, economics is one or part of one).

9 First appearing as Fine (1999c). Thanks to Costas Lapavitsas, other colleagues and referees, anonymous or otherwise, for invaluable comments on an earlier draft. This article was completed whilst in receipt of a Research Fellowship from the UK Economic and Social Research Council (ESRC) under award number R000271046 to study The New Revolution in Economics and Its Impact upon Social Sciences.

It is extending its methods as never before to analytical terrain that had previously been seen as lying outside its scope. It has redefined as economic or as subject to economic analysis what has been traditionally perceived, even by itself, as non-economic. In part, this has been based upon the simple extension of mainstream economics to the non-economic, as if the notion of rational agents beloved of neoclassical economics is universally applicable in all contexts. In this vein, both the economy and society more broadly can be understood as the outcome of the aggregated behaviour of otherwise isolated individuals, co-ordinated by the market or an "as if" market mechanism. Typically, in the new household economics, the new institutional economics and the new political economy, the domains of the family, institutions and politics, respectively, are reduced to as if market arenas and as the outcome of rationally optimising individuals.

In addition, however, these new developments within economics have added another twist to such economic reductionism. For, even on the continuing basis of optimising individuals, it has become possible to explain why economic and other social structures and institutions might arise. This has helped to bridge what has previously been the yawning chasm between economics and other social sciences as far as interdisciplinary endeavours are concerned. The economics of optimising individuals becomes enabled to address the social, rather than simply denying it or assuming it to be exogenously given, facilitating the flow of the so-called economic approach to previously non-economic subject matter. In short, as suggested in the concluding section, the future promises to open a new wave of interdisciplinary research with an enlarged economic content. If traditional methods within the social sciences are to prosper, it will be necessary for a non-individualistic political economy rather than for mainstream economics to provide that content.

Such is the constructive contribution offered. But it has in part been prompted by the wish to respond to the recent article by Grahame Thompson (1997). He has provided in informal terms a broad-brush landscape of the current progress of economics and its relationship to economic developments. In the next four sections, this chapter disputes this picture by presenting an entirely different assessment of what is going on within economics (and its relationship to economies) as outlined above and taken up in greater detail in the fifth and sixth sections. The difference with Thompson, however, is not merely one of emphasis on, or omission of, internal developments within the discipline. For, significantly, the major changes taking place within economics that are driving its shifting relationship with the other social sciences are totally overlooked by Thompson, even though most economists would recognise them to be at the research frontier within their own discipline.

2   Whither Economics?

There is a problem in defining what is meant by economics, even as an academic discipline, for it differs considerably at different levels – across both research and teaching. And there are different traditions both within and between countries. In addition, economics is taught (and deployed in research) within other disciplines, such as business and accounting, quite apart from the economic content of non-economic social science. Throughout this article, concern will usually focus on research within and around mainstream economics, primarily because this tends to lead and dominate the other aspects within the discipline. Further, it will provide a basis from which to judge the extent to which economics is or is not prospering at other levels or in its more heterodox versions.

Thompson's presentation of the current state of economics begins with methodology. He considers the methodological critique of mainstream economics to be bedevilled by lack of holistic alternatives and to have settled, possibly inevitably, on specific, minor skirmishes so that dissent has been fragmented and ineffective.

This involves a misreading and misjudgement of the status of the critiques of the methodology of mainstream economics. It has been established time and time again that mainstream economics is fundamentally flawed methodologically, certainly as understood and practised by the vast majority of academics. This is primarily a consequence of its being based on methodological individualism for which a science of the economy, or, indeed, of any social relation, is impossible except by arbitrary (and often concealed) assumptions of taking as given what is the object of study.[10]

There are other weaknesses in mainstream economics that might be defensible from certain methodological positions, such as the particular form taken by methodological individualism and its use of empirical evidence as data, externally given and used for testing theories. While the status of falsifiability remains subject to debate, in the form in which it is used and understood by mainstream economists, it is unacceptable. The behavioural assumption of utility maximisation and the exclusion of other motives are arbitrary or bordering on the tautological. The notion of data as neutral and external is

---

10   Most obviously in deploying ahistorical and asocial concepts, such as production function and utility, to explain historically and socially specific phenomena such as wages, prices, etc. For some critical commentary on neoclassical economics in the context of the current article, see Fine (1995 and 1997b). In the context of the theory of choice, see Hargreaves-Heap et al. (1992).

erroneous. Heterodox economists who are prepared to say this are increasingly thin on the ground and risk professional suicide to the extent that their scholarship seeks alternatives.

Paradoxically, although mainstream economics is in some respects thriving as a discipline, especially in terms of published output and self-confidence, it is currently characterised by a lack of dialogue with alternative approaches as never before. These are dismissed by the mainstream as woolly or non-rigorous if they do not draw heavily upon mathematical modelling and/or statistical estimation.

Indeed, a key feature of economics as a discipline at the moment is that it has become systematically more entrenched in its intolerance of alternative approaches. This is true of analytical substance as well as in professional practice. It is extremely difficult for any heterodox economist to survive, and even harder for a new generation to emerge through academic appointments, teaching and research.[11] In this light, it is not surprising that those in a position and brave enough to say "no" to the mainstream are induced in part to do so by sniping away at its margins on the basis of alternative methodologies which the mainstream studiously ignores. Thompson's overview is misleading to the extent that it reduces the alternatives to the mainstream to these so-called "epistemological critique" approaches. It is as if the various schools of political economy, Marxist, post-Keynesian or Sraffian for example, simply do not exist. In this respect, Thompson's analysis gives unwitting support to the hegemonising project of the mainstream. For he is little short of contemptuous of those who seek a "supposedly more 'scientific' set of assumptions", p. 600, and appears to look more positively upon texts where "the 'bits' of different economics are marshalled and assembled from different traditions", p. 601. More critically, Thompson refers to the mainstream being "under siege" from "rhetorical critique", p. 600, which originated and remains closely associated with the work of McCloskey (1986).[12]

---

11 Since the first draft of this article was completed, this view has been strikingly confirmed in the UK in the light of study of the impact of the Research Assessment Exercise on the discipline of economics. Lee and Harley (1998) suggest that non-mainstream economics could be eliminated from British economics departments within ten years!.

12 On a personal note, I taught a course on modern British economic history with Roderick Floud and McCloskey at Birkbeck College in the 1980s, when the now Deidre was Donald. I also crossed swords with or, more exactly raised mine against, McCloskey over interpretation of the economic history of the British Coal industry, both for reliance upon measurements of total factor productivity to gauge comparative performance with the USA and for neglect of the role of landed property on what factors (depth and thickness of coal seams, and degree of mechanisation) were deployed (Fine 1990).

A number of telling points need to be made about this critique and supposed siege. First, its impact upon the practices of mainstream economics has been negligible. Second, it has gained an airing in part because McCloskey is a well-established, committed and particularly aggressive neoclassical economist (working primarily in the field of economic history). Third, although McCloskey is a 'rogue', he, now she, still remains an elephant. His, now her, contribution heavily depends upon dismissing the scientific pretensions of neoclassical economics but still accepting not dismissing the beast itself.

Thus, if rhetoric is siege, it leaves the neoclassical walls unbreached, not least by McCloskey who continues to tell the same neoclassical stories as before, even if more entertainingly and often with tongue in cheek. Further, whatever the impact McCloskey has upon the practice of mainstream economics, and it is not great, the influence becomes even less as the methodological critique cuts deeper. Thompson, thus, neglects the single most important feature of methodology as far as current developments are concerned. This is the absolute intolerance of alternatives as a matter of professional demarcation of entry to the discipline. That lack of tolerance has itself led to the marginalisation of past as well as of current alternatives.[13] To make the point symbolically if, as cannot be emphasised too heavily, at the margins, consider the heterodox alternatives on offer. It is McCloskey who is seen as heterodox, more observed in passing than in use, rather than the likes of J.K. Galbraith, Joan Robinson and Nicholas Kaldor, let alone Kalecki, Baran and Sweezy, and Marx – who previously served as the reference point for alternatives to the mainstream.

Despite this commentary on the relatively limited impact on economics of debates around economic methodology, it is appropriate, paradoxically, to point to a blossoming of methodological debate from the 1970s onward. To a large extent, methodology has provided a refuge for those who wish to retain a dialogue with the orthodoxy but also to break with it. This has four effects that have already been observed. First, the agenda is heavily marked by issues set by the orthodoxy. As Maki (1993a, p. 5) puts it:[14]

---

13 See Gustafsson (1993) and Backhouse (1994), for example, who point to the emergence and growth of specialised journals and texts.

14 And continues: "It has been established by recent research in economic methodology that the Popperian principles do not hold in economics – descriptively, prescriptively, or both ... Even though Popperian falsificationism – the methodology of bold conjecture and critical refutation – is not practised or even practisable in economics, it (or a loose and more or less obscure version of it) nevertheless enjoys wide popularity in the metatheoretical commentaries by economists".

A Popperian dominance, a kind of Popperian mainstream in economic methodology has prevailed. It has been a dominance of certain questions and categories, such as whether economic theories are falsifiable and whether economists critically pursue falsifications, whether a given proposition belongs to the irrefutable hard core or to the revisable protective belt of a research programme, whether this or that episode in the history of economic thought is or is not progressive in the sense of providing increasing corroborated excess content, etc.

Second, mainstream economists generally ignore and/or are ignorant of methodological debates, and consider that it should be left to non-economists and/or constitute a separate arena of study (Caldwell 1993). Orthodox economists can and do safely proceed as if those debates in methodology do not exist. Third, nonetheless, the area does attract neoclassical rogues. Blaug (1980/92), for example, is credited by Backhouse (1994) with having set the agenda of falsification in the initial explosion of methodological literature.[15]

Fourth, even though the more recent literature is beginning to depart from that initial agenda, there are other rogues, such as McCloskey, to take Blaug's place. As Maki (1993b, p. 95) appropriately observes of McCloskey:

> Most of the time he appears to posit a sort of perfect market of economic ideas, an idea of unrestricted conversation with free entry, shared rules of the game, and evenly distributed power. The idea of institutionalized entry conditions ... does not fit this image neatly. For this reason, his work does not seem to be particularly useful for understanding the fate of dissenting ideas in economics.

Indeed, it is further argued that the conventional rhetoric of neoclassical economics has the effect of excluding the non-mainstream from participation, let alone being understood by the mainstream (Maki 1993b, p. 98). In this, the standards of axiomatic model-building and/or putative falsification have the effect of exclusion by the mainstream through claims of lack of rigour. If rhetoric is indicative of economics under siege, it is not the mainstream that is suffering the consequential starvation of resources and access to outlets.

---

15 See also Blaug (1998b) but Blaug (1994) for a continuing attempt to define falsification as being at the centre of economic methodology.

3 Economics and Economies

Thompson's misreading of the status of methodological critiques of economics is reinforced by his brief discussion of "history". Surprisingly, he appears to adopt a rather crude understanding of the relationship between economic events and economic theory. The content of economics is supposedly directed by the economy, as in the degree of internationalisation and the severity of business cycles. I would not wish to deny an influence of the economy upon economics but this relationship is complex, indirect and even perverse. Massive recessions can lead to the view that the market works well and that economics is concerned with the allocation of scarce resources between competing ends – the dictum initially posited by Lionel Robbins during the gross levels of unemployment of the 1930s. What economic events are picked up and how they are interpreted by economists is not pre-determined. It depends crucially upon the nature and dynamic of the discipline itself. Otherwise, economic theory would itself go through cycles and stages matching those of the economy. As his joint work, Hirst and Thompson (1996), has emphasised parallels in economic conditions between the current period and that of a century before, it would appear to follow that the economics ought to be similar also. With the end of the nineteenth century perceived at the time as a Great Depression and as a period of shifting economic competitiveness between nations, especially the UK, the USA and Germany, the economics of then and now ought to be identical in most respects.

Of course, they are not. For, to comprehend the current path of economics and its relationship to the economy, it is essential to take some view of the discipline's own history, certainly over the post-war period.[16] Thompson suggests a loss of "faith" in determinism, p. 602. But this is seriously misleading. Initially, the post-war period can be divided into two periods, the Keynesian phase up to the end of the post-war boom, and the subsequent period, marked in the first instance by the resurgence of monetarism, most closely associated, at least initially, with Milton Friedman. In the 1970s, economics as a discipline was suffering from its greatest internal crisis of self-confidence. Over the post-war period, microeconomics had developed ever-more sophisticated and esoteric models of the ideal conditions necessary for the existence and stability of a market economy based on optimising agents. Macroeconomics was thrown into disarray by stagflation, not least because the failure of Keynesianism and interventionism gave rise to the alternative of monetarism with its presumption that

---

16 For a detailed and fully referenced account of what follows, see Fine (1998a, Chapter 2).

markets work well if left alone – just as market economies were performing as badly as at any time for fifty years.[17]

The discipline was saved from its doldrums by the New Classical Economics. It draws upon a new technique, that of rational expectations, the idea that, in effect, each economic agent acts upon the same, consistent economic model, fully deploying the information available. This simple, wildly unrealistic, assumption gave rise to dramatic implications – that all previously estimated macroeconomic models were inappropriate for policy making, and government could not effectively and systematically intervene to shift the path of the economy.[18] Economic fluctuations became understood primarily as the consequence of responses to shocks by optimising and efficient economic agents who would neutralise systematic government intervention by anticipating its intended impact. It did not take long for the profession to embrace rational expectations which, for technical reasons, considerably ratcheted up the levels of mathematical and statistical techniques required. It was also realised that the results of the New Classical Economics depended less upon rational expectations as such and more upon the accompanying assumption of instantaneous market clearing in all markets – in other words, that supply and demand are brought into equality with one another at all times and at once by price movements (by analogy with the trading in foreign currencies through computer links). In the case of real business cycle theory, for example, fluctuations in (un)employment are freely chosen, with workers seeking to labour more (less) when productivity increases (decreases), and hence wages, are randomly higher (lower).

As a result of its content and results, the New Classical Economics served a number of crucial functions for the discipline. It rescued it from the analytical stagnation attached to the Keynesian/monetarism debate. On the one hand, it posed instantaneous market clearing as an extreme against which other models could react. On the other hand, it prompted the introduction of rational expectations into models that did not use this assumption previously.

---

17 Thompson does not analyse this initiative. However, he speculates on the reasons for lack of use of the term "post" to mark developments in economics and the apparent preference for the less dramatic notion of "new". Note that he makes no reference to post-Keynesian economics. Significantly, Stiglitz (1998) has posted a new era in appealing for a post Washington Consensus to replace the neo-liberal Washington Consensus, even though the novelty of analytical content in his proposed shift is entirely dependent on selected "new" developments in microeconomics.

18 In this vein, Friedman can be considered to have been too left wing in allowing for governments to be able to affect the level of employment if only at the expense of ever-accelerating inflation. See Fine and Dimakou (2016) for further discussion.

It pushed economics as a discipline further down the route of esoteric modelling in which mathematical and statistical technique prevails over conceptual advance. In addition, the New Classical Economics posed an intellectual challenge to its opponents in the form of explaining why prices might not adjust instantaneously in some markets. By resuscitating Say's Law of markets in the context of rational expectations, in a risky world subject to random shocks, the discipline established an extreme standard against and from which an agenda of less extreme mainstream alternatives has subsequently been able to prosper.

4   Standard Theory

Thompson does pick up on this last point as typical of new developments in economics. But he does so only in the context of oligopoly. It is true that oligopoly or imperfect competition is currently an element in economics along with game theory, economies of scale and scope, and other aspects of (imperfect) competition and potential for imperfectly working markets. But, apart from game theory and other technical advances, none of this is new. Nor is a focus away from perfect competition in any way novel. Many would doubt Thompson's (1997, p. 602) claim that "perfect competition is losing its centrality in economic analysis". For mainstream economics has always taken perfect competition as the ideal norm from which the economy is understood as a deviation.[19] Further, the acknowledgement of the problematic assumption of a single and stable equilibrium is not new. The conditions for this have long been known to depend upon highly restrictive and unacceptable assumptions. However, as in methodology, economics has a long tradition of simply setting aside whatever results, even within its own logic, it finds to be inconvenient.[20] Neither the use of oligopoly nor imperfect competition reflects any genuine intellectual novelty within economics, unless it be accidental and oblique. For, as suggested above in terms of the reaction to New Classical Economics, economics has been concerned at the microeconomic level with the rationale for non-market clearing. In doing so, it has drawn upon the presence of market imperfections in a way that is novel, obsessively drawing upon the idea of the availability of less than perfect information. More specifically, innovation within economics has been at the microeconomic level and has concerned the optimising behaviour of individuals in the presence of imperfect and

---

19 Hahn (1973) is the classic statement.
20 As in the Cambridge critique of (one-sector) capital theory, for example, and the continuing use of production functions, not least in the new growth theory (Fine 2000).

asymmetric information (you do not know everything and you know different from others). This is quite distinct from oligopoly. The early example is provided by Akerlof's "market for lemons", that the asymmetry of information between buyers and sellers in the second-hand car market leads to inefficient markets and even to their absence altogether.[21] The same principles can be extended to other markets, such as health insurance for the aged and infirm, or other similar principles can be applied to other markets such as the risk attached to loans and the qualities or work effort of workers. These theories of imperfect and costly information, which are not discussed by Thompson, are well-established within mainstream economics, relatively new and at the forefront of research.

Four features of this genuinely new theory are paramount. First, it is microeconomic in the sense of being based on the optimising behaviour of individuals. Second, such behaviour is taken as typical of the functioning of the economy as a whole subject to the market co-ordination of imperfectly informed individuals. Third, precisely because it is microeconomic in its starting point, new developments have been limitless in scope and, correspondingly, fragmented. Almost any idea concerning the imperfections of markets can be raised to the level of theory, especially if imperfect information is incorporated.

Fourth, a significant analytical effect of these new micro-foundations of macroeconomics, or new Keynesian economics, as it is known, is that it is able to construct social outcomes on the basis of individual optimisation. Costly transactions on the basis of imperfect information imply that individuals have an incentive to structure their activity between the market and the non-market (and hence create non-market institutions) and within the market itself. For the latter, for example, it makes sense to screen heterogeneous individuals in the labour market as if they were homogeneous on the basis of average characteristics (treat all blacks/women as having lower productivity since they do so on average), since the benefits of treating them as differentiated are less than the costs of finding the information to differentiate them.

In short, the most important analytical development within economics over the recent period has been in the microeconomics of market imperfections in which the consequences of imperfect and asymmetric information have been the source of genuine analytical originality – of whatever validity and relevance.

---

21   More generally, see Akerlof (1984).

5 Determinism

Paradoxically, the strengthening, even exclusive reliance, upon microfoundations has also allowed mainstream economics to be innovative in addressing the creation of social structures in the form of institutions or cooperative behaviour, albeit on an individualistic basis. The significance of this last result will be taken up later for, although the only major innovative aspect of recent developments within economics, it has had an even more profound impact on the relationship between economics and other social sciences. A symbol of its novelty is that recent Nobel prizes in economics have been awarded for quite limited contributions in this area, none for work on oligopoly at any time. For the moment, however, consider a number of other aspects of Thompson's account.

First, he claims that there is a loss of confidence in the deterministic content of mainstream economics. In support of this judgement, he offers commentary on theoretical and empirical developments within the discipline. For the theory, it is the recognition of multiple equilibria, complex dynamics and, hence, the impact of previous economic events on outcomes. In other words, the economy is path-dependent.[22] The equilibria to which or around which it is adjusting depend not only upon where it is but also on from where it is coming. The simplest illustration is mentioned by Thompson, that of hysteresis.[23] More specifically, as in the notion of the non-accelerating inflation rate of unemployment, NAIRU, the longer an economy has suffered high levels of unemployment, the more persistent is unemployment since workers lose skills and motivation, and employers lower their judgement of workers' employability. There is no doubt that economics has taken path-dependence more seriously, not least in the context of why some economies perform better than others despite the potential international mobility of capital and technology. However, this is not the same thing as abandoning deterministic methodology. What economics has done is to broaden the scope of outcomes that it can accommodate on the basis of a continuing deterministic methodology. Paths depend upon initial conditions and/or chance in the technical sense of risk, as understood by economics, in which all outcomes are knowable, if not known, in advance. The latter is analogous to tossing a coin to determine the path which will be followed by an economy. In all other respects, as Thompson

---

22   See forthcoming volume on (economics imperialism and) economic history.
23   Thompson's suggestion that this derives from new developments in quantum physics is incorrect. Hysteresis is a longstanding concept from electro-magnetism, with materials retaining their magnetism after the withdrawal of current.

acknowledges, the economy is pre-determined as before by the continuing shibboleths,[24] although the complexity of technicalities often requires some of these to be even more restrictive than before – as in all agents being identical or there being only one sector in the economy.

Thompson also suggests that there is a crisis of confidence in econometrics, or the statistical methods attached to economics. Multiple equilibria and dynamics do, indeed, create complex problems for econometric modelling. In the past, these have primarily been ignored. But it is misleading to suggest that they are now being taken into account as a sign of crisis of confidence in response to theoretical issues – multiple and unstable equilibria. These have long been known by the profession. A more adequate answer needs to incorporate another factor – the cheap and ready availability of computing power. In this light, *any* econometrics has been able to employ more complex statistical techniques on any number of data sets, varying the structure and specification of larger and more complex models at the touch of a switch or, more exactly, a keyboard.

Before addressing the implications of this for economics, it is worth drawing a sharp contrast with the situation prevailing just fifty years ago. Tobin (1997) tells the tale of being in Harvard and wishing to estimate one equation with four variables. There were no calculating machines in the economics department, other than the one he borrowed from an agricultural economist. It took him three days to undertake his statistical exercise. He wryly observes that the situation induced very careful consideration of model and variable choice.

Today, models of incomparably greater complexity can be estimated by anyone within seconds. There is no need to be careful about model or variable choice. One consequence, then, of the personal computing revolution is to give birth to an explosion of econometric studies on the basis of existing methodology. In fact, the mathematical and statistical content of such contributions is characterised by an upward spiral. This is far from signifying a collapse in confidence in statistical methods. However, the upward spiral has also spawned new developments in econometrics, especially those concerned with time-series and panel data.[25] At times, these do correspond to the issues

---

24 Given production and utility functions, etc.
25 Lawrence Boland argued that neoclassical economics was unfalsifiable because it was sufficiently flexible to be consistent with whatever the empirics. Upon reviewing reaction to this from the mainstream, he found it was a source of pride, look how great we are – even our critics say we cannot be proven wrong. Subsequently, on returning to the classroom, he found that the notion of model had gone through a far from subtle change. From being a theory to be tested, it had become a set of equations to be tested empirically with little or no regard for theory (Boland 2014).

of dynamics and multiple equilibria. Thompson suggests that these developments have been critical in undermining confidence within economics.

However, I suggest that exactly the opposite is the case. As indicated above, econometrics flourishes on the basis of its existing practices as well as opening up opportunities for more sophisticated contributions – even though these may be critical of, and even inconsistent with, previous conventional analyses. An excellent example is provided by new or endogenous growth theory.[26] The more advanced literature is entirely dismissive of the simple econometrics that has investigated whether and why growth rates differ. This new field, little more than a decade old, with journal and other contributions to be counted in the hundreds if not thousands, demonstrates how a more complex variety of determined, if probabilistic, paths is open both to mathematical modelling and empirical estimation. Only in the sense of building upon and generalising what has gone before can this be interpreted as a loss of confidence in deterministic models and empirical methods. It is as if nuclear weapons were understood to have undermined faith in conventional warfare and in warfare altogether.

Thus, contrary to Thompson's closing speculations, there is no "new scepticism among economists", p. 605. So there is only limited "opportunity for those advancing the 'rhetorical argument'" to undermine the "protocols of [economic] science". Nor do conceptions of biologization, therapeutization and securitization play any role on the margins let alone the forefront of economics. And the notion that ideograms, diagrams and simulations and chaos theory are at the frontiers of the new economics is very questionable if not fanciful, p. 605.[27] If there are virtual worlds and realities attached to economists, they remain those organised around laissez-faire and the imperative to make the world conform as far as possible to this figment of the imagination.[28]

---

26   For a critical assessment, see Fine (2000). Ultimately, with data fishing on speed, estimation of so-called Barro-type regressions led to millions of them being estimated over a weekend across hundreds of variables to tease out some results. Of course, even if the world were random, this would be bound to be successful. See Sala-I-Martin (1997).

27   Although this might be considered an accidental anticipation of the third phase of economics imperialism in which standard methods and assumption are suspended, see Fine (2019) and forthcoming second volume on economics imperialism.

28   See Carrier and Miller (1998).

6 Social Scientists: Beware Economists Bearing Gifts

The overview of economics provided by Thompson would scarcely be recognised by economists and is misleading to non-economists. For the latter, this is particularly damaging, as it leads to a misunderstanding of what is happening in the shifting relationship between economics and the other social sciences. In a nutshell, as argued elsewhere at greater length (Fine 1997a and 1999b), economics is currently colonising the other social sciences. This might warrant the designation 'revolution' since one central feature of the marginalist revolution of the 1870s is being reversed – the separation of the economy from society and, in parallel, the separation of economics as a discipline from any fruitful interaction with other social sciences. Traditionally, the strong barriers between social science and economics have primarily rested on the latter's peculiar form of methodological individualism (behaviour reduced to utility maximisation), analytical focus around equilibrium, and the uncritical use of ahistorical and asocial concepts (capital as physical object, utility, commodities as goods, production as technical relation between inputs and outputs, etc). Despite these continuing features, economics has long sought to colonise the other social sciences on the basis of its method by universalising what Gary Becker and his followers call "the economic approach" to any area of non-economic life.[29] Until recently, such attempts have met with only limited success, although the economic approach has occasionally arisen spontaneously within other social sciences, as in the theory of collective action based on the costs and benefits of acting alone or in concert.[30]

The most successful and longstanding example of colonisation is provided by the notion of 'human capital'. From a position of being treated with scorn, it is now well-established and deployed uncritically across the social sciences. As such, it points to some common features of the process of colonisation. First, it is often surreptitious and insidious, with the unacceptable origins of the ideas derived from within neoclassical economics simply being overlooked. Those using the notion in other social sciences forget that it involves

---

29 See especially Becker (1996) and his closest disciples' contributions in Tommasi and Ierulli (1995). As Ierulli et al (1995, p. 10, emphasis added) put it: "Economics has been widened, deepened and energized by Becker's writings and teachings. It has long been referred to as the dismal science; we (and he) prefer to call it the science of *human behaviour*".

30 Note, however, that Mancur Olson. who is most closely associated with the theory of collective action, was an economist by training. Note also that Olson headed the unit that was chosen to survey the social capital literature for the World Bank, out of which it became an academic enterprise, especially for Latin America (Fine 2023 and Fine and Ortiz 2016).

an understanding of the social construction of skills as a physical, capital-like, process, and also the reward, or return to those skills, as depending on a more or less perfectly working labour market.[31]

Second, the excessive formalism attached to human capital theory within economics does not have to carry over into other social sciences. Rather, the notion is taken as well-founded and, then, deployed in a variety of ways specific to the colonised discipline.[32]

Third, more specifically, the direct assault of economic theory upon non-economic terrains is heavily reductionist (to education as an investment in produced skills by optimising individuals), usually from a position of ignorance of, and contempt for, the contributions made from other social sciences[33] – the contempt for not relying exclusively upon the economic approach and, thereby, proving arbitrary and lacking rigour. Indeed, the new results to be found in economics are often well-known and more broadly founded in other disciplines – the better educated are paid more subject to residual discrimination. Consequently, when a concept such as human capital is used in other social sciences, it is open to refinement and manipulation according to the standards prevailing in its new analytical surroundings. The reductionism of the economic approach also encourages determinism, in which outcomes can be assessed by more or less simple statistical methods – usually with the use of additional social variables.

Fourth, this implies both methodological eclecticism within the recipient discipline and uneven reception of the economic concepts across disciplines, in extent as well as in content. Human capital can be used as an explanatory variable along with others to explain outcomes. The lack (of consideration) of conceptual consistency tends to be compensated for by the growing

---

31 As Becker (1993, p. xix) acutely observes of the academic and popular spread of the notion of "human capital", "a dozen years ago, this terminology would have been inconceivable".
32 Much the same is true of rent seeking and, as discussed later, social capital.
33 The reduction of social theory to a few explanatory factors is often parasitic upon other disciplines. Pick up one idea and run with it alone through use of the economic approach. Then treat the original source with contempt for lack of rigour. See Ingham (1996) for a similar view in the context of the new economic sociology and Toye (1996) for the new institutional economics. Where the economic approach is not even parasitic, speculative inventiveness is often the basis for proceeding. The new economics of crime, for example, appears to be based upon Becker's dilemma on whether to pay for legal parking or to park illegally. These processes are also admirably illustrated by the new growth theory and its explanation for productivity increase – strip out and isolate ideas from Schumpeter, for example, or simply speculate inventively about how technical progress might occur (see Fine 2000).

reliance upon statistical methods to demonstrate the salience of the variables concerned.

Fifth, and more positively, such developments from the influence of economics within other disciplines do induce a critical response, particularly where conceptual consistency is concerned. In the case of human capital theory, for example, the new branch of the economics of education went through a crisis of confidence in the 1970s, with devastating criticisms of the relevance and coherence of calculating rates of return to investment in education.[34] The outcome, however, has not been to inspire critical self-reflection, except among those who become marginalised, but rather to prompt the addition of extra variables in order to deal with empirical anomalies and/or theoretical and conceptual lacunae.

The preceding account is organised around human capital theory, the earliest and most advanced coloniser from economics in the recent period. As signified by the proliferation of the many "new" branches of economics – the new institutional economics, the new political economy, the new household economics, etc – similar paths have been trodden along other routes. The qualitative nature of this broader assault by economics upon other social sciences has also developed. As is made clear in Becker's own work, human capital is merely seen as one element in a broader category of what is dubbed personal capital. The latter includes the incorporation into the individual of what are generally freely-chosen experiences and which affect the capacity to generate and enjoy utility. Those with more experience of consumption, for example, have accumulated more 'consumption' capital and so know better what gives them pleasure and can also have gained more sophisticated tastes.[35]

The notion of personal capital, initially in the form of human capital, has spearheaded the assault of the economic approach upon the other social sciences. The encroachment has, however, been raised to another plane by the emergence of the notion of social capital to complement that of personal capital. From the perspective of neoclassical economics, social capital is simply the outcomes and influences that derive from interaction between individuals, whether freely chosen or the more or less accidental consequences of aggregated behaviour.

Interestingly, Becker and his followers seem to have been drawn into use of social capital as the spheres of application of personal capital became exhausted and faltered upon the glaringly unavoidable fact of the existence

---

34 See Fine (1998a, Chapter 3) for a discussion.
35 See especially Becker (1996) and, for a critique, Fine (1997b and 1998b).

of collective forms of behaviour and the presence of institutions and customs. The notion has, however, had independent origins derived from those previously mentioned, new developments within mainstream microeconomics. The latter through informational imperfections and asymmetries has been able to construct the social on the basis of individual optimisation. From an intellectual point of view, this has opened up the social sciences to economics as never before. For, even economists have adopted the view that the reductionism of Becker and his followers goes too far. Now, they are able to retreat to a more reasonable position in which the social is both incorporated and explained, often with a healthy dose of historical contingency.

And what is acceptable to more reasonable economists becomes equally so for other social sciences. For, the most significant barrier between them and economics has been that the latter's individualism has taken the social as given, unexplained and the appropriate subject matter of other disciplines. Now, economics can address the social both within its own discipline and in other disciplines. In doing so, it can draw upon the results to be derived from use of personal capital and add those attached to social capital. The outcome for the other social sciences is to intensify the features of economics' influence – the reductionism, eclecticism, empiricism, unevenness, ignorance, parasitism, contempt and critical, at times futile, conceptual reaction.

In short, my argument is that economics is colonising the other social sciences as never before with mixed and, as yet, uncertain outcomes. Many economists, especially associated with Becker, are explicit and fierce colonisers.[36] The volume edited by Radnitzky and Bernholz (1987), for example, is entitled *Economic Imperialism* and examines how economic principles are being applied across the social sciences. Swedberg's (1990) collection explicitly interviews leading economists and sociologists over whether they consider that economics has imperial designs over economics. His own conclusion is that, p. 5:

---

36   See the remarkable contributions to Tommasi and Ierulli (1995). My favourite from these is reminiscent of the joke about the economist who will not pick up a bank note from the pavement on the grounds that, if it were genuine, it would already have been pocketed. For Matsusaka (1995, p. 151), concluding on the economic approach to democracy: "Consider a policy that would make every single person in the country better off. Clearly there would be some pressure in favor of this policy, no pressure against it, and it would be implemented in short order. It follows that if there are any programs of this sort, they are already in effect". From different perspectives, see also Harcourt (1982), Buckley and Casson (1993) and Hodgson (1994) for discussion of economics as an imperialist social science.

> What is happening is very significant: the border line between two of the major social sciences is being redrawn, thereby providing new perspectives on a whole range of very important problems both in the economy and in society at large.

Indeed, Swedberg (1990, p. 14) traces the notion of economics imperialism back to the early 1930s. However, even as late as 1984, Stigler concludes (1984, p. 12–13) his discussion in terms of colonisation being prospective rather than achieved:[37]

> Heinrich Gossen, a high priest of the theory of utility-maximizing behaviour, compared the scope of that theory to Copernicus' theory of the movement of the heavenly bodies. Heavenly bodies are better behaved than human bodies but it is conceivable that his fantasy will be approached through the spread of the economist's theory of the behaviour to the entire domain of the social sciences.

Today, that prospect is matched by greater potential.

7 From Potential to Practice

The previous section has been primarily concerned with establishing how developments within economics have strengthened the potential for it to colonise the other social sciences. In brief, while it was always capable of colonising in principle, because of the universal principles of utility maximising upon which it is based, the potential to colonise is much greater today in the light of relatively recent developments in microeconomics. These, based on market imperfections in general and informational imperfections and asymmetries in

---

[37] See also Hirshleifer. (1985, p. 53) quoted in Heilbroner and Milberg (1995, p. 110): "There is only one social science. What gives economics its imperialistic invasive power is that our analytical categories – scarcity, cost, preferences, opportunities, etc – are truly universal in application. Even more important is our structured organization of these concepts into the distinct yet intertwined processes of optimization on the individual decision level. Thus economics does really constitute the universal grammar of social science" – if not the vision of society that leads Heilbroner and Milberg to entitle their critique *The Crisis of Vision in Modern Economic Thought*. Note that the presence of such a crisis does not, as some would suggest, imply that economics itself is in a crisis. Both internally and relative to other disciplines, it is stronger than ever before despite, even because of, its methodological barbarism.

particular, have allowed economics to address the social despite its methodological individualism. The social ranges over both structures and collective action, and historical contingency also plays a role, usually in terms of what economists address as the 'initial conditions' from which economies and societies evolve. The formal analysis involved remains extremely technically esoteric so that the form taken by colonisation is liable to be cut loose from its modelling origins within mainstream economics and become incorporated in more informal terms. As already observed, human capital and, more recently, social capital provide exemplary illustrations, respectively, of the old and new types of colonisation. Paradoxically, what has previously been taken as a weakness of economics from the perspective of other social sciences – its formalism and reductionism to remarkably few explanatory asocial factors – has become something of a lubricative strength in the process of colonisation. Precisely because of its analytical emptiness in most respects, there is a sense in which economics provides a blank sheet upon which other social sciences can revisit their own theoretical traditions. As already seen, social capital, for example, has origins within neoclassical economics as social experience and networks over which individuals can optimise. But it has also arisen separately in the work of sociologists at opposite ends of the methodological spectrum, namely Bourdieu and Coleman, the latter being the counterpart to Becker in applying rational choice to social theory.[38] Over the past decade, social capital has blossomed more generally across the social sciences, especially in political science through the work of Putnam (1993). It has already induced survey articles, such as Harriss and de Renzio (1997) and Woolcock (1998).[39] The latter identifies seven or more different areas of application – growth and development, (dys) functional families, performance in schooling, community life, (work) organisation, democracy and governance, and collective action – and provides a lengthy bibliography.

But does this represent colonisation by economics? Use of the notion of social capital has origins in other social sciences. It could even be argued that colonisation is running in the opposite direction as economists address the social, whether as 'capital' or otherwise. To some extent, answers cannot yet be given to these issues since the notion of social capital is still undergoing evolution. However, the present evidence strongly favours the colonisation

---

38   For critical assessment of the use of social capital by Bourdieu, Coleman and others, see Fine (2023), earlier chapters in this volume, and the later books, Fine (2001a and 2010a).
39   See also special issue edited by Edwards and Foley (1997) and Wall et al. (1998). The latter is unique, as far as I have discovered, in acknowledging the use of the notion of social capital in the theory of the fiscal crisis of the state, initiated by O'Connor (1973).

thesis. Despite its diverse origins, the concept is increasingly being deployed as an all-embracing factor that contributes to growth or other socio-economic objectives or outcomes. In this respect, where this is methodologically inconvenient, as in the work of Bourdieu for example, the response is to neglect the content of such approaches altogether or, if acknowledging them, to refer to them for authority despite their analytical dissonances.

However, the most telling argument in favour of social capital as an aspect of colonisation by economics is the way in which the notion has been picked up by the World Bank and deployed as the "missing link" in explaining economic development and performance – past, present and future. Oversimplifying, if not unduly, the social factors underlying economic performance are to be interpreted as social capital. In this way, issues such as the environment, community, gender, conflict, ethnicity, customs and culture are incorporated into economic analysis. The World Bank has even set up a website for social capital. It includes a bibliography of well over 500 items. Of these, a third or so explicitly refer to social capital, and it is easy to see how the concept is being used to project the non-economic onto the economic in on-going work. Even more remarkably, the other two-thirds of items in their bibliography do not refer to social capital but are interpreted as having done so.[40]

In short, social capital is colonising the theory of development just as economics is colonising the notion of social capital. The promotion of social capital by the World Bank is part and parcel of its move towards what has been termed the post Washington Consensus, a more state-friendly stance than the previous neo-liberal Washington Consensus.[41] Significantly, the new Consensus is being spearheaded by Joe Stiglitz, World Bank Senior Vice-President, one of the leading proponents of the new micro-foundations or information-theoretic economics as he dubs it. The example of social capital is highly, but not exclusively, dependent upon the initiative being taken by the World Bank. Outcomes across the social sciences will depend upon how individual disciplines respond. There is already plenty of evidence that there is a

---

40 My favourite example is the suggestion in an abstract of an article from the *Annual Review of Sociology* (Roy 1984) that the works of E. P. Thompson, Barrington Moore and Charles Tilly all "contain ample evidence of social capital, although this term was not in use at the time"! See Fine (2023).

41 For a critical exposition of the post Washington Consensus, partly in the light of the revolution around economics being posited here, see Fine (2001b). Note this is the introductory paper to a dozen or more seeking to show how the post Washington Consensus is colonising development economics (and studies) – just as previously the Washington Consensus dominated the analytical agenda in terms of market versus state, on which see Fine and Stoneman (1996) and Fine and Rustomjee (1997, Chapter 2).

general willingness to reinterpret and advance along the lines of social capital despite what is currently acknowledged as fundamental weaknesses in it as a concept. Before the World Bank's website became available, I argued that the theory of the developmental state was being re-run as, and reduced to, social capital (Fine 1999a). Now, it is clear that a much broader, even indefinite, agenda is involved.[42] However, social capital might not be considered to be of weighty significance or representative of other ventures in colonisation across the social sciences. As already implied, while the potential for colonisation has been enhanced by developments within economics, outcomes vary and will depend on how initiatives from within economics are received or embraced and incorporated in practice. On a personal note, the immediate reaction I have tended to experience in response to the hypothesis of colonisation is one of initial denial in general – but followed by a creeping acceptance and then the offering of illustrations with the passage of but a short period of time and reflection.

Nonetheless, the progress of colonisation can be illustrated from work that I have already undertaken.[43] One example is provided by endogenous growth theory (Fine 2000). This is an initiative that has its origins in seeking to explain why growth rates differ, given that orthodox economics would expect convergence of growth rates across countries, if not regions, with mobility of technology and capital. Extremely demanding mathematical and statistical methods have been employed but, more significant for the purpose here, the theory has increasingly made use of non-traditional variables to explain growth rates – how technological change is generated, political processes, stratification, etc. Consequently, it has become possible for non-economists to appeal to endogenous growth theory in order to be able to explain differences in economic performance by reference to their own preferred social variables.

Work on famine has recently been dominated by Amartya Sen's entitlement approach. This has generated both a positive and a critical response in the literature. This is usually interpreted as a debate between the entitlement approach and the FAD hypothesis that famine is due to food availability decline or fall in supply. I have shown that rather different tensions are also involved – between

---

42 See Fine (2001a, 2010a and 2023) for an account of the World Bank's prospective use of social capital as the key concept for promoting economics and reducing social science, even if some see it as the opposite. In addition, it is shown, contrary to my earlier view, that the World Bank at least does not appear to wish the use of social capital in order to raise or, more exactly, to erase the role of the developmental state.

43 That the hypothesis is taken seriously is indicated by the award of a two-year research fellowship by the ESRC to investigate it.

those who seek to explain famine on the basis of social theory as opposed to those who wish to build an explanation from the optimising behaviour of individuals grounded in mainstream economics (where entitlements become insufficient to prevent starvation) (Fine 1997c). Sen's own contributions might be considered to fudge this issue as classes are treated as individuals with insufficient entitlements. Not surprisingly, although not inevitably, the literature has not gone so far as to suggest that famine is the consequence of a large number of individual choices to starve oneself (although starvation has been recognised as a potential weapon of war). Consequently, as it currently stands, the literature reveals a remarkable compromise between a colonising economics, which perceives famine as a lot of people having no choice but to starve, and a more socially structured set of explanations, whether based on food entitlement, availability or other factors.

Not surprisingly, labour economics has become dominated by the revolution within economics, as labour markets are perceived to be particularly prone to informational imperfections – what work, motivation and skills are delivered and monitored. Consequently, much labour-market theory has become appropriated by the new labour economics, especially in the wake of efficiency-wage theory which is able to explain, on grounds of individual optimisation, why labour markets might not exist for certain strata, might not generate full employment even with flexible money wages, and might be structured and discriminatory. As argued in Fine (1998a, Chapter 6), this has had three effects. First, the radical versions of labour economics have been subsumed under the new orthodoxy.[44] Second, the same applies to much of the sociology of labour markets (Fine 1998a, Chapter 5). Third, the field of industrial relations has lost its radical content as the theory of class conflict around the workplace and has, instead, become increasingly transformed into the softer discipline of human resource development (Fine 1998a, Chapter 4) with corresponding absorption of Departments of Industrial Relations into business or management studies.

The field of economic history has long been subject to colonisation by economics as a result of the application of econometrics to it. A separate sub-discipline has been generated which is readily recognised as mainstream economics applied to the more distant past through use of formal models and statistics. More recently, however, economic history has drawn upon discursive accounts whose origins lie in the more informal appropriation of the results of the new developments within economics. More specifically, the new institutional economics (with its emphasis on transaction costs and property

---

44 See Spencer (1998).

rights) and the new political economy (with its notions of politics as economics by other means through rent seeking) have proved important. They provide examples of colonisation in their own right as well as for economic history through conceptual amalgams of initial conditions, path dependence, mutually determining evolution of the economic and the social, and so on.[45] The works of North and Williamson have been highly influential in setting such analytical agendas, in economic history and other disciplines.[46]

8 Concluding Remarks

The preceding section has drawn upon my own investigation, as an economist in a limited period of time, of the processes of colonisation. An overall picture is almost certainly beyond the capabilities of a single individual in the current academic climate of disciplinary boundaries and specialisations, neither of which is necessarily broken down by inter- or multidiscipliary research whether on the basis of economic colonisation or otherwise. Whether by discipline or topic, the process of colonisation warrants detailed study by those in a position to trace its path and significance. Pioneers and icons are readily identified, as in Olson and Putnam for political science, the latter in turn having drawn upon Coleman for sociology, and Posner (1998) plays the same role for law as an acolyte of Becker and Chicago more generally (Fleury and Marciano 2022).[47]

In these, and other cases, it is often extremes that are on offer from which a critical compromise or refinement does not negate but facilitates the incursion of what become heavily disguised postulates and concepts derived from mainstream economics. On the other hand, there are other areas in contrast to those just discussed in which, like the dog that did not bark, mainstream economics has not made any inroads. This is almost inevitable where the social is inescapably non-individualistic or analytically defended as such. The most natural examples are liable to be those in which meaning is itself a socially-constructed

---

45 In the light of the earlier discussion of methodology, Maki's (1993b, p. 98) observation is of relevance here in terms of the direction to be taken by the new institutionalism: "Much of the new institutionalism conforms more closely to the rhetorical conventions of the neoclassical mainstream than does the old institutionalism, therefore having fewer difficulties in finding receptive audiences".

46 For a brief critical review, see Fine (1998a, Chapter 4), but also forthcoming volume on economic history.

47 The orthodox economics literature is also marked by survey articles on the extent of its influence on other disciplines, as in recent issues of the *Journal of Economic Literature*.

object of scrutiny. Thus, the explosive interest in consumption across the social sciences has scarcely left its mark on economics, and vice versa, not least because the new literature tends to be interpretative where individuals or identity are concerned and systemic when seeking an understanding in the form of consumerism, consumer society or whatever.[48] Similarly, globalisation as a tendency or as a stage of development scarcely appears in the lexicon of mainstream economics, although the ideal notion of the boundary-less rule of markets does find its place in those non-economic understandings of globalisation that see it as undermining the nation state. With the questionable exception of rhetoric, mainstream economics and its incursions into other social sciences have been untouched by the otherwise widespread influence of postmodernism across the social sciences. Nonetheless, postmodernism in its various guises is an important factor in future developments, certainly as a catalyst even if by way of source for critical departure. For, if unevenly and in different ways, over the entire rhythm of its influence, the social sciences are retreating from the excesses of postmodernism and positively seeking a return to material realities of which the economic is a major part. Just as mainstream economics is at its strongest analytically for an assault on other social sciences, so the latter are at their most receptive to economic analysis.

The issue, then, is not whether economics has the capacity to colonise other social sciences but to what extent it has done so and how it has been and is being received. Traditionally, schools of heterodox and radical political economy have been more warmly received than mainstream economics both within the other social sciences and within mainstream economics itself.[49] With rapid decline, in the UK at least, of student interest in economics as a discipline,[50] there is a chance to strengthen non-mainstream understandings

---

48 For a critical overview of consumption across the social sciences and economics' place within it, see Fine and Leopold (1993) or revised edition of Fine (2002).

49 Nonetheless, there is a danger that all economics (mainstream and heterodox) is lumped together and dismissed by other social sciences – as appears to be the case for Zelizer (1988 and 1994) in her discussion of commodities and (personal) monies. For a critique of her position, see Fine and Lapavitsas (2000), who argue more generally in favour of the need for an appropriate political economy in order to be able to address such issues as raised by Zelizer within social theory. On a personal note, I had a telling response from Mary Douglas on the material culture of consumption of being dismissed purely for being an economist irrespective of commitment to political economy and interdisciplinarity.

50 There has been a dramatic decline in the popularity of economics as an A-level subject. Numbers declined by 20 per cent in 1997, to 20,873 from a peak of 46,144 in 1989, and a further 20 per cent drop is reported for 1998. I suspect that this does not reflect a lack of interest in economic issues in globalisation, famine and poverty, the collapse of the socialist economies, and the East Asian miracle and crisis, etc. Rather, potential students

of the economy within other disciplines from alternative economic perspectives. This has, however, to be set against the other developments within and around the discipline of economics – the mainstream's enhanced capacity to colonise other social sciences and, equally important, its capacity to colonise and exclude radical alternatives within economics itself. These processes are admirably illustrated by approaches based on rational choice in general and by analytical Marxism in particular. It is essential, then, that non-economists be critically aware of the significance of developments within economics even if not needing fully to absorb the protective belt of mathematical and statistical techniques with which they are surrounded. For, as cannot be overemphasised, the fate of the social sciences is by no means sealed. The alternative prospect in developing interdisciplinary research is to struggle for a genuine political economy, in which the 'social' and 'capital', and other such categories, are appropriately constructed and integrated.

References

Akerlof, G. (1984) *An Economic Theorist's Book of Tales*, Cambridge: Cambridge University Press.

Backhouse, R. (1994) "Introduction: New Directions in Economic Methodology", in Backhouse (ed.) (1994), pp. 1–26.

Backhouse, R. (ed.) (1994) *New Directions in Economic Methodology*, London: Routledge.

Barro, R. (2003) *Nothing Is Sacred: Economics Ideas for the New Millennium*, Cambridge: MIT Press.

Becker, G. (1993) *Human Capital: a Theoretical and Empirical Analysis, with Special Reference to Education*, London: University of Chicago Press, third edition.

Becker, G. (1996) *Accounting for Tastes*, Cambridge: Harvard University Press.

---

are intimidated by the technical requirements of the discipline, have justifiable doubts about its relevance to their concerns and, if vocationally oriented, can choose between a wide range of other subjects with an economics-like content, such as business studies and accounting. See also Blaug (1998a, p. 11): "A survey of graduate students in elite American universities ... revealed an appalling lack of interest among young would-be economists either in the economy or in the literature of economics. Success in the economics profession, they shrewdly perceived, came principally to those with a knowledge of mathematical economics and econometrics". Things have changed over the intervening years, not least as the worth of a degree in business/management/accounting as a vocational passport has been devalued by virtue of the extreme expansion of supply. As a result, there has been a resurgence in demand to study for degrees in economics as a passage into employment, especially for the financial sector.

Blaug, M. (1980/92) *The Methodology of Economics: How Economists Explain*, Cambridge: Cambridge University Press, 2nd edition, 1992.

Blaug, M. (1994) "Why I Am Not a Constructivist: Confessions of an Unrepentant Popperian", in Backhouse (ed.) (1994), pp. 109-36.

Blaug, M. (1998a) "Disturbing Currents in Modern Economics", *Challenge*, vol 41, no 3, pp. 11-34.

Blaug, M. (1998b) "The Problems with Formalism: Interview with Mark Blaug", *Challenge*, vol 41, no 3, pp. 35-45.

Boland, L. (2014) *Model Building in Economics: its Purposes and Limitations*, Cambridge: Cambridge University Press.

Buckley, P. and M. Casson (1993) "Economics as an Imperialist Social Science", *Human Relations*, vol 46, no 9, pp. 1035-52.

Caldwell, B. (1993) "Economic Methodology: Rationale, Foundations, Prospects", in Maki et al (eds) (1993), pp. 5-60.

Carrier, J. and D. Miller (eds) (1998) *Virtualism: the New Political Economy*, London: Berg.

Chester, L. and T.-H. Jo (eds) (2022) *Heterodox Economics: Legacy and Prospects*, World Economics Association Books.

Cord, R. (ed.) (2022) *The Palgrave Companion to Chicago Economics*, New York: Springer.

Damodaran, S., S. Gupta, S. Mitra and D. Sinha (eds) (2023) *Development, Transformations and the Human Condition: Volume in Honour of Professor Jayati Ghosh*, Delhi: London, forthcoming.

Edwards, B. and M. Foley (1997) "Social Capital and the Political Economy of Our Discontent", *American Behavioral Scientist*, vol 40, no 5, pp. 669-78.

Fine, B. (1995) "From Political Economy to Consumption", in Miller (ed.) (1995), pp. 127-163.

Fine, B. (1997a) "The New Revolution in Economics", *Capital and Class*, no 61, Spring, pp. 143-48. See also Chapter 4.

Fine, B. (1997b) "Playing the Consumption Game", *Consumption, Markets, Culture*, vol 1, no 1, pp. 7-29.

Fine, B. (1997c) "Entitlement Failure?", *Development and Change*, vol 28, no 4, pp. 617-47.

Fine, B. (1998a) *Labour Market Theory: a Constructive Reassessment*, London: Routledge.

Fine, B. (1998b) "The Triumph of Economics: Or 'Rationality' Can Be Dangerous to Your Reasoning", in Carrier and Miller (eds) (1998), pp. 49-74.

Fine, B. (1999a) "The Developmental State Is Dead – Long Live Social Capital?", *Development and Change*, vol 30, no 1, pp. 1-19.

Fine, B. (1999b) "From Becker to Bourdieu: Economics Confronts the Social Sciences", *International Papers in Political Economy*, vol 5, no 3, pp. 1-43. See also Chapter 5.

Fine, B. (1999c) "A Question of Economics: Is It Colonising the Social Sciences?", *Economy and Society*, vol 28, no 3, pp. 403-25.

Fine, B. (2000) "Endogenous Growth Theory: a Critical Assessment", *Cambridge Journal of Economics*, vol 24, no 2, pp. 245–65, a shortened and amended version of identically titled, SOAS Working Paper, No 80, February 1998, pp. 1–49.

Fine, B. (2001a) *Social Capital versus Social Theory: Political Economy and Social Science at the Turn of the Millennium*, London: Routledge.

Fine, B. (2001b) "Neither Washington nor Post-Washington Consensus: an Introduction", in Fine et al (eds) (2001), pp. 1–27.

Fine, B. (2009a) "Submission to the COSATU Panel of Economists on 'The Final Recommendations of the International Panel on Growth' (The Harvard Panel)", *Transformation*, no 69, pp. 5–30.

Fine, B. (2009b) "A Rejoinder to 'A Response to Fine's "Harvard Group Shores up Shoddy Governance"'", *Transformation*, no 69, pp. 66–79.

Fine, B. (2010a) *Theories of Social Capital: Researchers Behaving Badly*, London: Pluto Press.

Fine, B. (2010b) "Beyond the Tragedy of the Commons: a Discussion of *Governing the Commons: the Evolution of Institutions for Collective Action*", *Perspectives on Politics*, vol 8, no 2, pp. 583–86.

Fine, B. (2019) "Economics and Interdisciplinarity: One Step Forward, N Steps Back?" *Revista Crítica de Ciências Sociais*, no 119, pp. 131–48.

Fine, B. (2023) "Social Capital: the Indian Connection", in Damodaran et al (eds) (2023), forthcoming.

Fine, B. and O. Dimakou (2016) *Macroeconomics: a Critical Companion*, London: Pluto.

Fine, B. and C. Lapavitsas (2000) "Markets and Money in Social Theory: What Role for Economics?", *Economic and Society*, vol 29, no 3, pp. 357–82.

Fine, B., C. Lapavitsas and J. Pincus (eds) (2001) *Development Policy in the Twenty-First Century: Beyond the Post-Washington Consensus*, London: Routledge.

Fine, B. and E. Leopold (1993) *The World of Consumption*, London: Routledge, revised edition, 2002.

Fine, B. and J. Ortiz (2016) "Social Capital: from the Gringo's Tale to the Colombian Reality", SOAS Department of Economics Working Paper Series, no 195.

Fine, B. and Z. Rustomjee (1997) *South Africa's Political Economy: from Minerals-Energy Complex to Industrialisation*, Johannesburg: Wits University Press.

Fine, B. and C. Stoneman (1996) "Introduction: State and Development", *Journal of Southern African[Studies*, vol 22, no 1, March, pp. 5–26.

Fleury, J.-B. and A. Marciano (2022) "Richard A. Posner (1939–)", in Cord (ed.) (2022), forthcoming. Available at SSRN: https://ssrn.com/abstract=4145539 or http://dx.doi.org/10.2139/ssrn.4145539.

Gustafsson, B. (1993) "Preface", in Maki et al (eds) (1993), pp. ix–xi.

Hahn, F. (1973) *On the Notion of Equilibrium in Economics*, Cambridge: Cambridge University Press.

Harcourt, G. (1982) *The Social Science Imperialists: Selected Essays*, London: Routledge Kegan Paul.

Hargreaves-Heap, S. (1992) *The Theory of Choice: a Critical Guide*, Oxford: Blackwell.

Harriss, J. and P. de Renzio (1997) "'Missing Link' or Analytically Missing?: the Concept of Social Capital, An Introductory Bibliographic Essay", *Journal of International Development*, vol 9, no 7, pp. 919–37.

Harriss, J., J. Hunter and C. Lewis (eds) (1996) *The New Institutional Economics and Third World Development*, London: Routledge.

Hausmann, R. and D. Rodrik (2003) "Economic Development as Self-Discovery", *Journal of Development Economics*, vol 72, no 2, pp. 603–633.

Heilbroner, R. and W. Milberg (1995) *The Crisis of Vision in Modern Economic Thought*, Cambridge: Cambridge University Press.

Hirshleifer, J. (1985) "The Expanding Domain of Economics", *American Economic Review*, vol 83, no 3, Special Issue, December, pp. 53–68.

Hirst, P. and G. Thompson (1996) *Globalization in Question*, Cambridge: Polity Press.

Hodgson, G. (1994) "Some Remarks on 'Economic Imperialism' and International Political Economy", *Review of International Political Economy*, vol 1, no 1, pp. 21–28.

Ierulli, K., E. Glaeser and M. Tommasi (1995) "Introduction", in Tommasi and Ierulli (eds) (1995), pp. 1–14.

Ingham, G. (1996) "Some Recent Changes in the Relationship between Economics and Sociology", *Cambridge Journal of Economics*, vol 20, no 2, pp. 243–75.

Koshovets, O. (2019) "Neuroeconomics: New Heart for Economics or New Face of Economic Imperialism", *Journal of Institutional Studies*, vol 11, no 1, pp. 6–19.

Lee, F. and S. Harley (1998) "Peer Review, the Research Assessment Exercise and the Demise of Non-Mainstream Economics", *Capital and Class*, no 66, pp. 23–51.

Maki, U. (1993a) "Economics with Institutions: Agenda for Methodological Enquiry", in Maki et al (eds) (1993), pp. 3–44.

Maki, U. (1993b) "Social Theories of Science and the Fate of Institutionalism in Economics", in Maki et al (eds) (1993), pp. 76–112.

Maki, U., B. Gustafsson and C. Knudsen (eds) (1993) *Rationality, Institutions and Economic Methodology*, London: Routledge.

Matsusaka, J. (1995) "The Economic Approach to Democracy", in Tommasi and Ierulli (eds) (1995), pp. 140–56.

McCloskey, D. (1986) *The Rhetoric of Economics*, Brighton: Wheatsheaf.

Miller, D. (ed.) (1995) *Acknowledging Consumption*, London: Routledge.

Nielsen, P. and J. Morgan (2005) "No New Revolution in Economics? Taking Thompson and Fine Forward", *Economy and Society*, vol 34, no 1, pp. 51–75.

Nik-Khah, E. and R. Van Horn (2012) "Inland Empire: Economics Imperialism as an Imperative of Chicago Neoliberalism", *Journal of Economic Methodology*, 19, no 3, pp. 259–82.

O'Connor, J. (1973) *The Fiscal Crisis of the State*, New York: St Martin's.
Posner, R. (1998) *Economic Analysis of Law*, Boston: Aspen Law & Business, 5th edition.
Putnam, R. (1993) *Making Democracy Work: Civic Traditions in Modern Italy*, Princeton: Princeton University Press.
Radnitzky, G. and P. Bernholz (eds) (1987) *Economic Imperialism: the Economic Method Applied Outside the Field of Economics*, New York: Paragon House Publishers.
Roy, W. (1984) "Class Conflict and Social Change in Historical Perspective", *Annual Review of Sociology*, vol 10, pp. 483–506.
Sala-I-Martin, X. (1997) "I Just Ran Two Million Regressions", *American Economic Review*, vol 87, no 2, pp. 178–83.
Shiller, R. (2019) *Narrative Economics: How Stories Go Viral and Drive Major Economic Events*, Princeton: Princeton University Press.
Spencer, D. (1998) *Economic Analysis and the Theory of Production: a Critical Appraisal*, unpublished Phd thesis, University of Leeds.
Stigler, G. (1984) "Economics – The Imperial Science", *Scandinavian Journal of Economics*, vol 86, no 3, pp. 301–13.
Stiglitz, J. (1998) "More Instruments and Broader Goals: Moving Toward the Post-Washington Consensus", the 1998 WIDER Annual Lecture, January 7th, Helsinki.
Swedberg, R. (1990) "Introduction", in Swedberg (ed.) (1990), pp. 3–26.
Swedberg, R. (ed.) (1990) *Economics and Sociology, Redefining their Boundaries: Conversations with Economists and Sociologists*, Princeton: Princeton University Press.
Swedberg, R. (ed.) (1996) *Economic Sociology*, Cheltenham: Edward Elgar.
Thompson, G. (1997) "Where Goes Economics and the Economies", *Economy and Society*, vol 26, no 4, pp. 599–610.
Thompson, G. (1999) "How Far Should We Be Afraid of Conventional Economics? A Response to Ben Fine", *Economy and Society*, vol 28, no 3, 426–433.
Tobin, J. (1997) "Statistical Demand Functions for Food in the USA and the Netherlands – Comment", *Journal of Applied Econometrics*, vol 12, no 5, pp. 647–50.
Tommasi, M. and K. Ierulli (eds) (1995) *The New Economics of Human Behaviour*, Cambridge: Cambridge University Press.
Toye, J. (1996) "The New Institutional Economics and Its Implications for Development", in Harriss et al (eds) (1996), pp. 49–70.
Wall, E., G. Ferrazzi, and F. Schryeral (1998) "Getting the Goods on Social Capital", *Rural Sociology*, vol 63, no 2, pp. 300–22.
Woolcock, M. (1998) "Social Capital and Economic Development: Toward a Theoretical Synthesis and Policy Framework", *Theory and Society*, vol 27, no 2, pp. 151–208.

Zelizer, V. (1988) "Beyond the Polemics on the Market: Establishing a Theoretical and Empirical Agenda", *Sociological Forum*, vol 3, no 4, pp. 614–34, reproduced in Swedberg (ed.) (1996), pp. 298-318.

Zelizer, V. (1994) *The Social Meaning of Money*, New York: Basic Books.

Appendix

Auto-bibliography of Works on, or Related to, Economics Imperialism

Arestis, P. and M. Sawyer (eds) (2004) *The Rise of the Market*, Camberley: Edward Elgar.

Bayliss, K., B. Fine and E. Van Waeyenberge (2011) "The World Bank, Neoliberalism and Development Research", Bayliss et al (eds) (2011), pp. 3–25.

Bayliss, K., B. Fine and E. Van Waeyenberge (eds) (2011) *The Political Economy of Development: the World Bank, Neoliberalism and Development Research*, London: Pluto.

Bayliss, K. and B. Fine (2021) *A Guide to the Systems of Provision Approach: Who Gets What, How and Why*, Basingstoke: Palgrave MacMillan.

Birch, K. and V. Mykhnenko (eds) (2010) *The Rise and Fall of Neoliberalism: the Collapse of an Economic Order?* London: Zed Books.

Carrier, J. and D. Miller (eds) (1998) *Virtualism: the New Political Economy*, London: Berg.

Chang, H.-J. (ed.) (2003) *Rethinking Development Economics*, London: Anthem Press.

Chester, L. and T.-H. Jo (eds) (2022) *Heterodox Economics: Legacy and Prospects*, Bristol: World Economics Association Books.

Damodaran, S., S. Gupta, S. Mitra and D. Sinha (eds) (2023) *Development, Transformations and the Human Condition: Volume in Honour of Professor Jayati Ghosh*, New Delhi: Routledge, forthcoming.

Decker, S., W. Elsner and S. Flechtner (eds) (2018) *Advancing Pluralism in Teaching Economics*, London: Routledge.

Fine, B. (1997) "The New Revolution in Economics", *Capital and Class*, no 61, Spring, pp. 143–48. See also Chapter 4.

Fine, B. (1997) "Entitlement Failure?", *Development and Change*, vol 28, no 4, pp. 617–47.

Fine, B. (1998) *Labour Market Theory: a Constructive Reassessment*, London: Routledge.

Fine, B. (1998) "The Triumph of Economics: or 'Rationality' Can Be Dangerous to Your Reasoning", in Carrier and Miller (eds) (1998), pp. 49–74.

Fine, B. (1999) "From Becker to Bourdieu: Economics Confronts the Social Sciences", *International Papers in Political Economy*, vol 5, no 3, pp. 1–43. See also Chapter 5.

Fine, B. (1999) "A Question of Economics. Is It Colonising the Social Sciences?", *Economy and Society*, vol 28, no 3, pp. 403–25. See also Chapter 7.

Fine, B. (1999) "'Household Appliances and the Use of Time: the United States and Britain since the 1920s'- A Comment", *Economic History Review*, vol LII, no 3, pp. 552–62.

Fine, B. (2000) "Economics Imperialism and Intellectual Progress: the Present as History of Economic Thought?", *History of Economics Review*, vol 32, pp. 10–36, reproduced in Chinese in *Journal of Legal and Economic Studies* (*Hong Fan Review*), no 12, 2010, 269–307.

Fine, B. (2000) "Bringing the Social Back into Economics: Progress or Reductionism?", Department of Economics Research Paper, no 731, University of Melbourne, January.

Fine, B. (2000) "Endogenous Growth Theory: a Critical Assessment", *Cambridge Journal of Economics*, vol 24, no 2, pp. 245–65, a shortened and amended version of identically titled, SOAS Working Paper, No 80, February 1998, pp. 1–49.

Fine, B. (2000) "New and Improved: Economics' Contribution to Business History", SOAS Working Paper in Economics, no 93, February.

Fine, B. (2001) "Economics Imperialism as Kuhnian Revolution?", *International Papers in Political Economy*, vol 8, no 2, pp. 1–58. See also Chapter 6.

Fine, B. (2001) *Social Capital versus Social Theory: Political Economy and Social Science at the Turn of the Millennium*, London: Routledge.

Fine, B. (2002) "'Economic Imperialism': a View from the Periphery", *Review of Radical Political Economics*, vol 34, no 2, pp. 187–201.

Fine, B. (2002) *The World of Consumption: the Material and Cultural Revisited*, London: Routledge.

Fine, B. (2002) "Economics Imperialism and the New Development Economics as Kuhnian Paradigm Shift", *World Development*, vol 30, no 12, pp. 2057–70.

Fine, B. (2003) "New Growth Theory", in Chang (ed.) (2003), pp. 201–17.

Fine, B. (2003) "An Extraordinary Discipline", in Fullbrook (ed.) (2003), pp. 147–9.

Fine, B. (2004) "Economics Imperialism as Kuhnian Revolution", in Arestis and Sawyer (eds) (2004), pp. 107–44.

Fine, B. (2004) "Addressing the Critical and the Real in Critical Realism", in Lewis (ed.) (2004), pp. 202–26.

Fine, B. (2006) "Introduction: the Economics of Development and the Development of Economics", in Fine and Jomo (eds) (2006), pp. xv–xxii.

Fine, B. (2006) "The New Development Economics", in Fine and Jomo (eds) (2006), pp. 1–20.

Fine, B. (2006) "New Growth Theory: More Problem than Solution", in Fine and Jomo (eds) (2006), pp. 68–86.

Fine, B. (2006) "Joseph Stiglitz", in Simon (ed.) (2006), pp. 247–52.

Fine, B. and E. Van Waeyenberge (2006) "Correcting Stiglitz: from Information to Power in the World of Development", *Socialist Register*, 2006, pp. 146–68, London: Merlin Press.

Fine, B. (2006) "Debating Critical Realism in Economics", *Capital and Class*, no 89, June, pp. 121–29.

Fine, B. (2007) "Rethinking Critical Realism: Labour Markets or Capitalism?", *Capital and Class*, no 91, pp. 125–29.

Fine, B. (2008) "Vicissitudes of Economics Imperialism", *Review of Social Economy*, vol 66, no 2, pp. 235–40.

Fine, B. (2009) "The Economics of Identity and the Identity of Economics?", *Cambridge Journal of Economics*, vol 33, no 2, pp. 175–91.

Fine, B. (2009) "Development as Zombieconomics in the Age of Neo-Liberalism", *Third World Quarterly*, vol 30, no 5, pp. 885–904.

Fine, B. (2010) "Zombieconomics: the Living Death of the Dismal Science", in Birch and Mykhnenko (eds) (2010), pp. 53–70.

Fine, B. (2010) *Theories of Social Capital: Researchers Behaving Badly*, London: Pluto.

Fine, B. (2010) "Flattening Economic Geography: Locating the World Development Report for 2009", *Journal of Economic Analysis*, vol 1, no 1, pp. 15–33, http://users.ntua.gr/jea/JEA%20Vol.%20I,%20No%20I,%202010/jea_volume1_issue1_pp15_33.pdf.

Fine, B. (2010) "Beyond the Tragedy of the Commons: a Discussion of *Governing the Commons: The Evolution of Institutions for Collective Action*", *Perspectives on Politics*, vol 8, no 2, pp. 583–86.

Fine, B. (2011) "Whither World Bank Research?", in Bayliss et al (eds), pp. 263–84.

Fine, B. (2011) "Prospecting for Political Economy", *International Journal of Management Concepts and Philosophy*, vol 5, no 3, pp. 204–17.

Fine, B. (2011) "The General Impossibility of Neoclassical Economics", *Ensayos Revista de Economía*, vol XXX, no 1, pp. 1–22.

Fine, B. (2013) "Economics: Unfit for Purpose", *Review of Social Economy*, vol LXXI, no 3, pp. 373–89, shortened version of "Economics – Unfit for Purpose: The Director's Cut", SOAS Department of Economics Working Paper Series, No. 176, 2013.

Fine, B. (2015) "Neoclassical Economics: an Elephant Is Not a Chimera but Is a Chimera Real?", in Morgan (ed.) (2015), pp. 180–99.

Fine, B. (2016) *Microeconomics: a Critical Companion*, London: Pluto.

Fine, B. (2016) "The Endemic and Systemic Malaise of Mainstream Economics", FESSUD Working Paper Series, no 190, https://fessud.org/working-papers/#foresight.

Fine, B. (2017) "From One-Dimensional Man to One-Dimensions Economy and Economics", *Radical Philosophy Review*, vol 20, no 1, pp. 49–74.

Fine, B. (2017) "The Undead World of Mainstream Economics", SOAS Department of Economics Working Paper, no 206, translated as "Die Untote Welt der Mainstream-Ökonomik", *Zeitschrift für Kulturwissenschaften*, 2017, vol 11, no 2, pp. 85–102.

Fine, B. (2018) "*Collective Choice and Social Welfare*: Economics Imperialism in Action and Inaction", *Ethics and Social Welfare*, vol 12, no 4, pp. 393–399.

Fine, B. (2018) "In and Against Orthodoxy: Teaching Economics in the Neoliberal Era", in Decker et al (eds) (2018), pp. 78–94.

Fine, B. (2019) "Economics and Interdisciplinarity: One Step Forward, N Steps Back?" *Revista Crítica de Ciências Sociais*, no 119, pp. 131–48.

Fine, B. (2019) "Post-Truth: an Alumni Economist's Perspective", *International Review of Applied Economics*, vol 33, no 4, pp. 542–67, shortened version of, SOAS Department of Economics Working Paper No. 219, 2019, https://www.soas.ac.uk/economics/research/workingpapers/file139489.pdf.

Fine, B. (2022) "Towards Interdisciplinarity as Instinctive", in Chester and Jo (eds) (2022), pp. 290–325.

Fine, B. (2023) "Social Capital: the Indian Connection", in Damodaran et al (eds) (2023), forthcoming.

Fine, B. and O. Dimakou (2016) *Macroeconomics: a Critical Companion*, London: Pluto.

Fine, B., D. Johnson, A. Santos and E. Van Waeyenberge (2016) "Nudging or Fudging: the World Development Report 2015", *Development and Change*, vol 47, no 4, pp. 640–63.

Fine, B. and K. S. Jomo (eds) (2006) *The New Development Economics: After the Washington Consensus*, Delhi: Tulika, and London: Zed Press.

Fine, B., C. Lapavitsas and J. Pincus (eds) (2001) *Development Policy in the Twenty-First Century: beyond the Post-Washington Consensus*, London: Routledge.

Fine, B. and D. Milonakis (2000) "From New to Newest: the Economic History of Douglass North", mimeo, published in revised parts as "From Principle of Pricing to Pricing of Principle: Rationality and Irrationality in the Economic History of Douglass North", with D. Milonakis, *Comparative Studies in Society and History*, vol 45, no 3, pp. 120–44, 2003, and "Douglass North's Remaking of Economic History: A Critical Appraisal", *Review of Radical Political Economics*, with D. Milonakis, vol 39, no 1, pp. 27–57, 2007.

Fine, B. and D. Milonakis (2009) *From Economics Imperialism to Freakonomics: the Shifting Boundaries between Economics and Other Social Sciences*, London: Routledge.

Fine, B. and D. Milonakis (2011) "'Useless but True': Economic Crisis and the Peculiarities of Economic Science", *Historical Materialism*, vol 19, no 2, pp. 3–31.

Fine, B. and D. Milonakis (2012) "From Freakonomics to Political Economy", *Historical Materialism*, vol 20, no 3, pp. 81–96.

Fine, B. and D. Milonakis (2012) "Interrogating Sickonomics, From Diagnosis to Cure: a Response to Hodgson", *Review of Social Economy*, vol 70, no 4, pp. 477–91.

Fine, B. and E. Van Waeyenberge (2005) "Correcting Stiglitz: from Information to Power in the World of Development", in Leys and Panitch (eds) (2005), pp. 146–68.

Fine, B. and E. Van Waeyenberge (2011) "A Knowledge Bank?", in Bayliss et al (eds), pp. 26–46.

Fine, B. and Van Waeyenberge, E. (2013) "A Paradigm Shift That Never Was: Justin Lin's New Structural Economics", *Competition and Change*, vol 17, no 4, pp. 355–71; for longer version, "A Paradigm Shift that Never Will Be?: Justin Lin's New Structural Economics", with E. Van Waeyenberge, SOAS Department of Economics Working Paper Series, no 179, 2013, http://www.soas.ac.uk/economics/research/workingpapers/file81928.pdf.

Fulbrook, E. (ed.) (2003) *The Crisis in Economics, the Post-Autistic Economics Movement: the First 600 Days*, London: Routledge.

Lewis, P. (ed.) (2004) *Transforming Economics: Perspectives on the Critical Realist Project*, London: Routledge.

Leys, C. and L. Panitch (eds) (2005) *Telling the Truth, Socialist Register*, 2006, London: Merlin Press.

Milonakis, D. and B. Fine (2009) *From Political Economy to Economics: Method, the Social and the Historical in the Evolution of Economic Theory*, London: Routledge.

Morgan, J. (ed.) (2015) *What Is This 'School' Called Neoclassical Economics?: Debating the Origins, Meaning and Significance*, London: Routledge.

Simon, D. (ed.) (2006) *Fifty Key Thinkers on Development*, London: Routledge, second edition, 2019.

Index

Where terms appear continually throughout a chapter, they may not be (fully) indexed.

absolute
    fertility 28
    rent 30, 34–36
abstinence 33
abstractions
    ideal 83n24, 97
    timeless 83n24, 97
academic economists
    mainstream 131, 140, 162
academic life, my VII, IX, X, 2, 4, 14, 18–22, 72–74, 39–41, 46n7, 63–64, 74n4, 114–15, 131, 157–160, 163n12, 191–195
accountancy 71
accumulation 59, 83n23, 86, 89, 93n46
actors 96, 97n56, 98, 147n53
addiction 2, 67, 75, 77n12, 79
advantage
    comparative 80n20, 124n14
aesthetic 41n3, 89, 89n38, 130n23
Africa 35, 46, 73, 86, 93, 94, 100, 131, 141, 173n30, 184n50
Americanisation of economics 130
analogy 49n12, 89, 96n54, 97, 128, 158, 167
Anderson, P. 49n12, 142, 142n44, 149
Anheier, H. 94n49, 106
antithesis 136n33
apprentices 119
appropriate 19, 20, 35, 41, 67–69, 73, 75n6, 84, 84n28, 85, 95, 102, 105, 116, 118, 121, 133, 134, 135, 148, 164, 181, 183n49
arbitrage 139, 139n40, 140
Arestis, P. 15, 16, 149, 152, 191, 192
Argyrous, G. 116n6, 125n17, 149
aristocratic 88
arrogance, of mainstream
    economics 115, 121
Arrow, K. 105n75, 106
art 82, 93n46
Arthur, C. 79n15, 106, 107, 112
assault of economics 20, 65, 69, 100, 117, 174, 175, 183
assets 86, 88
associations 63, 94, 102, 143

atomised individuals 65, 120
austerity 12, 104
authoritarian 73n2
autonomy 89
axiomatic 7, 66, 165
Ayber, S. 149

Backhouse, R. 164n13, 165, 184, 185
Balakrishnan, R. 131, 132, 149
balance of payments 68
Balibar, E. 24n7, 36
Ball, M. 31n14, 35n21, 37, 59, 60
banana 98
Barbour, I. 119n10, 149
Baron, J. 11, 15, 97, 99, 100, 106
barriers, coal 48n9
Barro, R. 11, 130, 158n3, 172n26, 184
Barro-type regressions 11, 130, 172n26
barters 97
Bateman, J. 46n7, 59
Bates, R. 101, 106
Baudrillard, J. 78, 78n14, 84, 84n28
Bayliss, K. 2n3, 15, 78n14, 80n19, 103n72, 106, 191, 193, 194
Bebbington, A. 76n11, 106
Becker, G. 2, 3, 3n5, 3n6, 4n8, 8, 10, 12, 16, 67, 72–75, 75n8, 77, 79, 80, 87n33, 90, 91, 94–96, 97n56, 98, 98n57, 98n58, 99–101, 99n62, 100n63, 103, 106, 120, 127n20, 137, 138, 138n38, 141, 149, 173–178, 173n29, 174n31, 174n33, 175n35, 182, 184
behaviour
    collective 68, 176
    co-operative 170
    non-rational 121
    rational/optimising 3, 8, 65, 75, 87n33, 97, 97n56, 99, 103, 120, 121, 161, 162, 168, 169, 173, 173n29, 175, 177, 181
    sociological 99n61
    trade union 69
behavioural economics. *See also*
    neuroeconomics 141n42
Bentivegna, V. 59

Berman, M.   83*n*23, 106
Bernholz, P.   107, 112, 176, 188
Bernstein, M.   130*n*24, 149
Bernstein, P.   139, 149
Birch, K.   191, 193
Birkbeck College   163*n*12
Black Plague   129
blacks   40, 87, 169
Black-Scholes formula   140*n*41
Blaug, M.   116*n*6, 117*n*9, 125, 125*n*16, 129, 130, 141, 149, 150, 165, 165*n*15, 184*n*50, 185
Boland, L.   171*n*25, 185
Boulding, K.   34, 37
Bourdieu, P.   4, 4*n*8, 10, 12, 15, 16, 72–74, 77, 84–94, 84*n*28, 85*n*29, 86*n*30, 87*n*32, 87*n*34, 88*n*35, 90*n*40, 90*n*41, 92*n*43, 92*n*44, 92*n*45, 93*n*46, 93*n*47, 95*n*51, 95*n*52, 98*n*58, 99, 99*n*60, 99*n*62, 107, 108, 113, 178, 178*n*38, 179
bourgeoisification of Marxism   69
Bowden, S.   117*n*8, 150
Boylan, T.   123*n*13, 150
Brenner, R.   84*n*27, 107
Britain   22, 22*n*5, 36*n*22, 39, 39*n*1, 40, 42, 43, 45, 46*n*7, 47–49, 49*n*12, 57, 58, 58*n*23, 63, 142, 142*n*44, 163*n*11, 163*n*12
British coal   22*n*5, 36*n*22, 39*n*1, 42, 43, 47, 50
Bronfenbrenner, M.   116*n*6, 133, 150
Brown, H.   34, 37
Brown, P.   95, 107
Brunskill, I.   46*n*7, 60
Buchanan, D.   23–27, 23*n*6, 25*n*8, 25*n*9, 26*n*10, 29, 30, 32–34, 34*n*19, 37, 51*n*15, 60, 73, 73*n*2, 74, 117*n*8
Buckley, P.   176*n*36, 185
business cycle   36*n*22, 86, 157, 166, 167
business studies. *See also* management studies   71, 184*n*50

Caldwell, B.   165, 185
Calhoun, C.   85*n*29, 89*n*37, 90*n*40, 99*n*62, 107, 111
Callon, M.   147, 147*n*53, 150
Cambridge capital controversy   16, 21, 26*n*10, 56*n*22, 168*n*20
Campbell, M.   79*n*17, 107
cancer   40*n*2, 77*n*12
cannabis   77*n*12

capital   3, 5, 10–12, 21, 23, 25, 26*n*10, 30, 32, 32*n*17, 33, 35, 44, 45, 48, 49*n*12, 50–52, 50*n*12, 56, 56*n*22, 58, 59, 59*n*25, 63, 64, 68, 72–83, 72*n*1, 76*n*11, 77*n*12, 77*n*13, 80*n*18, 80*n*20, 83*n*23, 85–87, 87*n*34, 88, 88*n*35, 88*n*36, 89–95, 89*n*37, 89*n*38, 90*n*41, 91*n*43, 92*n*44, 92*n*45, 93*n*46, 93*n*47, 94*n*48, 95*n*51, 99, 100, 101, 101*n*65, 101*n*68, 104, 105, 138, 139*n*40, 141, 142, 148, 158*n*4, 168*n*20, 170, 173, 174, 175, 178, 179, 180, 180*n*42, 184
    academic   85
    and labour   5, 33, 63, 81
    and power   81, 86, 142, 142*n*44
    cultural   86–90, 87*n*34, 89*n*39, 90*n*40, 90*n*41, 92*n*43, 93, 94, 94*n*49, 99, 101, 101*n*68
    economic   85, 85*n*29, 86, 88–90, 89, 89*n*37, 92, 92*n*45, 93*n*46
    forms of   10, 81, 85*n*29, 86, 87, 89, 90, 92, 93, 93*n*46
    human   7, 11, 65, 67–69, 75, 79, 87*n*34, 90, 94, 95, 99, 100, 121, 138, 139*n*39, 141, 148, 173, 174, 174*n*31, 175, 178
    linguistic   87, 99
    natural   11
    personal   75, 80, 175, 176
    social   ix, 3, 10–12, 72, 72*n*1, 73, 75–77, 76*n*11, 77*n*12, 77*n*13, 80–85, 80*n*18, 87, 88, 88*n*36, 91, 94–97, 95*n*52, 96*n*53, 100–105, 101*n*65, 105*n*75, 127*n*20, 148, 158, 158*n*4, 173*n*30, 174*n*32, 175, 176, 178, 178*n*38, 178*n*39, 179, 179*n*40, 180*n*42
    symbolic   85–90, 87*n*32, 89*n*37, 98*n*58, 102
capitalism   9, 10, 12, 21, 23, 26, 30, 35, 36, 63, 74, 79, 80*n*20, 81, 82, 83*n*23, 83*n*24, 88*n*36, 148
capitalists   20, 27, 30, 30*n*13, 35, 35*n*20, 65, 78, 80, 89
career opportunities   70, 131
Carlton, F.   23*n*6, 37
Carrier, J.   107, 108, 137*n*35, 150, 151, 172*n*28, 185, 191
Casson, M.   176*n*36, 185
Catalano, C.   46*n*7, 58*n*23, 60
causation   27, 51, 51*n*16, 52, 53–56, 74, 83*n*23, 145

Chalk, A.   135n32, 150
Chang, H.-J.   191, 192
Chase, R.   116n6, 127, 127n21, 136n33, 150
Chester, L.   159n5, 185, 191, 194
Cheung, S.   36n22, 37
Chicago, University of   2, 10, 41, 72, 95, 139, 141, 182
children   67, 77n12, 85, 98n59, 100
choice
    rational. *See also* tastes and preferences   3, 67, 72, 75, 87n33, 96–99, 97n56, 99n62, 101, 135, 137, 178, 184
Christoforou, A.   76n11, 107
Christophers, B.   22, 37, 46n7, 58n23, 60
Church, The   46n7
Cicourel, A.   107, 111
circulation   59, 85, 89n38
citations, in and across economics   14, 100
Clark, J.   32, 37
classes   5, 20, 21, 25, 26, 26n10, 27, 30, 41, 64, 73, 78, 78n14, 81, 82, 87, 90n40, 94, 99, 139, 144, 158, 181
classical political economy   5, 19, 21, 25n8, 31, 64
classics of economics and sociology   7, 70, 116n7, 147
climate   VIII, 43, 80
    intellectual   43, 71, 76, 78, 129, 182
cliometrics   7, 14, 69, 143, 144
coal
    interwar   22, 39
    leases   44, 48, 48n9, 49
    mines   29
    price   29, 44, 49n10, 54
    royalties   6, 21, 22, 22n5, 39, 40–59, 46n7, 48n8, 49n10, 55n18, 56n21, 59n25, 59n26
    wayleaves   44, 48
Coasian   67
Coats, A.   116n6, 116n7, 130n24, 150
Coleman, J.   3, 10, 15, 72–74, 77, 79n16, 84, 93–96, 95n51, 95n52, 95n53, 96n54, 99, 100, 101n65, 107, 108, 178, 178n38, 182
collective   8, 68, 77, 79n16, 96, 101n65, 117, 121, 173, 173n30, 176, 178
colonisation by economics. *See also* phases of economics imperialism   1, 5, 7, 65, 67–70, 75, 77, 85, 93, 94, 99, 100, 105, 115, 117, 117n8, 120–122, 137, 138, 147, 148, 160, 173, 176–179, 179n41, 180–183
commercialisation   80, 83n24, 89n38
Commission, US Congressional on Fair Market Values Policy   39, 40
commodities   12, 23, 25, 26, 27, 31, 32, 35n20, 51, 54, 59n25, 73, 78–80, 80n19, 173, 183n49
commoditisation   89n38
community   13, 123, 127, 129, 135, 146, 147, 178, 179
comparative advantage   40, 58n25, 80n20, 124n14, 163n12
compensation   46n7, 54
competition   23, 25, 27, 36, 36n22, 43, 44, 47, 48n8, 58, 119, 124, 128, 129, 131, 132, 137, 148, 166, 168
computing   171
conceptual coherence   22, 122, 175
conflict   23, 33, 63, 69, 77, 89, 92n45, 102, 104, 147, 179, 181
Connell, R.   146, 150
conservative   36n22, 57, 70, 105
constructed. *See also* deconstruction   31, 32, 34, 58, 75, 80, 85, 95n53, 96n54, 98, 158, 183, 184
construction. *See also* deconstruction   13, 76, 118, 121, 137, 144, 158, 174
consumer   2, 26, 32, 34, 47, 52n17, 83, 183
consumerism   183
consumption   IX, 2, 2n3, 3, 13, 31, 77n12, 78, 78n14, 79, 80, 83, 83n26, 84, 84n27, 84n28, 101n67, 137, 175, 183, 183n48, 183n49
contemporary, the   X, 12, 19, 23n6, 39n1, 44n6, 63, 64, 78, 80, 92n43, 116n7, 123, 130, 148
Copernican   134n28, 135n30, 177
Cord, R.   185, 186
corn   28, 30
corporations. *See also* firms   21, 85, 89n39, 96
counterfactual   125
courtiers   88n35
Crafts, N.   142, 142n45, 150
credentialism   95
credit   80, 90, 94, 97, 132
Crilley, D.   102, 108
crime   2, 3n5, 68, 75, 174n33

crisis   VII, 133n26, 157, 171, 175, 177n37, 178n39, 183n50
   in economics   70, 166, 171, 175, 177n37
Crisis, Global Financial (GFC)   VIII, 9, 42, 64, 157, 157n2
crowding out   101n65
CSE, Conference of Socialist Economists   63, 66, 71
   Bulletin of   63
cultural. *See also* capital, cultural   2, 10, 20, 73, 79, 81, 83n23, 85–91, 87n34, 89n37, 89n38, 89n39, 90n40, 90n41, 91n43, 93, 93n47, 94, 94n49, 98n58, 99, 101, 101n68, 102, 144
culture   20, 78, 92n43, 102, 103, 143, 179, 183n49
cumulative   101n65, 119, 135n30, 144, 145
custom   75, 84, 103, 117, 120, 121, 137, 143, 148, 176, 179

Dammerer, Q.   17
Damodaran, S.   15, 16, 108, 109, 185, 186, 191, 194
Dasgupta, P.   57, 60, 106, 108, 112
Davis, J.   116n7, 134, 150, 153
de Grazia, V.   150
de Renzio, P.   76n10, 100, 104, 104n74, 110, 178, 187
de Vroey, M.   116n5, 116n6, 118n9, 150
deaf, dialogue of the   10, 52, 95n51, 159
Decker, S.   15, 191, 193
deconstruction. *See also* construction   14, 78
demand   7, 9, 20, 21, 23, 31, 32, 41, 51, 54–56, 58, 63, 65, 83, 84, 120, 143, 167, 184n50
democracy   176n36, 178
demography   67, 100
destructibility   33, 51, 53–55, 55n18, 56
determinism   18, 93, 159, 160, 166, 170, 172, 174
developed   66, 74, 75n6, 80n18, 92n43, 128, 129, 166, 175
developing   68, 104, 184
development   VII, 2, 3, 3n6, 4, 21, 22, 35n20, 41, 43, 45–47, 50, 57, 58, 65– 69, 72, 77, 82, 88n36, 103–105, 117, 127n21, 128, 128n22, 134n27, 142, 142n45, 144, 161, 169, 178, 179, 179n41, 181, 183
development economics. *See also* Washington Consensus and post Washington Consensus   2, 3n6, 65, 67, 68, 72, 117, 128, 128n22, 179n41
development studies. *See also* Washington Consensus and post Washington Consensus   2, 128n22
developmental state   77n13, 101, 103–105, 180, 180n42
dialectic   136n33
diamonds   40, 58n25
DiMaggio, P.   91, 91n43, 108
Dimakou, O.   2n4, 12n15, 17, 105n75, 109, 167n18, 186, 194
diminishing returns   31, 43
disciplines. *See also* individual disciplines   2, 4, 7, 9, 10, 12n15, 13, 13n16, 14, 19, 24, 65, 66, 70, 95n53, 115–119, 123, 125, 126, 128–131, 136–141, 143–146, 148, 157, 159–164, 163n11, 166, 167, 170, 173, 174, 176, 181–183, 184n50
discourse   VII, 3, 67, 78, 130, 181
discrimination   67, 174, 181
disease   77n12
disequilibrium   136
dismal science   105, 116, 173n29
distribution   4n9, 5, 21, 24–26, 32, 34, 41, 48, 58, 63, 89, 92n44, 94, 144
disutility   21, 33
dominance
   of mainstream   130n24, 160
   Popperian   165
Dow, S.   115n2, 116n6, 133n27, 151
durables
   children as consumption   100
   consumer   2
Durkheim, E.   147
dynamics   10, 13, 70, 72, 76, 95n53, 130, 147, 166, 170, 171, 172

East Asian miracle   183n50
eclecticism   76, 95n51, 100, 158, 174, 176
ecological   11
econometrics   12n15, 66, 122, 129, 130, 130n25, 140, 171, 172, 181, 184n50
economic approach. *See* Becker   72, 75, 95, 95n51, 100n63, 161, 173–175, 174n33, 176n36
economics of labour
   new   117, 181

economics, institutional   21, 68, 117, 158, 158n4, 161, 174n33, 175, 181
economies   82, 95n53, 145, 161, 168, 170, 178
  household   95n53
  market   167
  of scale and scope   124, 144, 168
  socialist   137, 183n50
  space   146
economism   90, 92
education. *See also* capital, human   10, 67, 73n2, 75, 80, 85, 87n34, 88n36, 93n46, 138, 141, 142, 174, 175
Edwards, B.   178n39, 185
Edwards, M.   59, 185
efficiency   7, 19, 31, 41, 67, 80, 89n37, 95, 115, 120–123, 126, 127, 140, 140n41, 167, 169, 181
elite   94n49, 130, 184n50
Elsner, W.   15, 191
embedded   20, 81n21, 94, 97, 98, 103, 132
empirical   42, 44, 45, 47, 48n8, 49, 58, 63, 66, 68, 76, 86, 92, 92n43, 93, 94, 114n1, 118, 119, 123, 130n23, 132, 133, 139, 147, 162, 170, 171n25, 172, 175
empiricism   176
employment   9, 26, 40, 43, 68, 89, 94n48, 130, 167, 167n18, 170, 181, 184n50
entitlements   180
environment   11, 78, 80, 82, 83, 101, 132, 136, 138, 179
epistemological   145, 163
equilibrium   7, 19, 24, 33–36, 36n22, 42, 43, 50–52, 56, 65, 66n3, 82, 97, 115, 120, 126, 128, 129, 145, 168, 173
  equilibria   41, 101n65, 129, 170–172
  general   20, 23, 24, 31–36, 42, 43, 50–52, 52n17, 53–56, 55n19, 66, 66n3, 123, 135n31
  partial   23, 33, 35, 36, 41, 50, 52–56, 52n17, 56n22, 58, 120
ethnic   94n48, 179
Evans, P.   101, 108
Evans, T.   49n11, 60
exchange   10, 25, 30n13, 43, 73, 75, 78–81, 83, 84n28, 89, 93, 96, 97, 97n55, 127
exemplars   13, 119, 126–129, 148
exhaustible resources   55n18, 55n20, 56–58, 58n25

exogenous   12n15, 52, 127
expectations   58, 134–136, 167
exploitation   81, 82, 94n48, 101n65
externalities   11, 58, 95, 96, 124, 135n31, 144
extraction, mineral   46

factor incomes. *See also* wages, profit, rent   32–34, 52, 53
falsifiability   122, 123n13, 125, 162, 164n14, 165, 165n15
family   x, 68, 85, 90, 94, 94n48, 161, 178
famine   180, 183n50
fascism   147
Fasenfest, D.   x, 151, 152
fatalism   77n12
female   2, 40
Ferrazzi, G.   188
fertility, of land   28, 28n12, 29, 30, 43, 45, 54
fetishism   12, 73
Fetter, F.   32, 37
feudal   23, 35n20, 57
field   4, 28, 45, 70, 87, 92n44, 140, 159, 164, 181
fields, disciplinary   2, 68, 70, 90, 100, 117, 125, 140, 147, 148, 158, 159, 164, 172, 181
finance. *See also* GFC   20, 22, 63, 71, 79, 85, 94, 115, 117, 130, 130n25, 131, 139–142, 140n41, 141n43, 184n50
financialisation   VIII, 12, 22, 74, 115
firms. *See also* corporations   67
Fischer, C.   135n31, 152
Fitoussi, J.-P.   IXn2, X
Flechtner, S.   15, 191
Fleury, J.-B.   3n5, 3n6, 17, 73n2, 109, 138n38, 152, 182, 186
flexible specialisation   84, 101n67
fluctuations, economic   136, 167
Flux, A.   54, 61
Foley, M.   178n39, 185
Folin, M.   59
food   2, 28, 30, 43, 80n20, 90n41, 125, 180
fortress, economics   6, 7, 9, 65–71
Fourcade, M.   115, 153
Frank, R.   95n53, 97, 110, 126n18
Frey, B.   117n8, 153
Fridell, G.   3n6, 17
Friedland, R.   108, 110
Friedman, M.   2, 3n6, 98, 103, 139, 141n42, 153, 166, 167n18

Friedman, R.   141n42, 153
Fukuyama, F.   102, 110
Fulbrook, E.   195
functions
   production   7, 10, 11, 19, 65, 81, 105, 115, 123, 126, 129, 139, 162n10, 168n20, 171n24
   utility   7, 95n53, 115, 124n14, 126, 171n24
fundamentals, in economics   126, 128
Furlough, E.   150

Gaffney, M.   61, 62
Galbraith, J. K.   66, 164
game theory   168
Garnett, R.   130, 149, 153, 156
Gaspar, J.   145n51, 153
GCC, global commodity chains   59n25
gender   179
General Strike   42, 49n10
geography   101, 101n67, 102n69, 117, 144–146, 146n52
Gerhards, J.   94n49, 106
Germany   45, 47, 94n49, 141, 166
Gerschenkron, A.   142
Glaeser, E.   187
Glennie, P.   101n67, 112
Glick, M.   84n27, 107
globalisation. *See also* GFC   12, 13, 73, 82, 104, 183, 183n50
Goodwin, M.   102, 110
Gordon, D.   116, 116n6, 116n7, 153
government   128, 129, 136, 142n45, 167
Granovetter, M.   91, 95n52, 97–101, 110
Gray, L.   55, 55n20, 58, 61
groups   86, 119, 124n15, 130
Grown, C.   131, 132, 149
growth   4, 12n15, 82, 105, 105n75, 140n41, 142, 164n13, 172, 178–180
growth theory   12n15, 105, 105n75, 180
   new   11, 12, 12n15, 117, 130, 130n25, 146n52, 168n20, 172, 174n33, 180
   old   12n15
Gu, G.   17
Guggenheim, S.   106
Gupta, S.   15, 108, 185, 191
Gustafsson, B.   164n13, 186, 187
Gutting, G.   116n6, 149, 153

Haacke, H.   84n28, 107

habitus   10, 93
Hahn, F.   126n18, 168n19, 186
Haldar, A.   72n1, 110
Hands, D.   141n42, 153
Hannan, M.   11, 15, 97, 99, 100, 106
Harcourt, G.   176n36, 187
Hargreaves-Heap, S.   187
Harley, S.   130n24, 154, 163n11, 187
Harris, L.   39n1, 61, 63, 63n1, 71, 142n44, 152
Harrison, P.   139, 140n41, 153
Harriss, J.   76n10, 100, 104, 104n74, 110, 178, 187, 188
Harvey, D.   83n23, 102n69, 110, 144n49, 153
Hausmann, R.   187
Heal, G.   57, 60
health   2, 40, 77n12, 131, 169
Heasman, M.   109
hegemony   64, 66, 76n11, 87n33, 163
Heilbroner, R.   177n37, 187
heterodox economics   VII, 1, 9, 10, 13, 13n16, 14, 18, 66, 83, 115–117, 118n9, 136, 159, 159n5, 160, 163
hierarchy   73, 88, 89, 158
Hildyard, N.   104n73, 110
Hirabayashi, L.   94, 110
Hirshleifer, J.   177n37, 187
Hirst, P.   160n8, 166, 187
historical and social   5, 7, 20, 41, 97, 121, 144
historical contingency   83, 176, 178
history, of economic thought   4, 4n9, 6, 20, 23, 24, 36, 115, 116n5, 118, 136, 165
history, social   142, 144
Hobson, J.   32, 37, 51n14, 61
Hodgson, G.   118n9, 130n24, 153, 176n36, 187
Hoff, K.   128, 155
Hollander, J.   24n6, 37
Hotelling, H.   55n20, 61
households   67, 69, 75, 80, 117, 161, 175
Hunter, J.   187
Hyland, M.   109, 110

identity, individual   124n14, 183
ideology   4, 7, 9, 70, 74, 82, 104, 116n7, 123, 142
Ierulli, K.   173n29, 176n36, 187, 188
illusion   10, 12, 32, 34, 77, 89n38, 102, 135
imperfections, market   1, 8, 9, 11, 72, 72n1, 77, 102n69, 114, 120, 121, 128, 132, 135–137, 141–143, 168, 177

incentives 72*n*1, 95, 127, 132, 169
indifference 83*n*26
individualism 5, 41, 65, 66, 68, 70, 90, 93, 94, 96, 97, 120, 122, 126, 137, 139, 162, 173, 176, 178
  individualistic 161, 182
  methodological 5, 41, 65, 66, 68, 70, 90, 93, 94, 96, 97, 120, 122, 126, 137, 139, 162, 173, 176, 178
individualistic 67, 69, 87, 87*n*34, 96, 115, 170
industrial relations, field of 69, 142, 181
inflation 68, 167*n*18, 170
Information
  asymmetric 8, 69, 75, 94, 100, 120, 127, 132, 136, 169, 176, 177
Ingham, G. 142*n*44, 153, 174*n*33, 187
innovation 13, 55*n*20, 67, 120, 122, 140, 159, 168, 170
institutionalism 182*n*45
institutions, social 97
interdisciplinarity 2, 4, 11, 66, 138, 146, 158, 161, 184
interdisciplinary 2, 4, 11, 66, 131, 138, 146, 158, 161, 182, 184
  boundaries 138, 139, 144, 146, 182
intervention, state 39, 74, 103, 104, 120, 136, 142, 167
Iraq 84*n*28
Italy 45

Jevons, W. 21, 24, 32, 37, 43, 43*n*5, 50, 51, 51*n*16, 61
Jo, T.-H. 159*n*5, 185, 191, 194
Johnson, D. 194
Jomo, K. S. 192, 194

Kähkönen, S. 117*n*8, 155
Kapur, S. 17
Karsten, S. 116*n*6, 136*n*33, 153
Kelly, M. 94, 111
Keynesianism 2, 3, 7, 114, 116, 157, 166, 167, 169
Khalil, E. 116*n*6, 117*n*9, 130*n*23, 136*n*33, 153
Kindleberger, C. 143*n*46, 153
King, A. 46*n*7, 88*n*35, 111, 113
Knorr-Cetina, K. 107, 111
Knudsen, C. 187
Kolankiewicz, G. 88*n*36, 111

Koshovets, O. 141*n*42, 153, 158*n*3, 187
Krugman, P. 102*n*69, 144, 145
Kuhn, T. 10, 12, 114, 115, 116*n*5, 116*n*6, 116*n*7, 118–120, 119*n*10, 123–126, 124*n*15, 129, 130, 132–134, 133*n*26, 133*n*27, 134*n*29, 136*n*33, 140*n*41, 147, 153, 154
Kuhnian approach 16, 24*n*7, 114–119, 123, 125, 134, 138, 146, 147
Kunin, L. 116*n*6, 134*n*29, 136*n*33, 154

labour markets 2, 3, 21, 40, 65, 79, 94*n*48, 120, 122, 132, 136*n*34, 141, 142, 169, 174, 181
Lakatos, I. 140*n*41, 153, 154
Lal, D. 74, 74*n*4
Lamont, M. 86*n*31, 90*n*40, 93, 94, 111
Lamoreaux, N. 143, 143*n*48, 154
landed property 6, 20–22, 30, 34, 35, 36, 36*n*22, 39, 40–42, 46, 48*n*8, 49, 49*n*12, 50*n*12, 57–59, 59*n*25, 163*n*12
  leases of 46
  ownership 22, 35, 39, 42, 44–50, 46*n*7, 57, 58*n*23, 59, 102
Lapavitsas, C. 74*n*5, 109, 117*n*8, 141*n*43, 149, 152, 160*n*9, 183*n*49, 186, 194
Lareau, A. 86*n*31, 90*n*40, 93, 94, 111
Larmour, P. 32*n*17, 37
Law, J. 51*n*14, 150, 168
laws, economic 32, 34, 51*n*14, 89*n*38, 92, 93*n*46, 150, 168
Lawson, T. 18, 18*n*2, 19, 37, 118*n*9, 125*n*16, 126, 126*n*18, 154
Lazear, E. 117*n*8, 123*n*12, 125, 126, 154
Le Mund, A. 111, 113
Lee, F. 13, 17, 130*n*24, 144*n*49, 154, 163*n*11, 187
lemons, market for 100, 127, 169
Leopold, E. 41*n*3, 61, 78, 83*n*25, 89*n*38, 109, 183*n*48, 186
Lewis, C. 187
Lewis, P. 152, 154, 192, 195
Leys, C. 17, 194, 195
Lindenberg, S. 99*n*61, 111
LiPuma, E. 107, 111
Livingston, J. 143, 154
location theory 36*n*22, 145, 146
Loury, G. 96*n*53, 111
Luxemburg, R. 80*n*20

macro as microeconomics 2, 65, 96, 169

Mader, P.   115*n*3, 154
mainstream economics   VII, IX, 1, 5*n*10, 6*n*11, 7, 9, 12*n*15, 13, 15, 18–20, 23, 33, 64–67, 70–72, 75, 75*n*6, 81–83, 95*n*53, 96, 97, 103, 105*n*75, 114, 115, 117*n*9, 120, 126, 128–130, 135, 137, 139, 144, 146, 157, 159–165, 162*n*10, 163, 163*n*11, 168, 170, 171*n*25, 173, 175, 178, 180–183, 182*n*47
Maki, U.   164, 165, 182*n*45, 185–187
management studies. *See also* business studies   131, 181
manufacture   26, 27, 44, 144
Marciano, A.   3*n*6, 17, 73*n*2, 109, 182, 186
marginalism   5, 6, 18*n*1, 20, 21, 25*n*8, 31, 33, 41, 43, 50, 51, 52*n*17
marginalist revolution   5, 7, 18–22, 18*n*1, 31, 41, 42, 50, 59, 64, 65, 66, 69, 80, 116, 117, 117*n*9, 146, 148, 173
marginalists   18, 31–34
Marshall, A.   20*n*4, 33–35, 37, 50, 54–56, 55*n*18, 58, 58*n*25, 61, 65
Martin, R.   145, 146, 154
Marx, K.   4*n*8, 4*n*9, 7, 12, 17, 18, 18*n*1, 31*n*14, 35, 37, 38, 49*n*12, 58*n*25, 61, 63, 70, 74, 78, 80*n*18, 83*n*23, 89, 90, 117, 147, 164
Marxism   VII, 40, 58*n*23, 63, 63*n*1, 64, 66, 69, 71, 86, 88*n*36, 99, 124, 159, 163, 184
Massey, D.   46*n*7, 58*n*23, 60, 102*n*69
Masterman, M.   124, 126–129, 154
material realities   VIII, X, 4, 7, 9, 12, 13, 73, 76, 78, 83, 83*n*23, 84, 89, 183
mathematical
   in economics   12*n*15, 51, 57, 65, 75, 131, 140, 146, 167, 168, 171, 180, 184
   modelling   7, 18, 122, 123, 163, 172
mathematical economics   3, 50, 130, 184*n*50
Matsusaka, J.   176*n*36, 187
Mavroudeas, S.   84*n*27, 111
maximisation   41, 116, 120, 124, 126, 162, 173
McCloskey, D.   125*n*16, 154, 163, 163*n*12, 164, 165, 187
McEwen, J.   61
McLennan, G.   93, 111
meaning, social construction of   13, 14, 57, 78, 79, 91, 92, 104, 121, 129, 137, 144, 147, 182
mechanisation, of mining   22, 42, 49, 49*n*11, 58, 163*n*12

media studies   2
Meek, R.   27, 30*n*13, 38
Mertens, D.   154
metaphysical   126, 128, 129
methodology. *See also* individualism, methodological   4, 10, 13, 65–67, 75, 78, 91, 92, 115, 118, 120, 123, 123*n*13, 125, 126*n*18, 126*n*19, 132, 133, 135, 159, 160, 162, 164, 164*n*14, 165, 165*n*15, 168, 170, 171, 182*n*45
microeconomics. *See also* macro as micro   103, 104, 120, 136, 138*n*38, 142, 142*n*45, 166, 167*n*17, 168, 169, 176, 177
micro-foundations, of economics   12*n*15, 117, 128, 136, 169, 170, 179
Milberg, W.   177*n*37, 187
Mill, J. S.   24, 25*n*8, 31, 38
Miller, D.   16, 107, 108, 111, 137*n*35, 139*n*40, 150, 151, 172*n*28, 185, 187, 191
Milonakis, D.   VIII, X, 5*n*10, 14, 17, 20*n*4, 38, 118*n*9, 143*n*47, 152, 154, 194, 195
minerals   40, 44, 45, 47, 53–55, 59*n*25
mines   22, 28*n*12, 29, 39, 43–48, 48*n*9, 49*n*11, 53, 54, 55, 57
mine owners   44, 46, 48
miners   40
Mirowski, P.   7, 17, 74*n*4, 111
Mishan, E.   32, 34, 34*n*19, 38, 55*n*19, 62
Mitra, S.   15, 108, 185, 191
model building   11, 67, 68, 75, 165, 172
modern   26, 31*n*14, 32, 33, 35, 55*n*18, 65, 83*n*23, 84, 101*n*67, 102, 129, 142, 142*n*45, 146, 163*n*12
modes of production   30, 35*n*20, 36, 42, 83*n*23, 84, 87, 119
Molho, A.   154, 155
monetarism   2, 7, 9, 114, 116, 166, 167
money   79, 81, 85, 85*n*29, 89*n*38, 97, 97*n*55, 101*n*68, 103, 135, 181
Mont Pèlerin   74, 74*n*4
Moore, B.   179
Moore, D.   109, 111
moral hazard   72*n*1, 127
Morgan, J.   14, 17, 152, 155, 159, 187, 193, 195
mother   77*n*12
multidisciplinary   131, 182
Munck, R.   109, 110
Musgrave, A.   153, 154

Mykhnenko, V.   191, 193

National Union of Mineworkers   40
nationalisation
  of coal   42, 49
Nee, V.   94, 95n52, 112
Nef, J.   57, 62
neoliberalism   VII, 2–4, 12, 13, 42, 73, 74,
   74n4, 137n36, 158n4
networks   59n25, 77, 85, 87, 88n36, 91, 94,
   94n48, 94n50, 97, 98, 101, 101n65,
   135n31, 141n43, 178
neuroeconomics. *See also* behavioural
   economics   141n42, 158, 158n3
Nielsen, P.   14, 17, 159, 187
Nik-Khah, E.   159n7, 187
norms   19, 135n31, 168

Offer, A.   117n8, 150
oil   40, 58, 58n25
oligopoly   168, 170
Ollion, E.   153
Olson, E.   106
Olson, M.   101, 101n66, 111, 155, 173n30, 182
ontology, social   18, 19
Orchard, J.   54, 62
organisational economics   158
Ortiz, J.   173n30, 186

Panitch, L.   17, 194, 195
paradigm   13, 24n7, 77m13, 114–116, 118, 119,
   121, 124–129, 127n21, 132–136, 133n26,
   134n27, 135n30, 135n31, 136n33, 138,
   146, 147
Parker, W.   153, 155
Perelman, M.   116n7, 117n8, 155
Pham, X.   17
phases of economics imperialism   19, 74, 158
   new (second)   13, 115, 127, 136, 137n36
   newer (third)   1, 12n15, 19, 64, 105, 172n27
   old (first)   13, 142
   pre-history   21, 22
Philo, C.   101n68, 102, 108, 110–112
philosophy   85, 123, 124, 134, 145, 159
physics envy   7
Physiocracy   23, 25, 26, 27, 29, 30, 30n13, 35,
   35n20, 36
Pincus, J.   109, 152, 186, 194

Plehwe, D.   74n4, 111
pluralism   9, 158–160
policy   VII, VIII, 3, 3n6, 4, 9, 11, 36n22, 40,
   42, 68, 70, 103, 104, 136, 144, 146, 146n52,
   158, 167, 176n36
political   20, 81, 116n7, 142
political science   100, 103, 178, 180, 182
politics   VII, 2, 59, 100n63, 101, 161, 182
Pollen, G.   103n71, 109
Popper, K.   125, 133
Popperian   125, 164n14, 165
Porter, R.   84n28, 111
positivism   123n13, 125, 145
Posner, R.   3n6, 182, 188
post Washington Consensus   3, 72, 77m13,
   103, 105, 128n22, 167n17, 179n41
post-Fordism   84, 84n27, 101n67
post-Keynesian   159, 163, 167n17
postmodernism   VIII, 12, 13, 73, 76, 78, 83–85,
   83n23, 83n24, 91n43, 99, 101, 101n67, 105,
   116, 118, 137, 138, 144, 148, 183
Postone, M.   86, 89n37, 107, 111
pragmatism   159, 160
Pratten, S.   20n4, 38
precapitalist   34, 81, 88
preferences. *See also* choice and tastes   2,
   52n17, 167n17
premodern   102
Prevezer, P.   39n1, 60, 61
Pribram, K.   36n22, 38
Primrose, D.   141n42, 155
privatisation   12, 40, 46n7, 80
productivity   22, 32, 33, 43, 52, 53, 79, 80,
   80n18, 80n20, 82, 127n21, 131, 138,
   139n39, 167, 169, 174n33
   total factor   142n45, 163n12
profit. *See also* factor incomes   20, 21, 27, 29,
   33, 52, 90, 92n45
property rights   29, 58, 97, 143, 182
psychology   2, 96n54
public goods   95, 96
Putnam, R.   3, 74, 101, 101n65, 111, 112, 148, 178,
   182, 188

quasi-rent   33, 35

racism   67
Radnitzky, G.   107, 112, 176, 188

INDEX

Raff, D.   143, 154
rationality   87n33, 97, 120, 134
real   12, 66n3, 78n14, 92, 124, 130, 140, 145, 146, 157, 167
real world   66n3, 84n28, 130, 140, 145, 146
realism   4, 126, 160
realistic   9
realities   9, 52n17, 73, 81, 84n28, 105, 116n7, 117n8, 118n9, 160, 172
reductionism   90, 92n45, 93, 122, 161, 174, 176, 178
regional science   67, 144, 145, 146
regressions   IXn2, 11, 130, 172n26
relation   27, 43, 49, 59, 59n26, 79, 80n18, 80n20, 82, 83n23, 85, 162, 173
relational   83
relations
  class   25, 81
  economic   24, 26n10, 36, 81, 82
relativism   78, 124n15, 135, 136
religion   94, 102
rent. *See also* factor incomes   5, 6, 21, 22, 23–36, 23n6, 25n9, 28n12, 31n14, 34n19, 36n22, 40–42, 44, 49, 49n12, 50–59, 51, 51n15, 52n17, 56n21, 56n22, 65, 68, 74n4, 121, 145, 174n32
reproduction, economic and social   IX, 10, 53, 59, 81n21, 82, 89, 90, 94, 99, 120, 139
restructuring, economic   22, 39n1, 42, 63
retreat, intellectual   70, 73, 76, 137, 138, 176
Reuten, G.   106, 107, 112
reverse economics imperialism   20, 41
Ricardo, D.   23, 30, 34n19, 35, 38, 49n12, 53, 54, 57, 62
rice   28
Richardson, J.   107, 112
rigour   90, 122, 123, 125, 147, 165, 174, 174n33
Rip, A.   150
risk   77n12, 124, 163, 169, 170
Robbins, D.   87n34, 112
Robbins, L.   166
Robertson, A.   108, 110
Robertson, M.   106, 110
Rodrik, D.   187
Rojek, C.   84, 111, 112
Rose, P.   139n39, 141, 141n42, 142, 152
Rothman, H.   130n24, 153
Roy, W.   179n40, 188

Royal Commissions, on coal   43
Ruccio, D.   123, 149
Rustomjee, Z.   103n71, 109, 179n41, 186
Ryan, B.   89n38, 112

Saad Filho, A.   4n8, 4n9, 17, 109
Sala-I-Martin, X.   172n26, 188
Samuel, H. Viscount   46n7, 48, 49n10, 62
Sanders, J.   94, 95n52, 112
Sankey, J. Sir   48, 62
Santos, A.   109, 112, 194
Sawyer, M.   15, 16, 149, 152, 191, 192
Schelling, T.   95n53, 98n57, 99, 112
Schmutzler, A.   144, 146n52, 155
school   23, 51n15, 52, 53, 56n22, 97n56, 101, 103, 119, 122, 141, 143, 163, 183
schools of thought   23, 51n15, 56n22, 101, 119, 122, 143, 163, 183
Schryeral, F.   188
Scotland   29, 46n7
Sedgley, N.   130n25, 156
  history, economic   VIII, IX, 14, 42, 69, 128n22, 142, 143, 143n47, 158, 163n12, 170n22, 181, 182n46
Serageldin, S.   106, 108, 112
Shiller, R.   158, 188
Simon, D.   16, 17, 106, 192, 195
Sinha, D.   15, 108, 185, 191
skills   75, 119, 130, 131, 170, 174, 181
Slater, D.   78n14, 89n38, 112
Smith, A.   23, 24, 26, 27, 28n11, 29, 30, 30n13, 34, 36, 38, 103, 116, 116n7
Smith, T.   84n27, 112
socioeconomic   12n15, 80, 87, 89, 94
sociological   20, 77, 91n43, 95, 98, 99n61, 126, 129
sociologists   3, 4, 72, 73, 77, 96
sociology, economic   91, 91n42, 94, 117, 174n33
Solow, R.   99, 105n75, 112
Sorley, W.   54, 62
South Africa   VII, 40, 158n4
special needs   VII
Spencer, D.   188
Sraffian economics   159, 163
stages of development   35n20, 74, 166, 183
Stanfield, R.   116n6, 155
Stanley, C.   83n23, 112

starvation 125, 165, 181
state. *See also* intervention, ownership, and developmental 39n1, 63, 68, 77, 80, 101n65, 102
stationary state 43
statistical methods 12, 75, 92, 94, 105, 122, 123, 129, 131, 140, 163, 167, 168, 171, 174, 175, 180, 184
Steele, H. 55n18, 62
Stigler, G. 2, 103, 117n8, 117n9, 133n26, 155, 177, 188
Stiglitz, J. 3, 3n6, 8, 16, 17, 72, 72n1, 73, 102n69, 103, 103n72, 110, 112, 127n21, 128, 128n22, 155, 167n17, 179, 188
Stilwell, F. 155
Stockhammer, E. 13, 17
Stoneman, C. 103n71, 109, 179n41, 186
stratification 93, 139, 180
structural 20, 83, 92n43, 137
structuralism 82
structure
 economic 67, 75, 120, 144
 social 69, 70, 81, 90, 102, 120, 121, 161, 170
students 3, 7n12, 9, 70, 71, 87, 114n1, 130, 183, 184n50
subjectivity 31, 76, 78, 83, 137
superiority, of economics IXn2, 29, 115, 130, 147
Suppe, P. 119, 155
surplus 26, 28, 32, 33, 34, 35, 55n18, 59, 79
 agricultural 26, 27
 consumer 26, 32, 34
 producer 33, 34, 55, 55n19, 56
suspension, in economics imperialism 7, 8, 19
Swartz, D. 94, 112
Swedberg, R. 15, 79n16, 87n33, 91n42, 95n53, 96, 96n54, 97n56, 98, 98n57, 100, 100n63, 101n66, 106, 108, 110, 112, 113, 149, 155, 176, 177, 188, 189
Sweet, C. 40, 62
symbolic. *See also* capital, symbolic 10, 65, 78, 85–87, 87n32, 88, 89, 89n37, 90, 92n43, 93, 93n47, 98n58, 101, 119, 129

taste. *See also* preferences and choice 67, 89, 89n38, 90n41, 124
Taussig, F. 55, 56, 56n21, 62
Taylor, A. 43n4, 62
teaching 4, 4n9, 8, 70, 162, 163

technical apparatus, TA1 7, 19, 83n26, 126
technical architecture, TA2 7
techniques 19, 50, 75, 92, 94, 126, 129, 131, 133n26, 134, 140, 167, 168, 171, 184
technology 13, 59, 63, 124, 128, 147, 170, 180
Teles, N. 109, 112
Temin, P. 143, 154, 155
tendencies 46, 57, 80, 82, 83, 105, 159, 183
Thatcher, M. 46n7
Thompson, E. P. 179
Thompson, G. 14, 17, 117n8, 155–159, 160n8, 161, 163, 164, 166, 167n17, 168, 170, 170n23, 171–173, 179n40, 187, 188
Thornton, T. 155
Thrift, N. 101n67, 112
Tobin, J. 171, 188
Tommasi, M. 75n8, 113, 173n29, 176n36, 187, 188
Toulmin, S. 119, 132–134, 135n30, 156
Toye, J. 174n33, 188
traditional 68, 70, 84, 99, 101, 102, 120, 122, 134, 142, 146, 161, 180
traditions 5, 7, 11, 20, 69, 70, 76, 95, 100, 121, 139, 145, 159, 162, 163, 178
transaction costs 67, 75, 181
transport 44, 48, 59n25
Truc, A. 141n42, 156
trust 101n65, 121
Turner, B. 84, 111, 112

UK 13, 13n16, 22n5, 39, 40, 46n7, 115n4, 157n2, 160n9, 163n11, 166, 183
unemployment 79n16, 120, 166, 170
USA. *See also* America 21, 39, 40, 74, 93, 94, 163n12, 166
Uzzi, B. 141n43, 156

Van der Zwan, N. 154
Van Horn, R. 159n7, 187
Van Waeyenberge, E. 3n6, 17, 106, 191, 192, 194
Veblen, T. 18
Veblenesque 19, 20
Velthuis, O. 156

Wacquant, L. 86, 86n30, 87, 87n32, 88n36, 90, 91, 92, 92n44, 93n47, 107, 113
wages 5, 20, 25, 27, 28n11, 30–32, 41, 49n10, 51–53, 51n14, 51n16, 56, 162n10, 167, 181
Wall, E. 178n39, 188

Wallace, P.   111, 113
Walras, L.   32*n*17, 50
Ward, B.   114, 116*n*6, 117, 156
Washington Consensus   72, 73, 103–105, 167*n*17, 179, 179*n*41
watershed, in economics imperialism   1, 15
wealth   54, 56, 79*n*16, 89, 90, 101
Weaver, F.   116*n*6, 134*n*29, 136*n*33, 154
Weegee   41*n*3
Wessel, R.   34*n*19, 38, 52*n*17, 62
Wible, J.   130*n*25, 156
Wills, J.   144*n*49, 154
Wood, G.   154, 155

Woolcock, M.   76, 76*n*10, 76*n*11, 100, 104*n*74, 106, 113, 178, 188
World Bank. *See also* Washington Consensus and post Washington Consensus   3, 3*n*6, 12, 12*n*15, 72, 76*n*11, 77, 77*n*13, 103, 104, 105*n*75, 113, 128*n*22, 173*n*30, 179, 180*n*42
Wright, J.   109
Wu, C.   89*n*39, 113

Zelizer, V.   91, 113, 117*n*8, 156, 183*n*49, 189
Zukin, S.   101, 113
Zupan, M.   135*n*31, 156

www.ingramcontent.com/pod-product-compliance
Lightning Source LLC
Chambersburg PA
CBHW060950050426
42337CB00054B/3876